W9-ABY-971

The Christian Pastor

The
Christian Pastor

REVISED AND ENLARGED EDITION

By

WAYNE E. OATES

THE WESTMINSTER PRESS

Philadelphia

PUBLISHED BY THE WESTMINSTER PRESS ®

PHILADELPHIA 7, PENNSYLVANIA

PRINTED IN THE UNITED STATES OF AMERICA

To My Wife and Sons
Pauline, Bill, and Charles

Contents

Preface

Many are the tasks into which circumstances press the Christian pastor, but he thinks of himself at his best as being a shepherd of his flock, a minister of reconciliation whose task is the care and cure of souls in the face-to-face relationships with individuals. This book is intended to serve as a practical guide for the average pastor in a specific church as he gives himself to this ministry.

Much that is valuable has been written on the important subject of the science of shepherding (as Washington Gladden called it, the "science of poimenics"). This book's claim to a hearing rests on its fivefold emphasis, which at the time of the first edition (1951) did not seem to be covered in the literature. These five emphases still need detailed attention, and the extensive literature on them since 1951 needs to be introduced to the reader. Yet patient research and study by others has served to confirm rather than invalidate the fivefold emphasis of the first edition. Therefore, attention is given, in the first place, to the historical role and function of the pastor as a "man of crisis." Secondly, the theological context for Christian counseling and pastoral work, which in other places has been treated philosophically at best, is here interpreted in the light of the functional role of the pastor as a "symbolic" representative of God the Father, God the Son, God the Holy Spirit — of God at work in the world through the church. Thirdly, the Biblical concept of the work of a pastor is brought into responsible and critical dialogue with the many helpful insights from the fields of psychiatry, psychology, and psychoanalysis. Great truths have a tendency to be very old. The Bible speaks in more familiar language of some truths to which scientific explorers of today have added fresh meaning for a psychologically oriented era of culture. The personal qualifications of a pastor, as set forth in the Bible, bring some of the values of these new fields of research into focus. Yet, in this revised and enlarged edition, a more mature recognition is given to the complexity of the world of today as contrasted with that of Biblical times. Ambiguities are involved in the too-easy assumption that the pastoral letters contain *all* that one needs to know today in order to be effective as a pastor. These letters will always be a " sure guide to faith and practice," but the peculiar dilemmas of the contemporary pastor are more clearly stated in this second edition.

Furthermore, the chapter on the " total task of the pastor " has been completely revised. The first edition of the book was written prior to the excellent work by Tillich in his book *The Courage to Be,* by Hiltner on the shepherding perspective of pastoral theology as an integrating theological point of view, and by Williams on the care of souls. Also, the work of Blizzard on the relationship between the working roles and the integrating roles of the minister had not yet been done. Nor had the study by Niebuhr, Williams, and Gustafson on the purpose of the church, its ministry and the advancement of theological education been produced. The first edition of THE CHRISTIAN PASTOR relied heavily upon theoretical models of personality that emphasize structural parts of personality, such as the unconscious and the conscious. Since that time much work has been published by Sullivan, Erikson, Havighurst, and Wheelis on the quest of man for integrity, identity, and relationship. Therefore, Chapter IV now lays hold of some of these more recent understandings and is entitled " The Identity and Integrity of the Pastor."

Fourthly, the conditioning influences that ordinarily go unspoken in most pastoral relationships were described in the first edition in order that a pastor might be freed of a slavish dependence upon any one or two techniques through an appreciation of the social context in which he functions. However, this revised and enlarged edition includes a sharpening of the statement of these conditioning influences and gives more detailed attention to them. Also, additional attention is given to the influence that a pastor's training, as such, has upon his identity and function as a pastor. This factor of discipline and education in both its formal and informal aspects underlies many of the other influences mentioned in this Chapter V. Moreover, training is the main factor of differentiation between the so-called layman, the uneducated preacher, and the educated minister. Whereas in 1951 there was a scarcity of opportunity for clinical pastoral education under competent supervision, in this volume the reader will be guided to the present-day abundance of opportunities both in this country and in the British Isles for getting such supervised education in pastoral care.

And finally, when the first edition of this book was written, the active pastor was ordinarily one who had not received courses in pastoral care and personal counseling while he was in seminary. Since 1951, four full generations of theological students have been receiving both required and elective work in pastoral care and personal counseling. These people need continuing education in this and other fields of study, but valuable journals such as *Pastoral Psychology, The Journal of Pastoral Care,* the *Journal of Religion and Health,* and the *Journal for the Scientific Study of Religion* have come into being in the last twelve years. Extensive surveys of the literature and opportunities for further training in clinical pastoral education are published each year in the January issues of *Pastoral Psychology.* These excellent journals are performing a function which this author anticipated in the first edition of this volume by publishing such data. The purpose of this revised and enlarged edition, therefore, is, at this point, to make use of these materials, to point the reader to them, and yet not to duplicate their efforts. Rather, the same space earlier devoted to that data, and more, will be used to pay attention to questions that pastors who have had courses in pastoral care are facing and to deal with some of the more precarious side effects that arise through the teaching of pastoral care itself. In other words, this volume will be more critically evaluative of pastoral care after the author's experience of teaching pastoral care for eighteen years. Shifts in the author's own perspective, and shifts caused by a change of national atmosphere from one of wartime, between World War II and the Korean War, to one of affluence and suspicion in the domestic situation and the international cold war, will emerge.

The title of this book, " The Christian Pastor, " was used in the late 1890's by Washington Gladden. The warm rays of the influence of this great pastor have given light and inspiration to me. I am indebted to him for his title, but I have sought to interpret this subject entirely afresh in the light of my generation's resources and needs.

I have been dependent upon others in writing these pages and my appreciation goes to many persons. My students have been fellow explorers with me, and this book is an attempt to express my gratitude to them. Their difficult questions and unfailing loyalty have made this work possible. My colleagues, Dr. Samuel Southard and Dr. D. Swan Haworth, professors of pastoral care and psychology of religion at the Southern Baptist Theological Seminary, have worked with me on the revision, and their suggestions appear throughout the book. My wife and two sons, Bill, fifteen, and Charles, nine, have made home a place of joyful companionship and secure affection for me as I have worked.

Further, I cannot name but can only express my devoted reverence for the many people who have sought my help as a counseling pastor. They have been my instructors in the ways of the human heart.

W. E. O.

Louisville, Kentucky

Part One

The Pastoral Task

Chapter I

The Crisis Ministry
of the Pastor

The pastor moves from one crisis to another with those whom he shepherds. In a single day he may visit the mother of a newborn baby, give guidance to a person who is becoming a Christian, talk with a high school or college graduate about his lifework, unite a couple in marriage, comfort a person who is bereaved, call upon a person who is confronting a serious operation, and listen to the last words of a patient who is dying. Two thousand years of Christian ministry have conditioned Christians to expect their pastors to be with them at these times of crisis. Therefore, the Christian pastor comes to his task in the strength of a great heritage. Even though he feels a sense of awe in the presence of the mysterious and tremendous crises of life, he also feels a sense of security in the fact that his people both want and expect him to be present at their times of testing.

The crises of everyday living — birth, redemption, work, marriage, illness, bereavement, and death — are the shared experiences of all people in one way or another. They are the common ventures of life in which " the whole creation has been groaning in travail together until now " (Rom. 8:22). The straitening anxieties of these times of crisis call for a reorganization of the total personality of an individual and his family, but the result may easily be disorganization. These crises either strengthen or weaken an individual personality; they are either-or situations which call for ethical choices, an increase

in emotional maturity, and additional spiritual resources.
Therefore the careful and considerate attention in these crises
of a skilled minister under the tutelage of the Holy Spirit often
makes the difference between a spiritually mature and mentally healthy person and a spiritually retarded and mentally
sick person.

Crisis, Continuity, and the Faithful Pastor

A Theological Perspective of the Crisis Ministry

As a pastor contemplates the meaning of crises in the life
of the local church, its individuals, and its families, he catches
a sense of the meaning of the theology of crisis for the life of
the church of Jesus Christ. Primitive religions tend to spring
from the periodicity of the life cycle from birth to death. The
Jewish and Christian faiths lose their intimacy with human life
as it is lived when their adherents ignore these common ventures of life or look upon them as "secular" concerns apart
from the struggles of man's crisis experiences. Paul Radin points
to the religious interpretations and customs associated with
marriage, birth, puberty, achievement of a professional status,
death, etc., as the way in which religious inspiration must
"gain its hold upon man's workaday life." Arnold van Gennep
describes these religious practices, customs, and meanings as
"rites de passage." Different "rites" help persons and groups
as they are separated from one era in human life, given support and challenge in the intervening time, and then brought
into full status in a new era of life. He classifies these rites as
"separation" rites, "marginal or intermediate" rites, and "reunion" rites.[1] Thus the spiritual community enables the individual to move from one stage of life to another without
breaking continuity with his former self. He is kept from being
isolated and from being left completely alone. With the inspiration of a new relationship he is born out of an old life and

---

[1] Paul Radin, *Primitive Religion* (Viking Press, Inc., 1937), p. 79;
also Arnold van Gennep, *The Rites of Passage,* tr. by Monika B. Vizedom
and Gabrielle L. Caffee (The University of Chicago Press, 1960).

passed into a new one. For example, the church and the school, particularly the college, as typified in the student religious organization, provide for the graduate of high school a commencement ritual, some sort of " going away to college " recognition, and a new " fellowship of believers " on the college campus. But one reason that student religious organizations suffer on the campus is that they too often simply perpetuate the same way of life, identity, patterns of behavior, and dependencies of the home church. Yet the young person sees himself as having " left " or " been separated from home." He sees college as a new identity, as indeed it should be, different from home and high school. But he needs some sort of intermediate relationship that will sustain him while he reunites with the larger family of mankind as represented in his college. Sometimes the dormitory group becomes this, or it may be the fraternity or sorority, or it may be the religious group which spontaneously forms of its own accord on a college campus. In every instance where a conventional religious organization really takes effect, one might safely hypothesize that the organization did *not* function as a smooth, unbroken reproduction of the kinship system of the college student's high school home and home church.

Anthropologists like Radin and Gennep are helpful in interpreting the cultural function of religion in the individual's maintenance of identity in the crises of the life cycle. Daniel Day Williams interprets the interrelatedness of the separate events of life in the context of the total destiny of the individual's salvation in God through Christ. He does so through what he calls " the principle of linkage in human existence." He says: " Man, God's creature, is the being who finds every part of his experience linked with every other part. . . . That man is a whole . . . is true, but too simply true. The real situation is that man is both whole and parts, mind and body, a flow of experiences, and is a responsible, searching self. What has to be recognized is the significance of the fact that every part of his being and experience is linked actually or potentially with every other part. A trivial incident may open the way for the first time to the discovery of oneself and of God." [2]

Two observations about Williams' statement need under-
scoring. First, he says that a _trivial_ incident may be directly
and causally or symbolically linked with the person's total
destiny and salvation. Thus, the pastor needs to avoid the fate
of paying attention to people _only_ on an emergency, crisis
basis. For example, it will be necessary for him to visit persons
when they are in a great crisis. This he cannot leave undone
and be a faithful pastor. But on the other hand, he needs a
regular program of visitation of his members as well as a carefully thought out appreciation of his very informal "marketplace" friendship with them. On the other hand, a pastor
learned three weeks after the crisis that an inactive member
of his church had broken her arm. He nevertheless visited her.
She considered her broken arm as "trivial," a thing that should
not attract notice, or "take up the pastor's time." But she was
gratefully surprised that he had visited. It became the occasion
for unburdening her spirit of feeling rejected by the church
and of expressing her need to heal this broken relationship.

The minister cannot allow himself to become so identified
with the great crises that people look upon him as a stranger
except in times of great emergency. Jesus, the Good Shepherd,
had time to notice children at play, acting out a funeral and
playing their pipes and dancing. He had time for a "break"
when he went home for a meal with a little man, Zacchaeus,
whom he noticed in a tree. In a time of great calamity, such
as an earthquake, a Japanese pastor has little time for anything but the ministry to the suffering. But when he visits in a
time of affluence, he may find the total redemption of a person
and his family to be linked with a harvest festival, the acqui-
sition of a new home, a new car, or a television set. The simplicities of going to market, paying the electric bill, or playing
with a child provide moments of involvement with eternity.
The Christian pastor weeps with those who weep, but he does
not do so at the expense of rejoicing with those who rejoice.

A second observation about Williams' statement needs un-

[2] Daniel Day Williams, _The Minister and the Care of Souls_, pp. 26–27.

derscoring. He says that every part of a person's total spiritual destiny is linked " *actually or potentially* " with every other part. The trivial and the tremendous crises of life are not *necessarily* religiously meaningful to a given individual. Karl Barth says that " it simply is not so that certain situations especially weighted in the negative, have, as such, a way of being the bearers of the mystery of transcendence and so of human existence. . . . The majority of men react to crises with notorious indifference." [3] One would challenge Barth's easy use of the word " majority " by facetiously asking if Barth has polled the whole human race on this matter and what his method of research was. Nevertheless, his point is well taken. Human crises are not *necessarily* but only potentially bearers of the mystery of the Eternal God. This distinction separates the sacramentally oriented pastor from the pastor who would insist that the meaningful personal participation of the individual and his group in a decisive and responsible commitment to God through faith turns a potentially religious crisis into an actual one. The " shaping environment " of the community of faith and its ministers — official or not — makes the difference.

As such, the religious meaning of the crisis ministry of the pastor becomes clear. He is known by his faithful exercise of concern for persons in the name of Christ whether their situation is critical or not. He is related as a teacher to people in their search for the meaning of their past histories, the nature of their calling in life, and the quality of hope that endows their ultimate concerns. As crises or trivial events of the day bring this meaning, calling, and hope to focus in the decisions of the person or persons, they are born out of the death of meaninglessness, purposelessness, despair, and sin, into the life of fellowship with God through the forgiveness of sin and the acceptance of this forgiveness through faith in Christ.

[3] Karl Barth, *Church Dogmatics*, Vol. III, 2, tr. by H. Knight and others (T. & T. Clark, 1960), pp. 135, 138.

A Developmental Perspective

The common crises of human life as men live in relation to one another provide a basis for understanding the total development of an individual amid his family and community. The pastor is not *just* an " emergency exit " for people when life becomes critical and unmanageable. He is a fellow participant with them as they move from one great era of life to another. He is faithful to them in times of crisis, and *between* crises as well. For these crises are not just isolated events in a person's life. A man is not bereaved of his child without at the same time having the time of the child's birth, the days of happy play with the child, and the way in which the child responded to his love called to mind. Nor do these experiences stand apart from his earlier choice of his wife as a mate and their commitment of their lives to each other. Each crisis lies upon the foundation of an earlier crisis, layer lies upon layer, precept upon precept, faith upon faith, distrust upon distrust, success upon success, failure upon failure.

The developmental psychologists have much to offer the pastor in his understanding of his crisis ministry as being not just an emergency " holding operation " but a participation in the spiritual becoming of those to whom he ministers. For example, Erik Erikson illuminates the *continuity of experience* which he calls a person's identity. At " any given stage of development " the individuality of the person is continued as a distinct identity, is added to, focused, and clarified, or is hindered, diffused, and confused, as the case may be. As Erikson says, " Through a series of crises the individual comes to feel most himself where he means most to others — to those others who have come to mean most to him." [4] This is obviously an intricate and lifelong process.

For example, the identity formation or diffusion of adolescence is only one of a series of crises that Erikson discusses at

[4] Erik Erikson, *New Perspectives for Research on Juvenile Delinquency*, Helen L. Witmer and Ruth Kotinsky, eds. (Children's Bureau, U.S. Department of Health, Education and Welfare, 1955), p. 4.

length in his monograph entitled *Identity and the Life Cycle*.[5]
In turn, Erikson sets forth another principle, which he calls the
"epigenetic principle." By this he means that "wherever something grows" the "growing is a differentiation of preplanned
parts during a given sequence of critical periods." [6] From his
point of view, both the task of the individual and his decisions
and the task of the shaping fellowship of other human beings
in relation to him is "together to maintain that continuity which
bridges the inescapable discontinuity between each one of
these stages. There is, for instance, discontinuity between the
trustful dependence of infancy and the stubborn autonomy of
early childhood, and the second depends upon the first." [7]

Robert Havighurst calls these critical moments "developmental tasks." The tasks arise "*at or about a certain period in
the life of the individual, successful achievement of which
leads to his happiness and to success in later tasks, while failure
leads to unhappiness to the individual, disapproval by society,
and difficulty with later tasks.*" [8] Each one of these tasks has
biological dimensions in the physical maturation of the individual, cultural dimensions in the needs of the individual to talk,
read, write, count, and accomplish many other expected skills
"at or about a given time," and ethical dimensions arising from
the personal values and aspirations of the individual. This concept of developmental tasks includes the layer-upon-layer principle, or the epigenetic principle, as Erikson calls it. These
tasks embrace what Havighurst calls the "teachable moment,"
or the concept of timing in education and spiritual guidance.
"When the body is ripe, and society requires, and the self is
ready to achieve a certain task, the teachable moment has
come," says Havighurst.[9]

[5] Erik Erikson, *Identity and the Life Cycle*, Psychological Issues
Monograph Series, Vol. 1, No. 1 (International Universities Press, Inc.,
1959).
   [6] *Ibid.*, p. 7.
   [7] *Ibid.*
   [8] Robert J. Havighurst, *Human Development and Education*, p. 2.
   [9] *Ibid.*, p. 5.

Thus a sense of timing within the continuity of one's pilgrimage of selfhood becomes an *epigenetic principle of pastoral care.* By this I mean that the *cardinal criterion of pastoral relationships is faithfulness in establishing and maintaining a durable relationship to individuals, small groups, and churches.* The pastor establishes a covenant of concern with them. He keeps these covenants. He measures his effectiveness and chooses techniques of care on the basis of both his and their willingness to initiate, maintain, and faithfully carry through a mutually responsible covenant of acceptance of the grace of God and respect for the laws of life. He is measured not by standards of success but by standards of faithfulness, which in turn determine whatever success he has. He and those who minister alongside him — parents, teachers, deacons, elders, stewards, vestrymen, physicians, social workers, lawyers, teachers, nurses, and statusless folk such as gardeners, lathemen, weavers, spinners, fishermen, and miners — are to be measured by their faithfulness in being on hand at the teachable moment, in standing by in the presence of success and failure, in being a bridge of continuity that arches over the discontinuities of the crises of life in which a person is thrust into the death of one era of his life and born into the life of a new era. In the agonizing test of a crucial hour, the pastor is called to have a sense of the hope for tomorrow and the capacity to evaluate the strength of yesterday. Thus he participates with the individual as he comes to grips with his history of past sin and failure, his sense of peril in the death of his old life, and his need for hope as he stands at the gate of a new era in his spiritual pilgrimage.

Consequently, the minister is called upon, not necessarily to do " some new thing," but rather to do more scientifically and accurately the work that has been expected of him and to which he has been commissioned by the living Christ since the beginning of the Christian era. In order to do this adequately in modern society, the pastor needs to take three practical steps: (1) He needs to include these crises in his total plan of visitation. He cannot safely or wisely restrict his visitation to these times of crisis. To do so would be to neglect people in their times of relative peace and serenity when their decision-making processes may well be functioning more effectively than during a crisis. Also, the minister should not neglect to equip his caring fellowship, the church, to take initiative and pay attention to those of their fellowship who are in crises. He cannot carry all the burdens of all the people all the time. He is called to be a pastor and a teacher, however, for the equipping of the saints for the work of the ministry. This is the " equipping responsibility " of the pastor. (2) In order to equip others, the pastor must equip himself with the devotional literature of the Bible and Christian history concerning these crises. (3) He needs to know the psychological significance of these crises in the developmental history of a person. Since the publication of the first edition of this book, the following authors' works on the psychological and religious development of the human person have exercised the most influence on the conceptions in this second edition: Harry Stack Sullivan, Lewis J. Sherrill, Robert J. Havighurst, Erik Erikson, and Søren Kierkegaard. Each author in his own way approaches the interpretation of the developmental pilgrimage of man uniquely. The Christian pastor will find a careful study of the works of these authors worthy of consecutive attention.

The pastor who visits his people when they need him saves much lost motion in aimless and meaningless visitation. Visiting them in crises lends purpose and warmth, meaning and value, to his call. Such calls establish a sense of rapport between him and his parishioners that serves as a foundation for all future pastoral care and personal counseling. The time that the pastor would otherwise spend in getting acquainted with people who ask for counseling help can be used for more meaningful purposes. Also, the informal ministry of a pastor during relatively quiescent times is enriched by his having been a faithful pastor to persons when times were not so good. These encounters become nonverbal bonds of satisfaction to the pastor when on a happy social occasion he sees laughter, joy, and fulfillment in the faces of those for whom he has cared in more difficult times. On the other hand, simple friendship and warmth with no purpose other than itself, and at times prior to any felt difficulty, has value for its own sake in the pastoral relationship, quite apart from any regard for the crisis ministry of which we are speaking here.

The equipment of Biblical and historical wisdom helps a pastor to deal with crises in his own life; with the patience and comfort of the Scriptures he has hope and can inspire hope in those to whom he ministers. The literature of the Bible and that of Christian history become pastoral aids in his hands, freeing him from hackneyed phrases and trite aphorisms that remind one of Job's comforters. Likewise, the simplicity of The Psalms and other hymnbooks of the ages purifies the pastor's speech of technical theological and psychological jargon which has a minimum of emotional strength for the average person.

However, a pastor cannot afford to be untutored in the science of human nature and behavior. He needs also to recognize the psychological significance of these everyday crises in the developmental history of a person and a community. He can best learn this by studying the results of research on each of these crisis situations: birth, conversion, vocational choice, marriage, illness, bereavement, death. Supervised clinical pastoral training in the care of persons most in need of help at such times is also a necessity. In these crises, a pastor can do much to promote mental health and to prevent mental disease if he has taken the time to learn the difference between mental health and mental disease. If he has not so equipped himself, he may even do much to cause mental disease by unwittingly misunderstanding the dynamics of personality formation and disintegration.

Therefore, both a thorough knowledge of the Bible and of Christian history and an empirical knowledge of the psychology of these crises are essential. But a "focused perspective" of the two is even more important. The art of living amid the everyday crises of normal growth is the province of common concern for both the pastor and the medical psychologist. In the reactions of people to these crises, the interests of religion and medical psychology intersect, both to meet and to part, in the mutually necessary emphases which they sponsor. In deed and in fact, when the religious and psychological points of view are focused upon each of these crises, the pastor gets a true-to-life, " polarized " perspective that has both the breadth of empirical research and the depth of religious experience and values. Such a perspective of the crises of birth, conversion, the choice of a vocation, marriage, illness, bereavement, alcoholism, marriage conflict, divorce, retirement, and death may be discussed suggestively here.

Some Common Crises and Pastoral Wisdom

Theologians (such as Carl Michalson in his book *Faith for Personal Crises,* Charles Scribner's Sons, 1958, and Lewis J. Sherrill in his book *The Struggle of the Soul,* The Macmillan Company, 1951) and developmental psychologists (such as Robert J. Havighurst in his book *Human Development and Education,* Longmans, Green & Co., Inc., 1953, and Erik Erikson in his book *Identity and the Life Cycle,* International Universities Press, Inc., 1959) tend to develop slightly different classifications of the psychosocial crises in the life cycle. However, these different approaches tend to operate from a common presupposition about life which Arnold van Gennep expresses: " The universe itself is governed by a periodicity which has repercussions on human life, with stages and transitions, movements forward, and periods of relative inactivity." [10] One might add, in agreement with psychoanalysts and other scientists of personality such as Arnold Gesell, that human life is also marked by periods of retrogression, retreat, and involution. The course of human life is not an inevitable evolution. The pastor is not only a *faithful* person, providing in himself and the church the bridge of grace for the inevitable chasms of separation in human life. He is also an informed, disciplined, and wise person who, as has been indicated, has through prayer and study discerned the mind of God and continues to learn how fearfully and wonderfully man is made and is being made

[10] Arnold van Gennep, *op. cit.*

by God in the crises of his process of becoming.

Therefore, the following discussion of some of the most common crises of life is an open-ended discussion. The astute pastor will, through his own study and reflection, want to add to it, change it about here and there, and possibly recast the whole understanding for himself. But in any event the objective of this writing will be achieved if the pastor takes this discussion as a starter for his own thought and develops his own heart of wisdom as he begins to number the days of human life.

The Birth of a Child

The home where a new baby has arrived is undergoing a crisis experience in which the pastors of all communions are expected to take an interest. This may be an occasion of great happiness and good fortune, or it can be one of tragedy and grief. At the very best, the birth of a child necessitates a total reorganization of routine in the home and brings about subtle changes in relationships between the members of the family. If the husband has been mothered by the wife, he now is displaced by one who really needs mothering. If the wife has been accustomed to going anywhere she pleases without regard to the needs of her husband, she now is tied down to the needs of the child. If there is another child in the home, the coming of this child means that the attention of the parents must be shared between the two children. From an economic point of view, the child increases the responsibility of the parents considerably and calls for a shift in their personal values. From a psychological point of view, the parents' concepts of themselves change perceptibly and they find it difficult to imagine what they were like before they had children. Therefore, parenthood may be either a cohesive or a disjunctive crisis in the life of an individual and a family.

In the affluent society of the present decade, several new dimensions of the crisis of birth have emerged.

First, the earlier marriage of young persons in high school, college, and professional school has presented the couple with the necessity for the deferment of parenthood in order that the wife might work to subsidize educational programs for the husband. This in turn has tended to confuse the roles of husband and wife at their formative stages. The fear of pregnancy and/or the apprehensiveness that the delay of the coming of children will result in their never having children causes both conflict and confusion between husband and wife.

Secondly, the necessity for birth control in such instances is specific, and at the same time preoccupation with multiple responsibilities for supporting the wife and any children who are born to the couple while they are in school produces fatigue and diffusion of identity. This in turn produces symptoms of sexual inadequacy in the husband as well as in the wife.

Thirdly, the exploding population is not all within the confines of marriage, for this decade continues to present unwed parents as persons who are denied the support, rituals, and respect which enable the wed parents to make more smoothly the transition into parenthood. In *Unmarried Mothers*, Clark Vincent tells us that in the United States from 1938 to 1958 the estimated annual number of illicit births increased from 87,900 to 208,700. The ratio of illicit births to total live births rose from 38.4 per 1,000 to 49.6 per 1,000, and the number of illicit births per year to each 1,000 unmarried women of childbearing age rose from 7.0 to 21.0. The families, the pastor, the doctor, the social worker, the home for unwed mothers, and the employers, are called upon to create a private society with rites of passage all its own for the care of the mother, the father, and the child. The adoptive parents stand in the wings of the stage on which this " audienceless " drama takes place, not able to see, but with everything at stake as to the outcome of the drama.

Finally, the church has tended to neglect the parents of the handicapped child. Destiny and desperation mingle indiscriminately with each other in these families. The literature of pastoral care on the care of such families in the crisis of birth has increased significantly since the publication of the first edition of this volume. Charles Kemp, *The Church: The Gifted and Retarded Child* (The Bethany Press, 1957), and Wayne E. Oates, *Where to Go for Help* (The Westminster Press, 1957), deal largely with the care of parents and their children. The winter issue, 1962 (Vol. XVI, No. 4), of *The Journal of Pastoral Care* is devoted to the religious nurture of disturbed children. The October, 1951, issue of *Pastoral Psychology* (Vol. 2, No. 17) deals with the relation between pastoral care and religious education and affords considerable insight into the pastor's relationship to children and their families.

The churches have always laid great store by the importance of children, and the Jewish and the Christian religions are as unique in their evaluation of children as they are in their concepts of God. As Luke describes the ministry of John the Baptist, the function of the prophetic religions has been "to turn the hearts of the fathers to the children" (Luke 1:17). Likewise, it may be said that the birth of a child has a way of turning the minds of some parents to a worshipful consideration of their own relationship to God. In other instances, the parents may become so emotionally involved with the child that they lose interest in everyone else. It is not unusual at all for a young couple to use the advent of a child as a reason for indifference to the church and other community activities. Such a family becomes ingrown upon itself, and the children themselves become objects of worship and in turn are expected to worship the parents.

Group instruction in family life education and individual pastoral attention can do much toward laying the foundation for a well-balanced parent-child relationship through the years. In fact, in all these crisis situations the church can effectively forestall undue stress and provide a common community understanding of the importance of crises through group work in the church. These groups also can be task-oriented groups, equipping the members of the fellowship to minister to each other and to those who are their neighbors, whether they are members of the church or not, during such times of stress. The April, 1955, issue (Vol. 6, No. 53) of *Pastoral Psychology*, edited by Paul E. Johnson, is devoted to the subject of group work in the church. Quite often a pastor is asked for specific information on child care and the emotional problems of children. Through close cooperation with his state board of health, the minister can have dependable insights and good literature to aid him in his pastoral care of young families. Pastoral visitation in the home and hospital, coupled with brief worship services of gratitude and dedication for parents and children, will be valuable for pastors in nonliturgical communions. In those communions where christening and baptism are used, the pastor will do well to lay hold of these significant occasions as opportunities to encourage the proper relationship between the child and his parents.

Religious Conversion

In the crisis of conversion the pastor serves as a minister of reconciliation, not between a child and his parents, but between an adult and the God and Father of our Lord Jesus Christ. Not all conversion experiences meet this definition; therefore, not all of them cause constructive changes in personality. Rather, many of them result in no changes at all, but merely perpetuate in different garb the same infantile character. In these cases, the conversion or pseudoconversion is an abortive, disintegrative miscarriage of creativity. It becomes a thorn in the flesh that cannot be assimilated into the rest of the personality, continuing as if it were entirely apart from the rest of the self. Such a projection of religious concepts into the mind, of religious practices into the habits, of religious values into the conscience, and of religious feelings into the affective depths of the personality increases the unhappiness and the lack of unity in the person. As one person has said, " My misery began when I was baptized."

But on the other hand, the fact remains that for many persons the conversion experience is the beginning of their true selfhood. They achieve spiritual autonomy by " getting their own religion " apart from that of their parents, which has been breathed for them in their mothers' lullabies. Their conversion points them into the direction of a happy vocational and marital choice and becomes that portion of their personality which arises at the very core of life. In a homely metaphor, this type of conversion experience becomes the stack pole around which the rest of the personality is organized. Allport has well described it by saying that such religious experience is a man's "audacious bid . . . to bind himself to creation and to the Creator, . . . his ultimate attempt to enlarge and to complete his own personality by finding the supreme context in which he rightly belongs." [11]

Probably the main determinant between these two kinds of conversion in any given case is the kind of spiritual relationship that existed between the person who is converted and his parents. Historically and psychologically the parents have always been the first pastors and priests of the individual. But next to the parents' determinative influence is the kind of pastoral care the individual receives from the minister of his church. The chaplains of state hospitals can tell the pastor a good deal about the part that pastoral neglect and malpractice can play in aggravating rather than healing mental disease at the crisis of conversion. No single factor is more determinative in quickening and strengthening personality growth and health than is the conversion experience that goes to the depths of the emotional life of a person. Wise pastoral care often makes the difference between an abortive and a creative conversion experience.

Since 1951 and the publication of the first edition of this book, considerable attention has been devoted to the pastoral care of persons at the time of conversion and the initial religious decision. This has been marked by a reappraisal of the evangelism that has characterized American Christianity in both its spontaneous and its institutional forms. One of the most used pieces of research has been Leon Salzman's article, "The Psychology of Religious Ideological Conversion," first published in *Psychiatry* (Vol. XVI, No. 2, May, 1953). He identifies two different kinds of conversion: (1) The progressive or maturational type of religious experience which "issues in the positive fulfillment of one's powers with self-awareness, concern for others, and oneness with the world." By "world" he means

[11] Gordon W. Allport, *The Individual and His Religion*, p. 142.

the realistic, everyday existence of human life. He does not mean " worldliness " in any moralistic use of the word. (2) The regressive, pathological conversion which is "a pseudo solution . . . brought about by increasing anxieties, and has a disjunctive effect on personality." This kind of conversion may either precipitate or be a part of a psychotic break with reality. Or, because of its defensive nature and the card of entry it gives to a similarly defensive religious group, such a conversion may ward off a psychosis.

Another group of studies of the care of religious converts was made by Harry M. Tiebout in his psychiatric treatment of alcoholics. In an article entitled " Conversion as a Psychological Phenomenon " (in the *Treatment of the Alcoholic*), Tiebout stresses the " conversion feature " in the recovery of persons in Alcoholics Anonymous. The positive function of religion is, he says, to " release the positive potential which resides in the unconscious." He says that an almost tangible wall, shell, or barrier " vanishes in [such] a conversion experience." Such an experience calls for the kind of " act of surrender " described in the Twelve Steps of AA.

During the fifth decade of this century, the study and application of pastoral care made two specific contributions to the ministry of evangelism itself. First, field studies of specific evangelistic crusades were made. This author did such a study of the Louisville Crusade of Billy Graham and his associates during the fall of 1956, where 439,859 persons attended and 8,189 commitments were made. One year later Palmer Bowers did a follow-up study of this group of commitments as a requirement for his master's degree in pastoral care. In 1960 Liston Mills studied a single church's evangelistic efforts more intensively as a part of his doctoral program.[12] Secondly, actual

[12] See *Evangelism and Pastoral Psychology*, Simon Doniger, ed. (Pastoral Psychology Press); Palmer Bowers, " An Evaluation of the Billy Graham Greater Louisville Crusade," unpublished master's thesis, Southern Baptist Theological Seminary, 1959; also Liston Mills, " Conversion Experiences in a Revival in the First Southern Baptist Church of Clarksville, Indiana," unpublished doctoral dissertation, Southern Baptist Theological Seminary.

clinical records of evangelistic work were made, evaluated, and
followed up carefully. The clinical method of teaching was
developed for the instruction and guidance of evangelists. William Oglesby published in the pamphlet *Evangelism and Pastoral Psychology* an article entitled "Evangelistic Results of
Effective Counseling," using the clinical record as a critical instrument for testing his approaches. John H. Boyle prepared a
master's thesis recording data on the pastoral care of new converts in a group situation.[13] The Presbyterian Church U.S.,
through its department of evangelism, developed a project for
the instruction of pastors in what was described as "personal
evangelism." The idea was to have small groups of pastors
study intensively actual interview material reported by the
pastors themselves in their evangelistic work.

These and many other studies in effective evangelism have
been made. One of the most comprehensive studies, however,
is that of Samuel Southard in his book *Pastoral Evangelism*. He
defines pastoral evangelism as the "dialogue in which the
Christian's actions and attitudes of loving care and righteous
discipline, empowered by the Holy Spirit, awaken a non-
Christian so that he will receive Christ as divine Savior and
Lord of his life in the Christian fellowship and in the world."[14]
This understanding of evangelism contrasts "instant evangelism" with the "pastoral patience" that takes into consideration
the total pilgrimage of the person, his history of encounter with
sin and grace, his family context, his vocational meaning in
life, and the durable relationships he builds with the fellowship
of believers of whom the pastor is one significant representative. Southard insists that the convert needs an adequate interpretation of his experience, recognition, and acceptance by
Christian people who become genuinely important to him, and
personal unburdening of the weights and sins that hinder him
as lively memories prior to his decision to be Christian. The

[13] John H. Boyle, "Group Dynamics in the Care of New Members,"
unpublished master's thesis, Southern Baptist Theological Seminary,
1955.
[14] Samuel Southard, *Pastoral Evangelism*, p. 8.

marriages tend to break up or the individuals within them become sick, depressed, or alcoholic. On the other hand, it is a
time of joy, celebration, and heartfelt achievement for those
who have effectively faced the previous developmental tasks of
life. The area of pastoral concern needs, for example, studies of
conversion in the age group of the forties and fifties similar to
those studies made by Starbuck with groups of college students.
The "late decider" for the Christian faith and the "late decider" for the Christian ministry offer fascinating areas of study
for a deeper understanding of the Christian faith. After all,
persons such as the apostle Paul, Augustine, Bunyan, George
Fox, and many other creative religious geniuses were in the
fullness of their years when they entered the depths of the
Christian faith.

In addition to the working mother and the couple whose
children are grown, the person facing retirement undergoes a
major crisis of separation, transition, and reunion in a new identity. Prior to World War II, retirement was a prerogative of the
privileged. The population was more distinctly rural. On the
farm, work in diminishing degrees is naturally possible. There
were fewer people who reached the age of sixty-five. But since
World War II, increasing numbers of persons from the upper-
lower, the lower-middle, the upper-middle, and the lower-
upper classes are retiring. Furthermore, by 1970 it is estimated
that more than 20,000,000 Americans will have passed the
sixty-five mark. For those for whom work has been the center
of meaning in life over and above the money that they earned,
the removal of work is the removal of meaning. This retirement
is for many today, especially in this affluent society where there
is a surplus rather than a wartime scarcity of working people,
a collapse of meaning and an encounter with nothingness. But
for those who have made adequate provision and preparation
for retirement, both spiritually and economically, retirement
can be a time of release, creative enjoyment, and productive
entree into the fruits of their labors. Effective pastoral care by
the fellowship of the church and disciplined understanding of
its ministers can make this difference.

The vocational heart of pastoral care addresses the most sensitive and perceptive emotions of the pastor to the quest for meaning in the lives of his people. He is concerned with what they are going to do with their lives at each point of arrival and departure in their developmental histories. He is concerned with the story of their manner of life in times past and asks them: " *Quo vadis?* " — " Where are you going? " The main direction of their lives as a whole is an ultimate concern, both to them and to their pastor.

Marriage

For people who take marriage seriously enough to consult a minister, it is a crisis. Traditionally marriage has been the concern of the churches, and even in the secular culture of today those who marry turn to pastors for religious sanction of the step they are taking. Marriage is a crisis, not only for the persons who are marrying but also for their parents and siblings. For this cause both the man and the woman leave their fathers and mothers, precipitating a radical reorganization of life both in their own lives and in the lives of the families from which they come. It seems almost ironical, but the family by its very nature was established with the ultimate biological and spiritual objective of being dissolved in order that new families might be formed.

Therefore all the early family relationships and parental training in religion are brought into focus at the time of marriage. The concept of the self of an individual undergoes marked changes. The routines of living of marital partners are transformed as they shift the centers of their attention from themselves to each other. Marriage brings religious values into bolder relief, and shows up the presence or absence of emotional stability with a fluoroscopic accuracy.

The minister may or may not function as a marriage and family counselor when young persons confer with him about wedding ceremonies. This depends upon his willingness to take the time to do so and his discipline of himself in the careful study of the principles and techniques of marriage and family counseling. When the pastor does this faithfully, he often makes the difference between a successful marriage and a failure. In other instances he can make the difference between an unhappy marriage and a happy marriage. The pastor who does not attempt to give family life education on a group level and marriage and family counseling on an individual level, however, has no right to preach against divorce. His own personal neglect may be directly responsible for the "hardness of heart" that made the writ of divorcement possible and even necessary.

The decision to marry is within itself a culmination of a series of meaningful and often joyful crises in itself. These crises are surrounded by many rites of separation, transition, and reunion. The process from friendship, through courtship, engagement, the wedding, and to the honeymoon represents the formation of a "covenant within a covenant." Here the individual moves into the crisis of what Erikson calls the tension between intimacy and isolation. The ministry to persons prior to the public announcement of an engagement and/or the wedding itself lays the foundation for effective pastoral ministry to couples in the more formal ministry of performing the wedding. The covenant of marriage is set within the covenant of the Christian faith itself when the wedding is performed as a ministry of the church and by the pastor as a representative of the church. Inasmuch as the church often has the families of either or both the bride and the groom in its fellowship, the minister has unique access to the whole fabric of the social relationships in which the marriage takes place.

Premarital pastoral care and counseling has moved through several stages since the early thirties. The depression years made the pastor exceptionally aware of the economic factors in marital happiness. The war years presented the strains of separation and impulsive decisions of young couples. The postwar years of inflation have presented the problems of the early marriage, the increase of premarital and extramarital sexual relationships, the social-status strivings of couples, and the conflict of marital aims with educational goals. Ministers have moved from the "bibliographical" approach to premarital counseling in which they asked for books on sex to hand to a couple. The doubtful value of this is becoming apparent to more and more ministers. They have tended in great numbers to lag in their progress by hanging on to the "statistical actuarial" approach to premarital pastoral care and counseling. By this I mean the use of sociological statistics which predict marital happiness on the basis of factors — such as differences of education, family background, social class structures, religious preference, and race — which have been demonstrated to be operative in much marital unhappiness. Increasing numbers of pastors, however, are beginning to probe the importance of less obvious factors that have the power to overcome even such differences as have been mentioned. Thoroughgoing education for marriage prior to marriage itself, submission to the disciplines of communication, creative clarification of an open covenant based upon an open-eyed awareness of each partner's weaknesses as well as his strengths, and a thoroughgoing commitment to each other in the context of a conscious commitment to Jesus Christ and the fellowship of believers are a few of these factors.

Likewise, the theological focus of the marriage relationship as the objective basis for a lasting covenant of marriage has become the predominant theme in pastoral approaches to the care of couples at the time of marriage. The work of D. S. Bailey, *The Mystery of Love and Marriage* (Harper & Brothers, 1952) set the tone for this approach. Gibson Winter, in his book *Love and Conflict* (Doubleday & Company, Inc., 1958) further enhanced this understanding with his discussion of "the covenant of intimacy." W. G. Cole presented a thorough historical analysis of the Christian understanding of marriage in his book *Sex in Christianity and Psychoanalysis* (Oxford University Press, London, 1955), and a similar study using the same historical approach as that of his previous volume was more recently done by D. S. Bailey in his book *Sexual Relations in Christian Thought* (Harper & Brothers, 1959). Two handbooks for ministers on premarital pastoral care and counseling were prepared, one by Granger Westberg, entitled *Premarital Counseling* and distributed by the National Council of Churches, and another by this author entitled *Premarital Pastoral Care and Counseling.*

The ethical and social dilemmas posed by the pastoral responsibility for the care of divorced persons, especially at the time of remarriage, have become an increasing concern of pastors in the last ten to fifteen years. Some of this concern has been spurred on by the conclusions of Kinsey and his associates as well as of Margaret Mead that one of the major forces in the development of divorce as a live option for the solution of marriage difficulties is the high degree of tentativeness with which people enter the covenant of marriage and the lack of simple determination to make this marriage work. Also, the studies of William J. Goode concerning 425 divorced women and the period following their divorces prompted closer attention to the pastoral care of divorced persons. Goode discovered a correlation in seven out of ten of the divorced women with the absence or brevity of an engagement period. He pointed out that first marriages are often training experiences in which people learn by trial and error how to make a second marriage a more effective one. In 84 percent of the cases he studied, the second marriage was apparently relatively stable and successful. Also, remarriage was demonstrated as a pattern, in that 94 percent of the divorced women aged thirty and below remarried within twenty-six months after divorce and 54 percent of the whole sample did so.[15] Seventy-one percent of the total sample received no counseling help at all.

Jesse Bernard also contributed to a realistic appraisal of the proportions of the problem of divorce in her study of remarriage. In her study, 14 percent of those divorced remained as a " hard core " of unassimilated, permanent divorcees, 33 percent were the " divorce prone " and were chronic recidivists in

[15] William J. Goode, *After Divorce* (The Free Press of Glencoe, 1956).

the divorce courts. But 53 percent remarried and demonstrated that they were "capable of at least average success in a marriage." [16]

The pastoral responsibilities for the divorced person become specific in the light of these studies: First, the church and its ministry are all the more responsible today for deepening a person's commitment, determination, and capability of establishing and maintaining durable, lasting human relationships of every kind, especially in the intimate covenant of marriage. Secondly, the church and its ministry are responsible for providing intensive preparation for marriage through carefully thought out plans of education, individual counseling, and forms of celebration of announcements of engagement, ceremonies of marriage, returns to the community after the honeymoon, the establishment of housekeeping either through renting or buying an apartment or house, and group fellowship during the critical first three years of marriage. Thirdly, the church and its ministry are responsible for developing a more private but nevertheless warm and accepting fellowship for persons who are divorced and prefer to remain this way rather than remarry. Fourthly, the church and its ministry are responsible for the rehabilitation of divorced and remarried couples in ways that neither compromise the integrity of the Christian ideal of marriage as a permanent covenant between two Christians nor consider the remarried persons as being sinners in a way that is either unpardonable or unique as contrasted with the other sinners in the fellowship of the forgiven. Fifthly, the church and its ministry are responsible for developing means of communication by which to discover marital discord before it has reached the point of no return, and for confronting persons who turn a second time to divorce, as a solution for marital trouble with their need for both personal repentance and professional therapy for the problems that beset them. In these latter incidences, the possibilities are high that marital discord is symptomatic of deeper personality disorders that are only further complicated by divorce. And, finally, the

[16] Jesse Bernard, *Remarriage*, pp. 107–108.

church and its ministry should be at work in relation to civil government and lawmakers in the development of civil laws that will contribute to the responsible solution of marriage difficulties by means other than easy divorce, such as requiring periods of waiting between procuring the license and marriage itself, and requiring a presentation of evidence of the absence of chronic mental disorders, chronic recidivism in the divorce courts, and such diseases as alcoholism, as well as other laws that would be devised on the basis of clinical studies such as those of Goode and Bernard.

Physical Illness

Sooner or later the crisis of illness enters most people's lives unless they die sudden or violent deaths. The physically ill person loses his independence and must lean on other people in a relative state of helplessness. He is shocked by the abruptness of pain, panicked by the thought of sustained helplessness or death, and confused by the opinions and procedures of the medical experts in whose hands rests his life. By his illness he may be isolated to a life of self-concern, and his mind searches in its loneliness for some explanation of the mystery of his suffering. He confronts the alternative of dealing constructively with these problems, or of adopting his illness as a chronic way of life. Here again is an either-or situation in which the individual and his family need the help of a skilled minister as they pass through the different stages of an illness.

The research of psychosomatically oriented physicians has established the fact that emotional tension and deeply rooted anxieties may cause, aggravate, or prolong an illness. Likewise, physical illness, even the sort requiring surgery, is often the prelude to psychotic disturbances.

The minister is expected to be a visitor of the sick, and the healing ministry is a part of the threefold commission of Jesus — to preach, to teach, and to heal. The Reformation marked the recovery of the preaching ministry from sacramentalism; the translation of the Bible into the vernacular marked the recovery of the teaching ministry from the monastery; now the development of clinical pastoral training and the closer cooperation of medicine and the ministry give promise to recover the healing ministry from the magic and superstition of relic worship and primitive faith-healing cults.

Many ministers look upon the visitation of the sick as a chore, dreading the discomfort of being around people who are helpless and in pain. But the minister who takes seriously the importance of physical and mental illness as spiritual crises of major proportions will find an effectual door of service and instruction set before him. He will become an original explorer into the laws of character that work themselves out before his eyes. He will be doing genuine laboratory work in the patient study of the facts of human nature.

1. *The separating power of illness.* The responsibility of the church and its ministry becomes most vivid in the care of the sick person in the decisive days prior to his hospitalization in a society in which going to the hospital has become a predominant pattern in the care of the sick. The patient-to-be is never diagnosed by the pastor, for diagnosis is the responsibility of those trained in differential diagnosis, i.e., the physician. However, the pastor is often a participant with the patient and the members of his family in evaluating whether or not the person is sick or well. This evaluation should be careful and specific. Determining whether a person is well or sick enough for a doctor to be called precedes medical diagnosis. The pastor can make this evaluation on the basis of careful observation of the basic functions of the person, i.e., working, eating, sleeping, accustomed daily routine, and effective communication with the significant persons in his realm of relationships. When a person ceases to work, eat, sleep, meet his scheduled appointments, and when he becomes isolated and uncommunicative with the significant persons of his life, such as father, mother, brother, sister, husband, wife, children, employers, one can safely asume that he is sick and needs a physician.

2. *The inner world of the patient.* A person is enabled to accept his identity as a sick person through all the rites of

separation that society uses to identify him as sick. He then has to come to grips with his own inner world as a sick person.

The minister who cares for physically ill persons quite often is a "stranger" to the inner world of the patient for whom he cares. He may not have ever had any severe illnesses himself, and may feel alien to the existing realities the patient is confronting. From my own experience as a surgical patient in something more than "routine" illnesses, and from my communication as a pastor and chaplain with many who have been sick, I would like to construct something of a descriptive psychology of the inner world of the patient who is suffering from real, organic physical pain.

The first thing to observe about any physically ill patient is that his normal life routine has been rudely disturbed by the advent of his disorder. Financially, his routine of earning and producing has been upset. Even if he is a salaried or professional worker whose "base pay" is not touched, in many instances those "extra sources" of income have been cut off. If he is a skilled laborer, working by the day, he is more seriously threatened financially. He may be quite concerned about his family, and even more agitated by his medical bills. On the other hand, if his basic desire is to avoid financial responsibility, he may cling to his illness as long as possible.

Furthermore, the life routine of a patient is disturbed in that he or she is separated from family and friends in an effectual and difficult way. The mother, or father, who has never been away from his or her children will find himself or herself at a loss without them. Homesickness, pure and simple, is one of the problems within the inner world of the patient.

The sexual routine of married patients is also interrupted. In short-term illnesses, this is not too serious, but it becomes acute in the long-term patient's life. He is thrown backward in his sexual adjustment. Patients in a tubercular sanitorium find themselves exceptionally concerned, for instance, as to what their wives or husbands will do, now that the sexual bond of their marriage has been severed for the duration of their illness. Victims of fatal diseases that cause them to linger, such as cancer and leukemia, realize with an inner sense of quiet desperation that the sexual part of their marriage is over. The advent of marital discord, infidelity, and even divorce in the midst of the illness of one member of the partnership is not an unusual thing as a result of this aspect of illness.

The untoward interruption of the routine of the individual reduces the physically ill patient to a state of helpless dependence. He may have been a person of great independence and one who carried an unlimited amount of responsibility. He may not have even been aware of his body, nor "have been sick a day in his life." He may have thought there was "no limit to the things he could do," and that he "could burn the candle at both ends," without penalty. But now "this thing" has "hit" him. He is rendered helpless and can only capitulate to the growing demands of a diseased body. He is now right back where he started as a baby — in a bed, made by a motherly and antiseptic nurse, unable even to feed himself and to control his own bodily functions. He resents this dependence at first and may become quite uncooperative and even obstreperous.

But as the heavy hand of pain, particularly in surgical operation procedures necessitating anesthetics and other drugs for the control of pain, clamps down on the patient, he becomes grateful for the right to this dependence. In the convalescent period, he may even hang on to his status as a sick person, reluctant to become the same independent person he always was. In a real sense, the physically ill patient undergoes some rather violent changes in his concept of himself. A man may be shaken in his self-confidence. He may, even after having returned to his normal routine, have an unsure hand as he makes decisions and accepts assignments in his work. A woman may become quite inadequate in her housework, in her care and control of her children, and in her role as a wife. A child may have disturbances in relating afresh to the play group and to the school situation.

The return to infantile dependence raises another constella-
tion of inner difficulties in the life of the physically ill patient.
States of unconsciousness, the effect of drugs, and the threats
to life all add together to cause old repressed and unsolved
emotional conflicts to return. In neurotic persons, the psychic
symptoms represent the return of the repressed difficulties. In
relatively mentally healthy persons, physical pain brings these
problems back. *Old* bereavements, *old* interpersonal aliena-
tions, *old* emotional deprivations come welling up for review.
Like the ghost of Hamlet's father, these problems "walk
again." As one patient told me, "All those people who have
long been dead are now alive again in my dreams." The listening ministry of a pastor or chaplain is of great value to the patient who feels the need to talk with an understanding person
as these remnants of old selves emerge for integration into the
conscious selfhood of the patient.

The core of all the inner struggles of the patient, however, is
the hard fact of physical pain itself. At this point, we are talking about primary pain, caused by real irritation of nerve endings, such as the pinching of central nerves by shattered verte-
brae. The cycle of pain needs careful attention from the point
of view of the patient's reaction.

The cycle of pain begins with the stimulation or irritation
of the nerve endings themselves. This is followed by shock:
pain hits the patient. It carries with it a stunning, blunting,
shocking effect. Theodore Reik says that shock is a primary
emotion, preceding others. Shock is followed by fear. The response of the patient is a fear reaction amounting to panic.
The whole emotional life of the patient is stampeded. This
reaction differs according to immediacy, amount of control,
and the degree of pain tolerance. The pain threshold in some
patients seems to be lower than in others. Some patients with
diseases accompanied by acute and prolonged pain seem to be
more aware of the pain than others. Prefrontal lobotomy, according to Donald Moore, M.D., of the Veterans Hospital,
Louisville, Kentucky, was given to sixteen patients in order to

lower anxiety over pain in incurable diseases.

The fear or panic reaction calls for a muscular tonicity of bracing against additional thrusts of pain. This tension predisposes the organism to more pain, finishing or closing the cycle: pain–fear–panic–tension–more pain. The need for relaxation is evident as a means of slowing down and eventually breaking the vicious circle. The importance, therefore, of a minister being a calm and steady presence for the patient stands out in bold relief at this juncture of his experience. All the means of relaxation at his disposal are of help to the patient.

Withal, the fact of pain brings to the patient's mind the possibility of death. The contemplation of death itself tends to populate the inner consciousness of the physically ill patient. He need not be seriously or critically ill; the illness itself is a reminder of his finitude, the shortness of life, the certainty of its end, and the necessity of its mortality. With many this contemplation takes on the character of an apprehensiveness, vague and undefined. With others it intensifies into a sense of dread and horror, and may even deepen into a panic that seriously militates against his recovery. With fatalistic persons, bludgeoned by circumstances or inner conflicts into a hopeless kind of despair, the thought of death may take on a definite intention *not to recover* at all. As many have said: "There is a line in most serious illnesses in which the simple will to live becomes a significant determinant of the prognosis of the patient."

The minister, representing confidence and hope that transcends even death itself, by incarnating that confidence and hope in his own way of life, can do much to alleviate the fear of death. As a representative of truth and reality, by being an incarnate spirit of honesty, he can give hope without glossing over the reality of death with superficial and banal reassurances.

The patient who knows intuitively that his minister is aware, if but tacitly aware, of the inner life which he must of necessity live feels understood. This understanding is the kind of redemptive presence that becomes in itself an aid to recovery.

The understanding *is* the therapy.[17]

The hospital is a specialized community for giving the patient a moratorium from the demands of society, for controlling the outside forces that affect him, and for bringing him into close supervision of doctors and nurses with the tools of diagnosis and therapy immediately at hand. A physician writing this would reverse this order of things. A minister, however, is concerned with the meaning of the spiritual moratorium of rest, protection, and freedom from demands which the hospital provides. A wise pastor has a high regard for the work of the doctors and nurses when he ministers to one of their patients. This specialized experience of the patient and his healing team, clearly focused upon the role of the pastor, has been dealt with at length, in detail, and with depth of perception in three important books: Richard Cabot and Russell Dicks, *The Art of Ministering to the Sick* (The Macmillan Company, 1937); Richard K. Young, *The Pastor's Hospital Ministry* (Broadman Press, 1954); and Joseph Fletcher, *Morals and Medicine* (Princeton University Press, 1954).

3. *The neglect of the convalescent patient.* Clinical pastoral education has emphasized the role of the pastor during the acute crises of the hospitalized patient's life. Not nearly enough attention has been paid to the more subtle situation of the patient who has reunited with his home, has begun to make decisions on his own about how much he will do, whether to follow his doctor's advice, and just how serious the illness was and is. This would be the time, also, when he would be free of the grogginess caused by anesthetics and pain-killing drugs, and the sense of helplessness that comes to people who are nauseated, running high temperatures, and unable to perform the simplest human functions of eating, excretion, etc., without the help of others. The convalescent period, for example, is a time of partial but limited functioning; many

[17] This material on the inner world of the patient was published as an article in the April, 1957, issue of *Pastoral Psychology* (Vol. 8, No. 73), pp. 16–18. This whole issue is devoted to "The Ministry to the Sick."

people do not assume that a psychiatric patient will need it just as surely as does a surgical patient. They will assume, and so will their families, that the psychiatric patient will be able to take up right where he left off before his hospitalization. The clinically trained pastor himself, not having seen these patients on a post-hospitalization basis, is likely to fall into this way of thinking. Yet the pastor is uniquely situated and responsible for developing rites of passage for the sick person as he moves back into the active community. He cannot, it seems, afford easily to neglect the patient when he is at home. Modern hospitalization procedures, for financial and other reasons, are at work getting the patient up sooner, and out more quickly. This means a longer time at home, when members of the family take over the nursing, the caring, the guiding of the patient.

Therefore, a church and its minister would do well to organize a close-knit study group of which the minister himself would be the teacher and leader. Carefully they can gather basic information as to the situation and needs of the patient. They can cooperate with the physicians of the patient; they can wisely plan as to the responsibility of the church and its ministry. More intimate consultation with the family as to their wishes and needs would be the work of this " task force " in the ministry to the sick. Other trained and specially skilled persons in the church, such as teachers, doctors, social caseworkers, nurses, and people who themselves have successfully dealt with major illnesses should be a part of this healing force. The patient at all stages of his illness could be undergirded by a known fellowship, guided by a more objective wisdom than his own, and reunited with his responsible community upon recovery. The amount and kind of visitation during his hospitalization could be governed more effectively for the patient's good and to the relief of doctors and nurses. The rites of reunion — such as preparation of meals by various families when the mother of a family happens to be the sick person; recording of worship services that take place at the church and can be brought into the home on a portable recorder; processes of more formal pastoral counseling with the individual by the pastor and/or other appropriate persons – can be developed by the caring community in bridging the gap between the person's identity first as a sick person and later as a recovered person.

Some would ask whether the psychiatric patient is not an exception to all that has been said here. The answer to this is no. All these things apply more especially to him or her and in greater degree. The basic principles of the caring community and the counseling pastor at work are the same. The rehabilitation of the mentally ill person is all the more significant. State departments of mental health are developing cultural "halfway" houses for bridging the gap between hospitalization and function in an open society. In the author's own city there is such an agency, known as Bridgehaven, where patients can work during the day and be cared for by doctors and nurses at night. Other facilities are available for caring for patients during the day and letting them spend the evening with their family. The church at work healing could do much more in the compassionate realization of the healing strength of a caring community in the transitional crisis of convalescent mentally ill persons. But the point here is that the basic issues are the same with people with all manner of function-interfering diseases. No clean line can be drawn between mental and physical illness. However, specific attention has been given by this author to the pastoral care of the mentally ill in his book *Religious Factors in Mental Illness*. Of course, the classical work on the care of the mentally sick is that of Anton Boisen, *The Exploration of the Inner World*. Both these books were based on research done within the confines of the hospital. What this decade most urgently needs is attention to the care of the mentally ill person who either never goes to a hospital, is under private psychiatric care on an ambulatory, outpatient basis, or has been to a hospital and has returned to the community. Here is the point at which the Christian pastor both sees the patient more often and therefore has more responsibility for his care.

Bereavement

Another crisis comes into the life of every person who takes the risk of loving someone other than himself. The course of normal grief at the loss of a loved one extends over a more lengthy period of time than is ordinarily assumed. It moves through stages of shock; numbness of feeling which seems to have organic involvements as well as psychic ones; a refusal to accept the reality of the death of the loved one; a period of semiconscious fantasy along with a selective memory of events that happened in relation to the loved one; a gradual return of feeling and a flood of grief; and a transference of feelings to a new object of affection.

The Christian community has intuitively provided ways and means of ministering to bereaved persons, and the pastor can depend upon the help of his congregation in the care of bereaved persons. Unusually powerful guilt feelings are quite often at work in bereavement, and subtle deifications of the dead loved one can cause the bereaved person to become mentally ill.

The pastor is the only trained person into whose hands the care of the bereaved is wholly committed at the time of the crisis. He has no competition here from other professions. His message of immortality and the transcendence of the eternal over the temporal is the only "renewal" of the minds of the grief-stricken that can transform them. The pastor becomes a traveler between life and death with his parishioners at these times, guiding them through the valley of the shadow of death. He cannot leave this ministry to professional mourners and morticians. He has been appointed "to comfort all that mourn; . . . to give unto them a garland for ashes, the oil of joy for mourning, the garment of praise for the spirit of heaviness; that they may be called trees of righteousness, the planting of the Lord, that he may be glorified" (Isa. 61:2-3, ASV).

One of the pioneer studies of grief that has been most used by pastors and professional persons of every kind was that by Erich Lindemann, a psychiatrist. This study was done during

World War II and made note of the "enormous increase of grief reactions due to war casualties." However, it was also based upon studies of civilian grief reactions after the death of over seven hundred persons in a nightclub fire disaster. Lindemann identified four basic principles in the life situation of the bereaved person: (1) Acute grief is a definite syndrome of both psychological and somatic symptoms. (2) These symptoms may appear immediately after a crisis, they may be delayed, or they may be exaggerated or apparently absent. (3) In the place of the typical syndrome, distortions may occur that represent one special aspect of the total malaise of the person. (4) Appropriate treatment can transform these distorted pictures of grief into a normal grief reaction with a creative resolution of the grief situation itself.[18] The pastor will appreciate the specific signs of pathological grief which Lindemann identified: unusual somatic distress, preoccupation with the appearance and image of the deceased, marked feelings of guilt, hostile reactions that are inappropriate, and a disruption of the basic patterns of conduct and routine of the individual.

An older study of grief, however, gives additional depth and breadth to the pastor's appreciation of the nature and importance of his ministry to the bereaved person. David Martin Fulcomer used the empirical case study method of research in his evaluation of the types of responses of seventy-two persons in various stages in the process of grief. He concluded that from a psychosocial point of view, there are four phases in the process of grief.[19] Fulcomer says that there are: (1) The immediate stage of grief, in which a person may react in any one of at least four different ways: dazed, stoic, lachrymose, or collapse. (2) The post-immediate stage, which begins with the funeral arrangements and continues until the end of the

[18] Erich Lindemann, " Symptomatology and Management of Acute Grief," *The American Journal of Psychiatry*, Vol. 101 (Sept., 1944), pp. 141–148.
[19] These phases, as will be noted, telescope and include the six phases mentioned earlier in this discussion and elaborated in detail in the book, *Anxiety in Christian Experience* (The Westminster Press), published by this author in 1955.

funeral service when everyone else has gone to his own home and left the person alone with his other family members and his regular routine of life to face. (3) The transitional phase, which begins after the funeral service and the return of friends and more distant relatives to their places and continues until acceptable adjustive patterns become established and integrated into the total pattern of life. Here the bereaved person may take a "trial and error" approach to adjustment, adopting one of several patterns in relation to his meaningful community: alternating (between participation and withdrawal, for example), enforced collaboration, or attention-getting. (4) The repatterning stage, which represents the formation of definite patterns of behavior of a durable and lasting kind.[20]

In these four stages, one sees the importance of the shaping environment of the Christian fellowship become evident. The church is a fellowship of celebration, comfort, thanksgiving, and confession and cleansing. It provides rites, customs, habits of helping, and through these protects the individual mourner and his family from isolation, meaninglessness, and impulsive decisions during each stage of grief. The basic premise of James N. Carlin in another depth study of practices of pastoral care in times of bereavement is that damage is done to persons when these rites and patterns of interpretation become stereotyped and standardized to such an extent that they produce a stalemate of ambivalence in the mourner rather than a spontaneous, growing experience of maturity through the freedom from idolatry of the dead. Ambivalence of feeling — i.e., contradictory emotions about the same person — is the key to understanding grief. If the person denies his negative feelings as well as extols his positive feelings toward the dead, he will develop stereotyped patterns of behavior that prevent his functioning in relation to both God and man. Therefore, the acceptance and encouragement of insight into these conflictual feelings by the pastor is a basic principle for the pastoral care of the bereaved. This more recent contribution makes more

[20] David Martin Fulcomer, "A Socio-Psychological Study of Bereavement," unpublished doctoral thesis, Northwestern University, 1926.

specific the previously well established principle of the care of the bereaved, namely, that it is a dynamic process and one that must be "worked through." [21] Paul Irion, in one of the standard works on the care of the bereaved, proposes the *personal* function of the funeral as one of the rites of passage that we use in the care of the bereaved rather than as a stereotyped ritual of an established order without due regard for the variable elements of the persons to whom it should be designed to minister.[22]

Yet in every funeral, there is one constant: it is the reminder that each one of us faces under God the crisis of death ourselves. In this, our universal kinship as human beings is most obvious. In this does the "eternal qualitative difference between God and man" become more than just a Kierkegaardian quotation. It becomes a matter of life and death.

Death

No one is exempt from the crisis of dying. The ministry to the dying, as they are surrounded by their family, is inseparable from the ministry to the bereaved. It, however, is one of the most intensely personal and individualized services that a pastor renders. The dying person's request for the pastor's time and attention takes precedence over all other requests, and the pastor should feel deep gratitude for the honor of being sent for at this final crisis of a person's life.

The minister needs to recognize the fact that many persons may be said to die mentally before they do physically. The presence of heart action and respiration are not indications of the presence of mind. The weight of sedation, the weariness of the struggle with pain, and the presence of infection in the organism militate against rationality in a dying person.

Furthermore, the person who is aware of impending death is quite often more concerned about his loved ones than about himself. Barriers that exist between him and those whose ap-

[21] James N. Carlin, "Grief Work and Pastoral Care Practices of Baptist Ministers," unpublished doctoral dissertation, Southern Baptist Theological Seminary, 1963.
[22] Paul E. Irion, *The Funeral and the Mourners,* p. 170.

proval he considers most worthwhile are problems to him. He is anxious about what will happen to them when he is gone, especially if some of them are small children.

Quite regularly the pastor is called upon to listen to the confession of the secret sins of dying persons, because they are concerned with middle walls of partition that separate them from God. The need for confessional ministry, although not formalized, remains an abiding reality in the spiritual hunger of the dying. Here, also, the pastor shares in the radiant pilgrimage that triumphant Christians make from mortality into immortality. To him are granted glimpses into eternity, in spite of his childlike blunders in the use of God's instruments of redemption.

In his ministry to the dying, the pastor drives a hard course between being evasive, dishonest, and falsely reassuring on the one hand, and leaving the patient to carry his possible awareness of the imminence of death all alone, on the other hand. The pastor walks an equally narrow ridge between being candid, honest, and open with the patient about the seriousness of his condition, and speaking with authority and assurance on an issue of which he is not certain. In doing the latter, he may remove every vestige of hope the patient has for continuing to live. Thus this ministry calls for some basic principles that take into consideration the ambiguities that have just been mentioned. These principles have been developed in careful studies by pastors and teachers with much patience in the face of death.

The first principle is close cooperation and dialogue with members of the family. They should be taught to listen carefully to what the patient says and to follow the lead of what he himself says and surmises about his condition. They can admit with the patient that the situation is critical and serious without simply throwing away every semblance of hope. The second principle is an even closer dialogue with the physicians caring for the patient. They can provide the minister with a clinical understanding of the particular patient's personal and medical history, his capacity to accept the realities of life and of death, and his basic patterns of emotional reaction. The particular patient may be depressed, hostile, withdrawn, apathetic, suspicious, dependent, ambition-driven, etc. The effects of these emotional reactions to the knowledge of the nature of his disorder and the shortness of his remaining life must be assayed clinically in consultation with the physicians. No static, inflexible rule of thumb should be applied in caring for a dying person. This is one time when a person has a right to the dignity of his own individuality and to the integrity of his own selfhood.

A third principle of the pastoral care of the dying involves the *private* relationship of the pastor as a representative of the people of God to the dying person. Groups can do much for the person: a Sunday school class can write notes, the care of the children of a young mother can be scheduled, protection can be provided from the disorder of many well-intentioned but undisciplined visitors who insist on being morbid, etc. The family can be pulled together or apart by such a crisis, particularly if they are anxious for the goodwill of the person toward them concerning his or her " last will and testament." People in the place of employment can provide security in terms of attention to the ongoing care of the family, etc., or they can be in deadly competition with one another for the man's place at work. But the sensitive and wise pastor needs to copy the approach of the Lord Jesus Christ, who often even sent people out of the room when he cared for critically ill persons. This can be arranged ahead of time, in order that people will know that a pastor wants to talk with the person alone. In this atmosphere of privacy, apart from the ears of those whom he or she loves, fears, or feels totally responsible for, the person can tell the pastor how he or she feels, what intimations of life and death have come to him or her. In these quiet moments of self-confrontation I have discovered that persons facing death drop many of the cultural subterfuges of life and communicate with the pastor concerning their deepest thoughts, their past history of fulfillment and failure, and their personal attitudes toward God. Therefore, the creation of a permissive privacy is a basic principle. Arnold Hutschneker quotes a surgeon, Dr. Frank Adair, with whom I would also agree: "The dying patient usually knows his condition and at the end is glad to go. This seems to be especially true of those patients who have deep religious convictions." [23]

Finally, the epigenetic principle of pastoral care is never more vivid than in the care of the dying. A pastor cannot make up to a dying patient for the absence of relationship in previous years by becoming compulsively concerned about his salvation all of a sudden. This has been tragically reflected in the reports of attempts to convert Adolf Eichmann, which appeared in the public press on March 2, 3, and 4, 1963. The dismal results of these efforts point to the absence of confrontation at major teachable moments in the spiritual pilgrimage of Eichmann.

From birth to death and at every significant point between, the Christian pastor is commissioned by Christ and expected by his community to bring the mind of Christ and the reality of the Holy Spirit to bear upon the crises that people face. Several crises have been described here. Others, less universally confronted, but nevertheless acutely meaningful to those who do experience them, could be named. Social crises of war, famine, flood, and fire assail people en masse. Divorce and mental illness are crises of family and personal disorganization that are increasing in prevalence.

The pastor, along with all others engaged in humanitarian tasks, is a man of crisis for such times as these. Having inherited such a ministry, he can conserve his birthright and add to it his own personal spiritual fortune by assimilating all that modern research has to offer him in discipline and technique and by understanding Biblical truth in terms of human needs. Thus he "brings out of his treasure what is new and what is old" (Matt. 13:52).

[23] Arnold A. Hutschneker, "Personality Factors in Dying Patients," *The Meaning of Death,* Herman Feifel, ed. (McGraw-Hill Book Co., Inc., 1959), p. 238.

Chapter II

The Symbolic Role
of the Pastor

The Christian pastor enters the responsibilities of his crisis ministry in the strength of the oldest calling among men. His role and function as a minister have been, through centuries of Christian culture, bred into the deeper levels of the consciousness of those whom he serves. Therefore, he has symbolic as well as personal influence, and the symbolic power of his role gives him a strength far beyond that of his own personal appeal to people. Paul described it well when he said, "We are ambassadors for Christ, God making his appeal through us" (II Cor. 5:20). The pastor represents and symbolizes far more than himself. He represents God the Father; he serves as a reminder of Jesus Christ; he is a follower of the leading of the Holy Spirit; he is the emissary of a specific church; and he symbolizes the caricatures of the Christian faith to those who are hostile, suspicious, and/or detached from the Christian faith, but nevertheless he is a shepherd to the non-Christian as well as to those who are in the church.

This symbolic influence elevates the importance of the unique structure and function of a pastor's interpersonal relationships with people. It places in proper perspective the specific techniques of pastoral care and personal counseling and reveals the inadequacy of stereotyped advice in given situations. The careful, intelligent, and devoted management of the unique interpersonal relationship of a pastor to an individual or group becomes the normative definition of pastoral care and

43

personal counseling. As such, the pastoral task is the participation in the "divine-human encounter."

All this implies a Christian context of basic theological axioms for pastoral care and personal counseling. The sovereignty of God, the principle of incarnation whereby the Word was made flesh, the activity of the Holy Spirit in contemporary living, and the function of the church as the body of Christ — these are the realities that the pastor symbolizes and represents. In pastoral care and personal counseling they become functional realities rather than theoretical topics of discussion. The analysis, therefore, of the symbolic role of the pastor provides an interpretation of his relationship to people in terms of his relationship to God. Such an approach gives a *theological framework for pastoral care and personal counseling.* Such a framework is needed lest the strength of secular concepts of counseling and psychotherapy force the pastor into a role and a relationship that are foreign to his unique place in society and in history.

Since the publication of the first edition of this book, much attention has been directed toward the theological foundations of the role and function of the pastor. The church has been described by H. Richard Niebuhr as a community of memory and hope sharing in the memory of Jesus Christ and of the God of Israel, " united by its direction toward one God, who is Father, Son, and Holy Spirit." [1] The purpose of the church and its ministry is " the increase of love of God and neighbor," and the pastor both embodies and communicates that love. This love is a rejoicing and celebrating of the presence of both God and neighbor. It is gratitude for God and neighbor. It is reverence that " keeps its distance even as it draws near, neither seeking to absorb the loved one nor being willing to be absorbed by the loved one." This love is loyalty, i.e., the " commitment of the self by a decision of self-binding will to make the other great." But the pastor does not have this kind of love to offer apart from the grace of God that bestows God's own unmerited love

---

[1] H. Richard Niebuhr, *The Purpose of the Church and Its Ministry,* p. 23.

upon the pastor. The reality that holds the pastor together as a person and keeps him at his task is the generative love of God. As Niebuhr says, "Love to this God is the conviction that there is faithfulness at the heart of all things: unity, reason, form, and meaning in the plurality of being." [2]

Yet when we say that the pastor is a "man of God" and an "ambassador for Christ," what kind of authority does this give him and how shall it be exercised? How can he exercise this "authority" without either losing his sense of urgency and commitment, on the one hand, and without becoming an authoritarian "pusher" of the ecclesiastical trappings of his social position? The authority of the minister does not arise from his relation to civil government, from his accrued education, or from his participation in a certain social class. These are incidental to his real authority as a representative of God, of Christ, and of the Holy Spirit. Rather, as Niebuhr again says, "Ministers have derived their immediate authority to preach and teach, lead worship, care for souls, and perform their other offices from the church and from Scripture." [3] But more basically than this, they derive their authority from having experienced themselves the gospel as the good news of God in Jesus Christ and, in a sense, from being eyewitnesses of that which they declare to others.

It is one thing to discuss authority and its sources in the minister's life, but it is another to see this functionally. Just how does the minister exercise this authority as a "man of God" and as an "ambassador of Jesus Christ"? He does so as a man of faith, who has evidence for things that are not seen, the things which, amid the shaking of the foundations of men's lives, remain as that which cannot be shaken. The actual power of his identity arises, not even from the conferring of status by the church or from some factual knowledge of the Scripture, although neither of these is to be considered lightly or indiscreetly. Rather, as Daniel Day Williams says: "The authority of the Christian . . . to speak and act as a representative of

[2] Ibid., p. 37.   [3] Ibid., p. 70.

God's forgiveness and his healing power, is given only through the actual exercise of the pastoral office. Real personal authority arises out of the concrete incarnation of the spirit of loving service which by God's help becomes present in the care of souls. And this means that ministerial authority can be lost as well as won." [4] This was the witness of our Lord Jesus Christ, the Good Shepherd, when the disciples of John asked if Jesus were " he who is to come." Jesus said: " Go and tell John what you hear and see: the blind receive their sight and the lame walk, lepers are cleansed and the deaf hear, and the dead are raised up, and the poor have good news preached to them." (Matt. 11:2-6.) The very authority of a minister, then, rests in his exercise of his office, and, as with his bodily health, he loses this authority unless he participates in the full exercise of his preaching, teaching, and caring ministries. Let us consider the dimensions of these exercises of the man of faith.

The Pastor as a Representative of God

Late one evening a minister received a call to come to a ward in the local hospital. Upon arrival he found an elderly farmer who had just been admitted. The man looked frightened and lonely, but a natural sense of humor welled up from beneath his anxiety. The minister introduced himself, and the patient said: " I heard that you would come if I asked for you. It's mighty kind of you, because I need you. You have heard that story in the Bible about how some fellows was cutting wood one day and the ax flew off the handle and fell in the river. They had to call the man of God to help them get it out. Well, I sure have had the ax to fly off the handle with me. I never been sick a day in my life, and all of a sudden things went wrong and they told me that I have cancer of the colon. I got to be cut on Monday morning. The ax has come off the handle with me, and when the nurse told me that a man of God was close by, I sent straightway for you to help me get the ax out of the creek."

[4] Daniel Day Williams, *The Minister and the Care of Souls.*

People like this man still search out Christian pastors when they need friendship, encouragement, guidance, reconciliation, and relief from guilt. They seek their pastor because he is the man of God; he symbolizes the presence of God as a loving Father and as the center of all moral rightness. People of every condition turn to the minister because he represents the universal gospel of the eternal God. This universality means something more than geographical inclusiveness; it also means that *all* manner of people come to the Christian minister with *all* manner of problems. The Christian pastor, therefore, cannot select his clientele; he cannot eliminate those whose plight does not come under the classification of his speciality; neither can he pass hopeless cases to someone else. Regardless of the other ministers to humanity who may be serving his people (whether those servants be doctors, nurses, lawyers, social workers, psychiatrists, welfare workers, or public-school teachers), the pastor, by virtue of his role as a man of God, can never consider his people as being some other person's responsibility to the exclusion of his own. *He cannot pass his ministry to anyone else.* This is the distinctive difference between the Christian pastor as a servant of men and other people who are also engaged in humanitarian helpfulness.

The Christian pastor, then, is a representative of God, commissioned to bring the ruling sense of the presence of God to bear upon the conflict-weary lives of men and women. He is an apostle of redemption and reconciliation, a practicer of the art of communion with God (II Cor. 5:20). As such, the pastor is concerned with the salvation of the *whole* personalities of his people through an effective relationship to God in Christ rather than with the readjustment of this or that part of their lives.

As a representative of God, the minister is a reminder of all the parental training in the ways of right doing that his people received in childhood. These precepts, regardless of their truth or error, have become incorporated parts of their psychic lives. Consequently, the minister may find persons reacting to him in much the same way they did to their parents, and equating the precepts of their parents with the wisdom of God. The minister confronts the task of disentangling the good gifts of parents to their children from the much more excellent gifts of the Heavenly Father that are available through a personal experience of the Holy Spirit. Through this personal experience, religious experience becomes firsthand and intimately personal rather than traditional and customary.

Again, the minister, as a representative of God, becomes a visible embodiment of *conscience*. Therefore many will draw the fig leaves of respectability over the naked places of their souls lest their minister come to know them as they really are. By its very nature, the role of the minister is a judgmental role, and he cannot avoid the fact that a moralistic connotation is placed upon his presence. Every pastor, therefore, needs to avoid the error of thinking that the persons with whom he counsels appear in the same spiritual clothing to him that they do to those to whom they are more closely related. The minister's task is to discover the real selves of his people and to be the kind of minister with whom they can associate without pretension. At the same time, suffice it to say, the quiet dignity of a minister's own presence is often more of a rebuke to his people than any verbal censure he could pour upon them.

The strange power of a judgmental presence reminds the Christian pastor of his ever-present temptation to *supplant* rather than to represent God. A minister may easily be lured into substituting his own sovereignty for that of God, " in order that the excellency may be of himself rather than of God." The matchless insights of Hawthorne in *The Scarlet Letter* and Maugham in *Rain* are subtle reminders that the minister too is human and not divine. His relative degree of authority is derived by reason of the One whom he symbolizes; therefore his greatest temptation is to assume that it originated with himself, to confuse the symbolism of his role with the reality of God.

Within the personality of every individual who turns to the pastor for help is the active tendency to make a god out of the minister, with an unconscious need to idolize and desecrate him at the same time. This has been called the " unreal need for a god in human form." [5] One way the minister may give in to this idolatrous demand is to require strict conformity to his will and to the ideas that he gives to his people in the form of advice. A very common daydream of ministers is that of seeing their people do just as they want them to do, seeing their own wills incarnated in the lives of their people. As Oscar Wilde describes this feeling, " There is something enthralling in projecting one's soul into someone else's gracious form, and letting it tarry there for a moment, to hear one's own intellectual views echoed back; to convey one's temperament into another as though it were some strange and subtle perfume." [6]

Another way a minister may substitute his relative authority for the sovereignty of God in the lives of his people is to use them as means for his own chosen ends rather than treating them as ends in themselves by reason of the fact that they are sacred human personalities " for whom Christ died." Thus the pastor may let his function as an administrator, a builder of an organization, a promoter of a budget, or the leader of a crusade come into conflict with his representation of God. He must become a god himself in order that he may manipulate his people toward his own predestined goal.

This is simply one form of idolatry. Charles Stinnette has related the problem of idolatry to the care of disturbed and unhappy persons in a precise way. He says: " Polytheism was the conscious problem of the ancient world, and it is the unconscious problem of our age. In the necessity of living through anxiety, man seeks the god of his salvation; and the crucial question is whether he worships idols or that God alone who saves him by restoring him to genuine freedom and selfhood in relatedness." [7] The bereaved husband or wife makes an idol of the departed loved one. The husband and wife who cannot

[5] Otto Rank, *Will Therapy; and Truth and Reality* (Alfred A. Knopf, 1945), p. 63.
[6] *The Picture of Dorian Gray* (The World Publishing Company, 1942), p. 38.
[7] Charles Stinnette, *Anxiety and Faith* (The Seabury Press, 1955), p. 178.

have children become obsessed with this inability to the point that the whole organism is out of balance. The person who has been fired from his job organizes his life around the failure to win his point. The professional person makes his profession his god, spirit, and church. In each case, the life is thrown into shock from the wrongness of its center. Also, the moralistic systems of a legalistic faith can become a possessing idol. To someone with this faith, the minister represents the "seared" or "darkened" conscience.

Also, a minister may yield to pressure and make his people's decisions for them; in doing so, he, like Jiminy Cricket, becomes their official conscience for them. He takes responsibility away from them, which means that he takes their freedom from them and enslaves himself with them. The minister's task is to cooperate in the growth of human personalities that have been born of God. An individual does not become a person in his own right until he has exercised his own free powers of decision, and accepted the responsibility for the consequences of his decisions. As the Christian pastor stands in the holy of holies of men's souls, they may say to him, "You tell me what to do, and then I know it will be right." If the pastor gently but firmly moves this responsibility back to them and increases their confidence in their own ability to find the way of God, later he may have them come back and say to him, "All my life I have had people tell me what to do, and when they did, it seemed that almost against my own will I found myself doing just the opposite from the advice they gave me."

Something strong in human personality reaches out for an idol, but something eternal in human personality that outlasts both the idol and the desire for the idol says, "Cast down imaginations and everything that exalts itself against the knowledge of God." The unreal need for a god in human form clutches at the minister's desire to supplant God, but if he yields himself to this need, he in turn becomes an idol cast down when those whom he exploits discover that he also is human.

Therefore, the Christian pastor's objective is to free persons from bondage to their own self-reflections in the mirrors of their chosen idols and to bring them into a life-giving loyalty to Christ. In this drastic cutting of affectionate bonds, they are likely to shift their idolatry to the pastor, saying as did the people at Lystra and Derbe, " The gods have come down to us in the likeness of men! " All the while they may still be sitting on their own household gods just in case they are wrong. Thus a person's own attitude toward the concept of the sovereignty of God becomes a continuously thrown down gauntlet before the minister. If he lets it go unchallenged and accepts the dependent worship of the person, the last state is worse than the one before. If the minister accepts the challenge and refuses the prerogatives of God, then he faces a struggle with his own childish desires for omnipotence.

To symbolize the reality of God, therefore, calls for a unique kind of dedication. The Christian pastor knows that he has the treasure of his ministry in an earthen vessel. Insight into the earthenness of his own humanity prompts him to confess that the excellency of the power is of God and not of himself. David E. Roberts clarifies the issues confronting the pastor when he says:

> The danger of " playing God " in the lives of people, which certainly must not be minimized, should not blind us to the fact that men can be instruments in the service of healing power. The endowments and skills of the therapist as an individual are immeasurably enhanced by the fact that he is the symbol of something much greater than himself — namely, the drive toward fellowship, wholeness, and honesty which is deeply rooted in human life.[8]

The security of the pastor arises out of his dependence upon the Chief Shepherd rather than from the completeness of his knowledge, the power of his own personality, or the cleverness of his techniques in dealing with people. He finds guidance for his pastoral practice in the Chief Shepherd, " who, though he

[8] David E. Roberts, *Psychotherapy and a Christian View of Man*, p. 53.

was in the form of God, did not count equality with God a thing to be grasped, but emptied himself, taking the form of a servant, being born in the likeness of men. And being found in human form he humbled himself and became obedient unto death, even death on a cross" (Phil. 2:6-8).

Just such a renunciation lies at the base of all effective representation of God. Paul describes it best when he says, "We have renounced disgraceful, underhanded ways; we refuse to practice cunning or to tamper with God's word, but by the open statement of the truth we would commend ourselves to every man's conscience in the sight of God" (II Cor. 4:2).

The Pastor as a Reminder of Jesus Christ

"God . . . has shone in our hearts to give the light of the knowledge of . . . God in the face of Christ." (II Cor. 4:6.) The pastor is related to people "as though it were in Christ's own stead." It is his personal motive to have in himself the mind that was in Christ Jesus. The request of the Greeks when they said, "We wish to see Jesus," is the unspoken need of those to whom the Christian pastor ministers. He symbolizes and reminds them of Jesus Christ. More recently, the Christological heart of pastoral care has taken precedence in the theological discussions of pastoral care. Daniel Day Williams says that the objective reality "which stands between persons is God made personal and available to us in Jesus Christ." In the pastoral relationship, both pastor and parishioner seek a true knowledge of who they are. As Williams says, "Christ is the person who discloses us to ourselves." More than this, Christ is the New Man "who opens the way to what we can become. . . . Christ is the Third Man in every human relationship." [9] He is the One who relates us to our individual and corporate sin, confronts us in our personal decisions about what we are doing with our lives, and separates us from sin, transiency, and disillusionment through the challenge of the power of his death, burial, and resurrection. Christ is the one through whom the minister is

[9] Daniel Day Williams, *op. cit.*, p. 67.

emboldened to exercise his office as a caring pastor. He bears witness, not to his own somewhat meager powers to accept, but to the acceptance he has received and can now communicate to the person to whom he ministers in Christ's name.

The sacrifice of Christ as our High Priest both creates and re-creates right relations between God and man. Christ's sacrifice removes what wastes away man's integrity, namely, his sin. Because of this forgiveness, the pastor is able to minister in Christ's name. As Hebrews puts it:

> For every high priest who is chosen from among men and appointed to act for men towards God, offering gifts and sacrifices for sins, is able to deal gently with the ignorant and the mistaken, because he himself is ringed around with weakness. And for this reason he must make offerings for sins, not only for the people but for himself also (Heb. 5:1-3, Williams Translation).

But this affectionate permissiveness does not mean that there is no serious confrontation, honest criticism, and appeal to a higher source of judgment. The Christian fellowship, of whatever denomination, rests upon a covenant. This covenant is the horizontal dimension of the basis of our mutual judgment of one another's acts. Within this covenant, there is a *ground* of communication for developing mutually understood personal covenants with individuals and small groups. These covenants are made, revised, and renewed through the processes of human life and interaction. But underneath all of them is the basic covenant in which we are *bound* to treat each other as "persons for whom Christ died." Christian love within this covenant can become cleansingly but not painlessly honest, as the instructions for Christian conversation set forth in Matt., ch. 18, reveal. But the whole pastoral relationship is, as Eduard Thurneysen says, "characterized by a movement of accepting and taking away, of comprehending and apprehending and analyzing the human facts and submitting these facts to a wholly new judgment surpassing any human judgment." [10]

[10] Eduard Thurneysen, A *Theology of Pastoral Care*, p. 132.

And, as Thurneysen says further, "We accept the facts in the secure knowledge that the forgiveness of sins through the Word of God must become effective in these facts." [11]

Thus we come to look upon ourselves as reminders of the Word of God, Jesus Christ, who is not just an example to be emulated under vastly different and impossible circumstances, but a living Christ who has returned to us in the gift of the Father of the Holy Spirit. Therefore, the central objective of all *pastoral* care and personal counseling is that "Christ be formed" in the personality of the individuals who seek help.

Therefore, the principle of incarnation in continued action requires that the Christian pastor be a man of faith, "working through love." Hereby the minister becomes a permissive shepherd who loves his sheep rather than a pseudosovereign who rules his subjects. The pastoral task is a voluntary relationship of shared affection.

Because of this affectionate tie of personal goodwill and loving identification, people can trust the motives of the minister and confide in him at times when they would be suspicious of their own family, their employer, or their physician. This may be called "the relationship of a trusted motive," whereby the pastor, by reason of the Infinite Love that he symbolizes, is given access to the holy of holies of men's confidence. This is an indispensable necessity in the relationship of a pastor to anyone whom he helps.

Therefore, the Christian shepherd must be continually at the business of examining his own motives for his face-to-face ministry to his people. He cannot hide tawdry motives of financial greed, love for domination, or erotic concern from those to whom he seeks to minister. The demons of fear, suspicion, greed, hatred, and exploitation know their own kind before they see them coming. Unconscious needs meet unconscious resistances, and nothing is hidden that is not revealed in the intimacy of the pastoral situation. A relationship of a trusted motive prevails only when a Christian pastor voluntarily accepts and effectively carries through with his role as a repre-

[11] *Ibid.*

sentative of the love of Christ. He is a servant of men for Jesus' sake. The effectiveness of all pastoral procedures depends upon the singleness of this motivation, and the ineffective use of the best techniques of counseling can be explained by the adultera- tion of this motive.

Other names have been given to this relationship of a trusted motive by explorers in the field of pastoral care and personal counseling. Rollo May calls it " empathy," whereby the pastor " feels his way into " the life situation of the person who seeks his help. Russell Dicks in his earlier works called it " rapport," by which he meant a positive emotion of " good will, confi- dence, trust, affection, and in its deeper sense . . . love." [12] R. H. Edwards, in his book *A Person-minded Ministry* (The Cokesbury Press, 1940), describes it as a " sense of together- ness" which exists between two people because they share confidence in mutual values, goals, and loyalties. However it is named, this relationship of a trusted motive is actually the power of " faith working through love " to heal humanity's hurt, to cast out fear, and to break down middle walls of parti- tion that separate helpless people from sources of divine strength.

The psychological fact under consideration here is called " identification." This is the process whereby one person takes into himself the character traits of another because of his con- fidence in him, his love for him, and his desire to be like him. The law of identification on the divine-human level and in terms of religious psychology is known as worship. Personality takes the form of the object of its adoration; therefore it is formed and transformed through the power of love.

The earliest illustrations of this power are found in the parent-child relationship, whereby the character of a child is formed into a positive likeness or a negative reaction formation of the actual character of his parents. The character formations of children are largely the result of the personal behavior pat- terns of their parents and are only remotely related to the

[12] Russell Dicks, " Current Trends in Counseling: A Symposium," *Marriage and Family Living*, Vol. III, No. 4.

moral preachments and oral instructions of their parents. As the
wisdom of Whitman suggests:

> There was a child went forth every day,
> And the first object he look'd upon, that object he
> became,
> And that object became part of him for the day
> or a certain part of the day,
> Or for many years or stretching cycles of
> years. . . .
> His own parents, he that had father'd him and
> she that conceived him in her womb and
> birthed him,
> They gave this child more of themselves than
> that,
> They gave him afterward every day — *they and
> of them became part of him* . . .
> These became part of that child who went forth
> every day, and who now goes, and will al-
> ways go forth every day.[13]

The process of identification works in the pastoral relationship to groups and to individuals in much the same way that
it does in the parent-child relationship. The Word becomes
flesh through the power of faith working through love; insofar
as the minister participates in the mind of Christ toward people, the pastoral relationship becomes the transmission line of
the character of Christ. Therefore, the able minister of the new
covenant of the love of Christ does not look upon his work as
the scribes did, i.e., as orally transmitting a literal law that is to
be carried out legally to the last iota; but the minister looks
upon his work as the effective manifestation of the Spirit of
Christ. He is a minister, " not in a written code but in the
Spirit; for the written code kills, but the Spirit gives life " (II
Cor. 3:6).

The pastor is confronted with the practical task of finding
out what is bothering the persons who come to him. He must
first be a student of the person in the privacy of his own mind

[13] From *Leaves of Grass.*

before he can be a teacher of the person in the interpretation of his difficulties. Also, the minister must have a certain amount of knowledge of ways of dealing with specific difficulties. In both instances (in the minister's knowledge of the private secrets of his people, and in his knowledge of how to deal with them) the pastor faces the practical application of the principle of the love of Christ.

In the first place, people will not tell their pastor — or anyone else, for that matter — their inmost problems *for fear* they will be condemned. Also, they will not tell these noisome troubles *for fear* they will be exposed to others and confidences betrayed. These are the two great hindrances to the establishment of a relationship of a trusted motive. The process of reconciliation goes on between pastor and people as he gradually impresses them that Christian love lies in knowing each other even as they are known of God, and yet accepting each other as they are, because God has so accepted them. Such love casts out fear. Therefore, love has no meaning apart from their personal knowledge of each other and from an ethically severe kind of forgiveness of each other's frailties. Jesus set the Christian fellowship in this framework when he said, " I am in my Father, and you in me, and I in you." Paul aligns perfect love and perfect knowledge in the thirteenth chapter of I Corinthians, and in Phil. 1:9 he prays that " love may abound more and more, with knowledge and all discernment." Karl Menninger lays his finger on the same understanding when he says:

> Love is impaired by dread, more or less dimly felt by everyone, lest others see through our masks, the masks of repression that have been forced upon us by convention and culture. It is this that leads us to shun intimacy, to maintain friendships on a superficial level, to underestimate and to fail to appreciate others lest they come to appreciate us only too well. Love is experienced as pleasure in proximity, a desire for a fuller knowledge of one another, a yearning for mutual identification and personality fusion.[14]

[14] Karl Menninger, *Love Against Hate* (Harcourt, Brace & Company, Inc., 1942), p. 272.

Furthermore, the pastor's relationship may be impaired also if his parishioners suspect that he is using them as psychological cadavers on which to demonstrate his counseling techniques, rather than caring for them as a good shepherd does his sheep — with love and simplicity of motive. His very knowledge of human nature, if used as an end in itself, may become an impediment to his usefulness. *Every knowledge of the human heart, every skill in dealing with human problems, is as dangerous as it is useful, and ordinarily it is the presence or absence of the love of Christ that makes the difference.*

The knowledge of the inner lives of the persons who seek the pastor's care, however, is always imparted to him in the context of the Christian community, not in isolation from it. When he feels that he should be related to persons on a *clandestine* and irresponsible basis, he should peg these feelings as real danger signals of irresponsibility in himself. On the other hand, when persons seek to develop a relationship to him that is *totally* secret, and which at the same time involves other people, such as wives, husbands, children, parents, and fellow church members, the pastor must be realistic about so-called *confidential* relationships. The experience of the author since the writing of the first edition has taught him to make covenants of communication with individuals. This is thoroughly discussed in the more recent volume, *Protestant Pastoral Counseling.* But suffice it to say here that the minister builds a covenant of communication in which he promises to be fully responsible to the person in the use of facts that the person gives him. For example, he can promise not to communicate this information without first consulting with the person himself and working out a plan with him as to how the information shall best be used. In return, he can expect and require this same kind of responsible action from the other person: if the parishioner is planning to talk with other persons about what the pastor has said to him, about the fact that he has talked with the pastor, the parishioner should first confer with the pastor in such a way that everyone concerned can be edified and not torn down by the conversation. The pastoral conversation does not happen in a vacuum but in a dynamic society in which words are the main instruments of helping and hurting people.

Yet the focus of the pastor's identity and the end of his conversation with those whom he would serve is incarnate in Jesus Christ, the Word of God. Both he and those whom he would serve are on a pilgrimage of selfhood, the end result of which is either a self *in* Christ or a self apart from Christ. The encounter of redemption is initiated, neither by the pastor nor by the parishioner, but by God. This is the thrust of my own effort to portray in detail the nature of Christian selfhood in a serious theological frame of reference. In the book *Christ and Selfhood* the point is made that "by his own decision, God has in Christ chosen to come out on the road of life and meet man where he is. . . . We cannot let the emphasis rest upon ourselves as chosen people but upon God as a choosing God who has decisively acted in Jesus Christ." The Christian pastor does not move on the basis of some grandiose feeling that he has been chosen above all other men. Rather, he lives in steady gratitude for his own association with the living Christ in participation in the body of Christ, the church, and for his instruction in the record of the revelation of God in Christ. As he faithfully exercises his gratitude, he is among men one who calls Jesus Christ to their remembrance that they may be confronted by him.

The Pastor as Follower of the Leading of the Holy Spirit

"While they were talking and discussing together, Jesus himself drew near and went with them." (Luke 24:15.) Jesus as the living Christ manifests himself vitally in the presence of the Holy Spirit. The Christian pastor does well to think of his face-to-face ministry to people as a form of prayer. As he and his people talk and discuss together, or for that matter simply sit in silence together, Jesus himself in the presence of the Holy Spirit according to his promise draws near and goes with them. This is a more adequate understanding of the place of prayer in pastoral work than to think of it as being limited to those formal occasions when the pastor reads a part of the

Scripture and bows or kneels in prayer with a person or a group of persons.

Such a feeling of being a continual instrument of the Spirit of God lends reverence to the pastor's interpersonal relationships, and naturalness and spontaneity to those special occasions when formal expressions of prayer are appropriate. Ministers who are allowed access to the secrets of human hearts are not immune to developing a raw sense of familiarity with the crudity and frailty of their fellow human beings. Likewise, ministers who are continually called upon for formal prayers are often led to the edge of profaning this holy experience by entering into it lightly, inappropriately, mechanically, and by carrying through with it without depth, sensitivity, or dignity. Furthermore, the seething mass of detail that calls for the concern of a busy pastor often disperses his attention in such a way that his pastoral work becomes corroded with a creeping sense of fatigue that brings inattention and boredom.

The promises of Jesus concerning the Holy Spirit dispel all doubt concerning the intention of the Master. He wanted his disciples to depend upon the Holy Spirit's fellowship with them in both the creative and the destructive tensions of their work. Pastors often long for a never-failing technique which they can use with success in any situation. Likewise they want to know *one* procedure to follow in dealing with all people who have a similar grouping of difficulties — such as divorcees or alcoholics. But each testing situation calls for different measures, indicated only by the pastor's sensitivity to and grasp of the need of the moment. The appropriateness of the moment determines what needs to be said and how it should be said. But it takes a restful relaxation given only by the Holy Spirit to lay aside all preconceived approaches. This may be a glimmer of the brilliant light that Jesus gave his disciples in his assignment of pastoral duties. Obviously, the tenth chapter of Matthew was written against the backdrop of persecution, for the Lord tells his disciples that he sends them out as sheep in the midst of wolves and that they will be hauled into court and made to testify, with their very lives at stake. Such elements of risk and jeopardy of life have too often been removed from the sense of identity that reigns in the lives of contemporary pastors. But the conflicts of contemporary life provide a testing arena for the willingness of Christian pastors to witness. Theological disputes, racial strife, far-right and far-left brainwashing attempts, and economic exploitation and graft offer abundant occasion today where, in the privacy of men's offices, pastors are in another kind of court. Times of testing are just as severe, and no rules of thumb are available today. Nor can someone a thousand miles from the scene of action speak with any intelligence as to "what we shall speak." In our own way and in our own day, we too must be suspicious of stereotyped ways of dealing with such crucial situations. We must depend upon the Spirit of our Father speaking in us.

This was the kind of crucial situation in which a certain young minister found himself. His name is not mentioned because he has never sought any publicity for the things he said, nor did he pose later as someone's martyr with special stigmata of his own. But when mobs sought to prevent Negro children from going to the public school according to the order of the courts, this pastor, a white man, went early in the morning and walked to school with the children. He was beaten by a mob on one morning. But the most significant thing is that he remained as pastor of his church without conflict until years after the incident.

Since the publication of the first edition of this book in 1951, the Korean conflict, the racial strife because of the 1954 Supreme Court ruling, widespread theological controversy in more than one denomination, the replacement of hot wars of bullets with cold wars of ideas, the advent of pressure groups of extremists, have all had considerable impact on the identity and function of the Christian pastor. These forces have removed the "middle ground" from many areas of controversy, and the intent to be a minister of reconciliation, concerned with the resolution of conflict by effective communication and by the power of the Holy Spirit, is likely to be understood as compromise and cowardice. Mass media of propaganda are used to sharpen and spread biased interpretations of situations, and face-to-face involvement of contending parties is avoided. The Christian pastor, however, is committed to the tutelage of the Holy Spirit and to following the leadership of the Holy Spirit. The Holy Spirit, in the name of Jesus Christ, gives gifts to men, and the pastor and teacher is committed to the use of the gift of this ministry in the equipment of God's people for the work of ministry for the building up of the body of Christ. This edifying ministry cannot be forsaken in behalf of any pressure group, however worthy their temporal objectives.

Since the publication of this book in its first edition, I have given attention in two volumes to the work of the Holy Spirit. In the book *Christ and Selfhood* full attention is given to the work of the Holy Spirit in the personal and social conflicts of men. The Holy Spirit focuses the conflictual issues of identity at the growing edge of personality, both individual and corporate. This growing edge is often characterized by conflict and suffering. The Christian pastor participates in this growth, and, as Regin Prenter says, "the place where we may learn to know the Holy Spirit is in the school of inner conflict." [15]

Furthermore, the Holy Spirit functions as Creator of community (as Luke puts it: "All who believed were together") as a result of the action of the Holy Spirit bringing about a sense of belonging and shared meaning between a pastor and his people. The Holy Spirit is the comforter who strengthens, given that he might "be with us." The Holy Spirit is the instructor, given that he might "teach . . . all things." The Holy Spirit is the convicter, who convicts "of sin and of righteousness and of judgment." The Holy Spirit is the healer who makes men whole by bringing to remembrance those spiritual reserves for combating psychological diseases. And finally, the Holy Spirit is the co-worker, who is with us always in the commissioned tasks of Christ.

These functions of the Holy Spirit become the task of the minister, under the guidance of the Holy Spirit, in his inter-

[15] Regin Prenter, *Spiritus Creator*. tr. by J. M. Jensen (Muhlenberg Press, 1953), p. 208.

personal relationships. At one time the minister is the *under-standing friend* who works in the processes of fellowship, creat-ing a sense of community, breaking down the middle walls of partition, and developing a sense of togetherness with other-wise isolated, withdrawn persons who have been cut off from the land of the living. At another time he is the *comforting strength* of a person in the midst of a bereavement, a frustrated or broken love affair, an unbearable pain because of the sins of parents, or the heavy demands of war. The isolating power of suffering is met by the knowledge of the Holy Spirit that gives the sufferer access to " the whole creation [that] has been groaning in travail together until now," and it is the same Spirit that gives expression to those " groanings which cannot be ut-tered " (Rom. 8:26, ASV). The pastor's knowledge of the wis-dom and feelings of the ages that are stored in the Bible will make it possible for him to express his people's inmost feelings *for* them.

Again, the pastor functions as a *teacher* who informs an ig-norant mind, or who supplies the missing piece in a confused perspective. Here he accepts as a fact the religious illiteracy of the average person and draws upon his total store of knowl-edge: the rudiments of his own experience, the patience and comfort of the Scriptures, the example of great personalities, and his systematic knowledge of literature and human nature. At another time he is the *spiritual confidant* and parent con-fessor to whom the fearful and guilt-laden person confesses his intimate sin, thinking all the time that it is unbelievable that another human being can look with compassion upon him, to say nothing of receiving God's forgiveness.

Or, to those individuals who are enthralled in the worship of themselves, the pastor becomes the one who unshackles their experience of God from their concepts of themselves and sets them on the path of progressive spiritual growth. At even an-other time the pastor functions as the *healer* who helps uncover and bring to remembrance those buried memories of the past which nevertheless create blind spots in the person's present view of life and cause him to stumble in his way. Here the pastor functions as a reconciler of paradoxical and conflicting desires, and helps his people to assimilate undigested and unacceptable past experiences in such a way as to profit by them rather than become enslaved to them. Finally, the pastor functions alongside his people as a *co-worker* in the great enterprise of the Kingdom of God. He is a "comrade in a radiant pilgrimage" in which the special relationship between "those . . . of the household of faith" sustains him. Thus, all his planning, meeting, experimentation, and ways of doing things become the instruments of "insightful" relationships to people. As Paul put it, "What you have learned and received and heard and seen in me, do; and the God of peace will be with you" (Phil. 4:9).

These functions of the pastor serve to alternate with one another from time to time. The spiritual appropriateness of this or that function is largely a matter of timing the needs of each psychological moment. Ecclesiastes has a remark about this time (ch. 3:1-11):

> For everything there is a season, and a time for every purpose under heaven: a time to be born, and a time to die; a time to plant, and a time to pluck up . . . ; a time to kill, and a time to heal; a time to break down, and a time to build up; a time to weep, and a time to laugh; . . . a time to rend, and a time to sew; a time to keep silence, and a time to speak; a time to love, and a time to hate. . . . God . . . hath made everything beautiful in its time: also he hath set eternity in their heart.

And the capacity to fit eternity to time depends upon the total store of accrued knowledge and experience of the minister, his intuitive insight into the basic difficulties the individual is up against, and the degree to which he has yielded himself to the Holy Spirit for spiritual sensitivity and understanding.

Thus the interpersonal relationships of a pastor with his people in the times of their suffering become a continuous experience of prayer. In this experience, the inner life of those to whom he ministers is continually being opened to the healing love of God as the personality of the minister is continually being yielded to the working out of the purposes of God. Thus the minister of the healing redemption of the gospel goes about the task of bringing its marvelous light to darkened consciences, its fortifying strength to those who are weak and have no might, and its releasing freedom to those who are clutched by fear, consumed in wrath, and enslaved by inordinate affections.

Then again, in *Protestant Pastoral Counseling*, I discussed the role of the Holy Spirit as Counselor, as the name of the Paraclete is translated in the Revised Standard Version. Colleagues of mine such as Seward Hiltner and Richard Goodling have pointed out to me that this was not a satisfactory discussion to them. I readily admit that of the discussions of the Holy Spirit in which I have engaged either by the spoken word or the written word, none of them has ever been satisfactory to me. Much of what is real in the work of the Holy Spirit is indescribable, reaching beyond the ken of the spoken word. However, I am compelled to continue to try to be articulate and would ask Professors Hiltner and Goodling to help me. I am eagerly awaiting their discussions of the ministry of the Holy Spirit, and not only theirs but those of other teachers and pastors who have begun to take the work of the Holy Spirit seriously. Intensive attention to this is the wave of the future in pastoral care. In this we can learn much from the mystical frames of reference of men like Douglas Steere in his book *On Listening to Another*, in which he challenges the caring relationship of every kind by saying that any such friendship, regardless of how deep, bears with it "the seeds of tragedy unless both persons have opened their lives to a power that is infinitely greater and purer than themselves." [16] This power is the Holy Spirit.

[16] Douglas Steere, *On Listening to Another* (Harper & Brothers, 1955), p. 27.

The Pastor as a Representative of a Specific Church

"Then after fasting and praying they laid their hands on them and sent them off." (Acts 13:3.) A mixed emotion of uneasy satisfaction comes over most ministers when they realize that they symbolize and represent a *specific congregation of people*. The definite form of a pastor's ministry is affected greatly by the history, the traditions, the personal opinions, and even the passing whims of this group of people. The Christian pastor is called, not only to speak *to* this congregation in his preaching ministry, but also to speak *for* them in his individual and group counseling. He cannot go " off duty " from this responsibility; it is a twenty-four-hour-a-day, seven-day-a-week ministry. He finds also that he must represent his congregation to the rest of the community, and occasionally protect his members from the rest of the community. He uses his staff of guidance on his flock, and quite often must use his rod of protection upon attacks from without. His problem is to know *when* to use *which* upon *whom!* No veteran minister will call this an easy problem.

Therefore a Christian pastor, being invested with such a responsibility, must have confidence in his congregation; he must believe in their essential integrity. He must be committed with a clear conscience to the major objectives, principal teachings, and operational strategy of the church to which he accepts a call. The time to clarify this loyalty is *before* he agrees to become their leader. The wise pastor, upon having received overtures from a new congregation, seeking that he become their pastor, will take pains to acquaint himself with the history, traditions, and practices of the church. He will decide in advance whether or not he can be the community advocate for such a congregation. More care and concern at these formative stages of the relationship between pastor and church will lead to more wholeheartedness of service in the days to come. Such precautions will serve to prevent disillusionment among ministers and confusion in congregations.

This does not mean that a pastor should assume that he will

not relate himself to a church that does not sign a "dotted line" agreement to all his expectations. Rather, it means that he is willing to cast his lot with the people as he finds them and to give himself to them in a loyalty that makes room for the progressive development of their corporate life together. This implies that the pastor needs a working concept of what a church actually *is* as well as an ideal concept of what a church as the body of Christ *can* be.

The Christian pastor not only represents the welfare of the Christian community; he also is a sponsor of the individual rights and needs of the persons within the community. One of the unique distinctions of the work of a minister is that he represents *both* the individual *and* the social good of his people at the same time. Individual interests often threaten the safety of the group, and the corporate selfishness of the group often oppresses the welfare of the individual. The sensitive pastor is conscious of the power of the church to isolate an individual, and also of the intentness with which some individuals dominate the church until they must be isolated in order that the community may survive. Therefore the good minister repeatedly evaluates afresh the resources and liabilities of his congregation. He understands the dynamics of group behavior as well as the motives of individual conduct. The opportunities for personal counseling that come to him will arise most often in connection with groups with which he has met. And, too, the structure of his relationship to an individual is greatly determined by the kind of affiliation that person has with the church that the pastor represents.[17]

A pastor, by virtue of his personal as well as economic dependence upon his congregation, ordinarily gives preference to persons and groups who belong to that fellowship. The next group in order are the close relatives and friends of members

[17] See Rudolph Wittenberg, *So You Want to Help People* (Association Press, 1947), pp. 61–121; J. W. Klapman, *Group Psychotherapy; Theory and Practice* (Grune & Stratton, Inc., 1946), pp. 8–11; Murray G. Ross and Charles E. Hendry, *New Understandings of Leadership; A Survey and Application of Research;* and Paul F. Douglass, *The Group Workshop Way in the Church.*

of his congregation, regardless of their connection with his church. The pastor is most often criticized in this connection for being absent from his pulpit and community in order to do this or that service for some other church or organization. He may also be attacked for spending so much time in individual counseling with a few persons who may or may not be concerned with the life of the church that he neglects the needs of the large number of people who are members of his church. The ethical decisions that a pastor must make as to the use of time and energy along these lines are legion in number. But the way he makes these decisions is the stream bed along which his usefulness to his people either flows or evaporates.

The Pastor as a Shepherd of the Non-Christian

The contemporary pastor does not care only for those who are safely within the confines of his church, or of Christendom as a whole, for that matter. He is a shepherd to those on the outside as well. He functions as a symbol, as an interpreter, and as an evangelist. The persons with whom he associates may be apathetic and indifferent to the Christian faith. They may be suspicious and distrustful toward both the Christian community and the Christian faith. They may be directly hostile toward and reject the Christian faith. Yet the minister is responsible, as a witness to the gospel, for relating himself in some challenging and dynamic way to these persons.

The pastor functions as a symbol to the non-Christian. He symbolizes authoritarianism and dogmatism to many who are hostile toward any authority, especially that which their religious parents exercised over them. In dealing with the person who is hostile, the pastor must meet the stance of atheism. The person may insist, in a more passive kind of rejection, that he is not an atheist but a devout agnostic. In either instance the Christian pastor symbolizes the domination and dogmatism of which the person wants to be free. He is stereotyped in his reactions and *all* ministers are alike to him. If the pastor can be permissive enough to establish a dialogue with this person,

warmth and acceptance begin to flow, not necessarily for the
Christian faith, but for the minister himself as an exception to
the rule the person has made about ministers. However, this
blanket judgment of *all* persons as looking upon *all* ministers
as authoritarian is in itself a stereotyped kind of thought. Seward Hiltner and Lowell G. Colston made a careful contrasting
study of counseling done in a psychological counseling service
with counseling done in a local parish situation by a pastor.
They arrived at a startling conclusion:

> The psychologically sophisticated person might predict that
> the person coming to the church for counseling would expect
> authoritarian guidance while he who came to the counseling
> center would be democratic and expect to work out — with
> help — his own problems. This was not our finding. Whatever
> religious or pastoral authority may mean to people these
> days, with our parishioners it did only rarely carry author-
> itarian overtones. And whatever the actual objectivity of
> science and psychology, the prevailing aura over the counsel-
> ing center, it did not prevent many people from expecting
> it to produce answers in what they would be shocked to hear
> called an authoritarian fashion. Religion must continue to
> work on the problem of authoritarianism, but our experience
> suggests that science and psychology have it in even larger
> proportions.[18]

Therefore, the Christian pastor today may be in a position
to explore with the person who is hostile toward the Christian
faith the personal spiritual history that lies behind his need to
rebel against Christianity. He may find that the gospel has
been communicated to the person with such heavy distortion
that even the minister himself would reject the caricature of
the Christian faith that the person has thrown overboard as
invalid for his life.

In the second place, the minister may be a symbol of insincerity and hypocrisy to the person on the outside of the Christian fellowship. He and all professing Christians may be " pho-

[18] Seward Hiltner and Lowell G. Colston, *The Context of Pastoral
Counseling*, p. 37.

nies" to the suspicious and distrustful person. From Carl Sandburg's "Contemporary Bunk Shooter," to Sinclair Lewis' Elmer Gantry, to J. D. Salinger's Holden Caulfield, the Protestant pastor has been made uncomfortable by the implication of phoniness, insincerity, and dissimulation. The pastor, on the other hand, is burdened with a sense of guilt for having to play a role, wear a mask, and be "nice" to everyone. But the Biblical image of the shepherd is that of a person who is disarmingly honest. He is forthrightly freed by the grace of God in Christ to activate his identity as a pastor through confrontation as well as through the solicitous comfort and support of those both inside and outside the church. Consistency and candor supply security once the shock of the first encounter with such a minister subsides. People suddenly realize that his yea is yea and his nay is nay, and that much more than this is evil.

But more subtly than either the hostility or the suspicion is the fact that the minister symbolizes commitment. He is a man with his mind made up and fixed. He will be asked by persons who are outside the orbit of the Christian community: "Where is it that you will not bend?" At the same time, commitment itself removes the luxury of indecision which is often mistaken for open-mindedness. Commitment removes the spiritual bachelorhood that majors on uninvolvement and detachment from any durable relationship. The pastor represents this kind of decisive commitment and durable covenant of a faith community. His efforts to establish a durable relationship to persons whose way of life is detachment and avoidance of responsible involvement may be met with an intricate number of rebuffs, unfulfilled covenants, and unproductiveness. The detached person finds responsible involvement with any committed person, regardless of what his commitment may be, to be an uneasy friendship. As Mr. Faithful said to Christian concerning Mr. Talkative (in Bunyan's *Pilgrim's Progress*): "He would rather have done with your company than to change his ways."

The atmosphere of contemporary culture is such, however, to cause the pastor unwittingly to assume that those on the outside of the church are invariably hostile, suspicious, or uncommitted as far as the Christian faith is concerned. One reason for this is that he is likely to be institutionally oriented to people rather than personally related to them for their own sakes and not as a means to his institutional and " churchly " objectives. For example, the purpose of his visitation may be first, last, and always to get them to be more active in the church. Even when he visits them when they are sick, he may use the situation to promote the church. When he has once caught the vision of caring for people as ends within themselves, of losing himself in the center of their " thrown situation," then he discovers them to be less hostile, suspicious, and detached. He finds at the core of countless numbers of people an estrangement, a loneliness, a feeling that no man cares for their soul, and a querulous sense of strangeness that anyone could genuinely take time to listen to and understand them without having some " sales pitch " or ulterior motive in mind. That someone could is such good news that it is unbelievable! In fact, even when they begin to believe it, the pastor has to call upon the independent action of the Living God to help them to believe it! When we see people from this perspective, Christian pastors take a new look at the internal meaning of hostility, suspicion, and detachment. We have begun to be schooled in the kind of compassion that only the Good Shepherd can generate, because it was he of whom it is said: " When he saw the crowds, he had compassion for them because they were harassed and helpless, like sheep without a shepherd " (Matt. 9:36).

Chapter III

The Personal Qualifications
of the Pastor

The representative of God, the ambassador of Christ, the follower of the leading of the Holy Spirit, the emissary of a
church, and the shepherd of non-Christians must have unusual
spiritual equipment and emotional stability.

The writers of the New Testament were zealous and enthusi-
astic when they spoke of the necessity of a man's being called
to the ministry, but they were equally exacting in their requirements of those who were chosen for the task. It could be fitly
spoken of the early churches that *many* were called to the task
of an overseer of souls but few were chosen.

Early Christians were not vague in their statement of the
personal qualifications of those into whose hands was committed the care of the flock of God. They did not leave this important decision entirely to the sentimental whims of men who
aspired to the office. The responsibility was laid upon and
taken seriously by the churches themselves. The writers of the
pastoral epistles and of I Peter felt it necessary to describe in
minute detail the qualifications that they themselves sought to
incorporate into their own way of life and the high standards
that they held for those who became their fellow workers. They
were convinced of the nobility of their task.

Consequently, churches today have at hand in the New Testament (I Tim. 3:1-7; Titus 1:5-9; I Peter 5:1-4) the standards
whereby they may judge a man's fitness as their pastor, and
aspiring candidates for the ministry may judge themselves.

" Above Reproach "

A pastor should be a person who has earned the respect of his community; that is, he is above reproach, not having been laid hold of for disorderliness, indecency, and immodesty. This is not merely a matter of having kept up appearances before one's neighbors, but rather that a person has proved his own work before his community and actually merits the approval and acceptance of those about him.

Especially important is it that a man have the respect of non-Christians. First Timothy states it: " He must be well thought of by outsiders " (ch. 3:7). The purpose of this requirement is made plain: " In order that he may not be publicly exposed to abuse and affliction and fall into the snare of the slanderer." The man who is to bear witness to those who are outside must have lived convincingly before them, be above their reproach, and have their respect if he is to have any influence over them. This requirement points not only to the positive witness of the church to those outside but also to the need for protecting the flock of God from those on the outside.

Of course, it is a common saying that unless a minister is maligned by sinners, and persecuted by the unrighteous, he does not truly have the first fruits of being called to the ministry. The " persecutory passages " of Scripture and the fact that the Chief Shepherd was criticized for eating with publicans and sinners are cited as supporting evidence. Nevertheless, the fact remains that it was the religious people of Jesus' day who criticized his behavior, and not those who believed on him or those who were publicans and sinners. Those who were on the outside, the lost sheep of the house of Israel, never accused him of being one of them. Among these groups he was " above reproach."

The ever-present fact of gossip and slander in a community hovers like humidity over the face-to-face ministry of a pastor to his people; he may be unaware of it, but he is never free from its influence. It necessitates his being above reproach himself; he must have brought his whole life under a finely balanced discipline lest he himself become a castaway.

Not a New Convert

The New Testament says plainly that a pastor should not be a new convert, a novice, a neophyte. Rather, he should be a seasoned veteran of the Christian way of life. No specific length of service as an active Christian is stated, but experience taught these early churches that a "newly planted" Christian had to be put to the test of time before being given the responsibility of the care of others.

One clear reason for this requirement was stated: " In order that he may not become puffed up with conceit and fall into the condemnation of the false accuser." The literal phrase for " puffed up with conceit " is " to be wrapped up in a cloud," or "beclouded with conceit." This word is used again in I Tim. 6:4-5: " He is puffed up with conceit, he knows nothing; he has a morbid craving for controversy and disputes about words, which produce envy, dissension, slander, base suspicions, and wrangling among men who are depraved in mind and bereft of the truth, imagining that godliness is a means of gain."

Accordingly, then, the course of experience through which a novice goes when he attempts the work of a pastor is after this order: He first is overwhelmed by the new sense of importance of the role into which he has been cast. He gets the same sense of competitive victory that made Paul feel that he had advanced beyond many of his own age, and caused him to become " extremely zealous." Then the new convert begins to realize his inadequacy and becomes very insecure in trying to discharge the new responsibilities that bear so heavily upon him. This prompts him " to put up a front," and to try to cover his ignorance with high-sounding words and obscure intellectualisms that confuse his listeners and hide the simplicity of the gospel. This cloud of confusion brings on divisions and wranglings among people who are also babes in the way of Christ. Party cries begin to be heard, and the more emotionally unstable people of the community begin to use the situation of godlessness to see who can gain his own personal ends.

Such Biblical understanding merits the conclusion that one of the explanations of " split churches " and a multiplying number of rival sects in Christendom today is the spiritual immaturity of carelessly chosen pastors and leaders. They are cakes not turned, burned on one side and raw on the other. Attempts therefore to unite Christendom without getting back to this source of its divisions are futile indeed. These groups are set into motion by spiritually adolescent leaders with a thirst for power, and these leaders can do more to shatter the unity of churches in a short while than mature leaders can undo in a long time.

This does not mean that a person's age should be the sole determinant of his selection as a pastor, for the Scriptures do not refer merely to chronological age, but to spiritual maturity. It does mean, however, that a man should have achieved a sufficient degree of full-grownness as a Christian not to get lost in the cloud of his own conceits.

" The Husband of One Wife "

Two of the pastoral epistles (I Timothy and Titus) require that the pastor be the husband of one wife. This may be interpreted several ways.

First, polygamy and concubinage were prevalent practices in the communities of which the early churches were a part, and the writers evidently were insisting that their leaders be an example of the Christian principle of monogamous marriage. They looked upon singleness of devotion to one marital partner as essential to the integration of personality alongside the necessity of singleness of devotion to one God. These two distinctives set the Christians apart, in glaring contrast, from their neighbors who practiced both polygamy and polytheism.

Secondly, this passage may be interpreted less directly to mean that the early Christians preferred a married minister to a single one. This was evidently prior to the ascetic development of a celibate ideal for pastors, and one wonders what a Catholic priest thinks when he comes to this text. Social pressures among Protestant churches today almost demand of a minister that he be married. So universal is this demand that occasionally theological students depend upon this external motivation for the selection of a mate rather than upon inner devotion to the woman they marry. Likewise the pressure for a certain kind of woman, with ability to be a sort of " assistant to the pastor," occasionally dominates the marital choice of ministers to such an extent that affection becomes a secondary consideration. Nevertheless, the main intention of the Scriptural requirement seems to be that a minister *needs* a wife as his companion in the work of the gospel, as his partner in the enjoyment of their mutually expressed sexual powers, and as his comrade in the adventure of parenthood.

Thirdly, this passage may be interpreted in the light of another prevalent social problem at the time of the writing: divorce. At this point the application becomes most pertinent to present-day practice. Divorced men are, in increasing numbers, applying to theological seminaries for admission, in order to prepare for the active pastorate. This poses a thorny ethical problem for the individual men involved, for theological faculties, for ordination councils, and for churches in need of pastors.

The statements of Paul in I Cor., ch. 7, reflect that the early churches were very tender and sensitive to the plight of people who became involved in pagan marriages prior to having become Christians. They most certainly did not consider divorce or even remarriage as an unpardonable sin for which they would break fellowship with an individual Christian. The New Testament ideal for all marriages is complete chastity prior to marriage and complete faithfulness to one's marital partner after marriage until death. This ideal is implicit in the statement that a minister shall be " the husband of one wife." The New Testament does not hold forth a double standard, one for ministers and one for other people. But today, one divorced minister (anonymous to this author) was right when he wrote:

"The minister certainly does have to face up to many risks resulting from divorce that other men do not have to face. Whether we like it or not, there is a sort of double standard, one for the minister and one for the non-minister, in the public mind."[1] This poignant statement needs to be set against the New Testament times when the cleavage between standards for ministers and other persons within the church was not nearly so great. It is an open question as to how much of a paid, professional ministry existed at the time of the writing of these pastoral epistles. The ministry as an employment situation did not exist as we have it today. Another divorced minister said: "I did delay my decision [to be divorced], not because I doubted the need for a divorce, but because I was not prepared to do any other kind of work and I hated to give up the ministry."[2]

This is vastly different from the situation that existed at the time of the writing of the pastoral epistles. Yet this double standard does exist today. Some ministers who are divorced are able to carry through with a ministry that is effective insofar as their churches allow it. Others are completely closed out of the ministry. All sorts of casuistic explanations of these differences can be developed. None of them succeed in equating the New Testament situation with present-day conditions. Nor do present-day conditions remove the validity of the New Testament ideal for marriage for all people. The main ethical issue that the problem of divorced ministers presents is the way in which the church, especially American Protestant denominations, neglects the spiritual guidance of the whole church in terms of educational preparation for marriage among Christians. As Goode pointed out (see Chapter I), pastoral care of couples at crucial junctures of their marital pilgrimages was nonexistent in 74 percent of the cases he studied. From a Biblical and theological point of view the problem of the divorced minister is not materially different from that of the divorced

[1] Seward Hiltner, "Divorced Ministers," *Pastoral Psychology*, Vol. 9, No. 87 (Oct., 1958), p. 19.
[2] *Ibid.*, p. 20.

Christian generally. Yet the divorced minister spotlights the timidity and pastoral neglect with which Christian denominations approach making requirements and providing preparation for the marriage of all Christians. In the absence of this kind of ethical seriousness, the church shifts from one stance of sentimentality and unrealism to another of harshness and unreasonableness in dealing with ministers who themselves become divorced. Consequently, the minister as a public figure is dependent upon a vote of confidence of a given congregation that in one week can spend several hours in adulation of film heroes and heroines who practice the consecutive polygamy sometimes mistaken for divorce and yet at the same time expect their minister to be completely untouched by such cultural fallout in the ethical atmosphere. The attitudes of congregations toward divorced ministers vary from one educational level to another, from one part of the country to another, and from one denomination to another. The ethical relativism of Christians validates the need for reaffirmation of the Christian ideal set forth in the New Testament for the marriage of all Christians. At the same time, the compassion of Jesus Christ makes imperative the necessity for careful clinical study of a given divorced minister's situation as he seeks the guidance of the Holy Spirit for his calling under God.

Finally, clinical experience in marriage and family counseling with ministers and their wives teaches one more thing about how a pastor shall be related to the woman to whom he is married. He is to be her *husband* in the fullest sense of the word, and to set an example before the men of his community in the way he loves and cares for his wife. He is to be related to his wife as a husband, and not as a little child is to his mother. He is to be related to her as a husband, and not as a father is to a little daughter. They should be related to each other as man and wife, and not as pastor and parishioner who are continually reminding each other of their rank. They should be related to each other as man and wife, and not as separate members of the staff of a church. These other functions certainly condition the life of a minister and his wife together, but in no instance should any one of them become the determinative pattern of their relationship.

The work of Wallace Denton on the role of the minister's wife has been a unique contribution to the understanding of the minister's responsibility to and for his wife. He conferred directly through controlled interview procedures with a cross section of Protestant ministers' wives. He found that these women felt that they were scarcely any more active in church work than any other active laywoman. "However," Denton says, "by virtue of her role as minister's wife what she does is different from what the other women do. On the other hand, the wives think of themselves as being vitally involved in their husbands' work on the home front. They see their chief contribution as being supportive, one that includes hearing him out, sharing ideas with him, and providing the type of home atmosphere to which he may retreat as a refuge from a busy and hectic schedule. This encompasses the primary thrust of their role and they give evidence of accepting it with relative ease and comfort." Yet, Denton observes, they experience loneliness in their separation from other women in the church and, one might add, in that a double standard is applied to them as is to their husbands.[3] Thus, both the condemnation of the incidence of divorce in the minister's life and the isolation of his wife even when she is happily married portray a decline of the application of Christian ethics to all Christians alike. Likewise these two phenomena represent a decline of the application of the doctrine of the priesthood of all believers shown by the separation of the clergy from the laity in standards for their homes, especially for their wives and children.

Good Manager of Own Household

The New Testament writers seem to assume that if a pastor is the "husband of one wife," he will also be the parent of children. One of their criteria for judging the fitness of a man for

[3] Wallace Denton, *The Role of the Minister's Wife* (The Westminster Press, 1962), p. 86.

the ministry was his success as a parent. They required of him, therefore, that he should have a finely balanced control of his own home, because " if a man does not know how to manage his own household, how can he care for God's church? " (I Tim. 3:5).

Many pastors have interpreted this to mean that they are to rule over their children with an iron hand, the clutching authority of which is never to be relaxed. Such men are often embarrassed to find late in life that their children rise up in rebellion at the tyranny of their father and reject not only him but his religion. Certainly the writers of this passage of the New Testament meant something more than and different from this interpretation. The larger Biblical context reveals a more adequate understanding.

In the first place, the patriarchal type of family organization in which these early Christians participated had its beginnings in the early Hebrew period when the father of the family was the only priest of the family. He was the representative of God to the family, and all that has been said concerning the pastor as a representative of God applies also to his relationship to his family. Accordingly, the exhortation found in I Peter 5:2-3 may be paraphrased and applied to the pastor's relationship to his children without doing violence to the total Biblical context: " Act as a shepherd to your children, not as lording it over them, but as an example before them." In other words, the power whereby a minister maintains control over his children is the strength of the child's natural need to become like his father. He depends more on the persuasive pull of this need than he does on the coercive demand of an infallible parental authority.

Again, the Greek word for " manage " is derived from a word that means literally " to stand over." It is followed in the text by a term that is translated " with all gravity." This word is derived from another word which means " to worship." The interpretation of the law of identification set forth earlier is applicable here. On the human level, the character of the child is shaped by the tie of identification between him and his parents. If this goes either to the extreme of stark fear of the parent or abject servility to the parent, the father, for all practical purposes, becomes the god, the object of the infantile worship of the child. Therefore, the child is instructed by Paul, " Obey your parents *in the Lord,* for this is right " (Eph. 6:1). The pastor rules over his children as a representative of God and " in the Lord," not capriciously and by virtue of his own infallibility. In so doing, he serves as a " molding influence " upon the life of his family. He depends more upon affectionate management in his own relationship to his children than he does upon " pulling his rank " as a preacher.

Not only does the pastor exert a molding influence over his family by maintaining a loving tie of identification between himself and them, but he also serves as a " sieve " to protect his family from destructive outside influences. The children of a pastor can very easily become confused by the many voices of the congregation who seek to direct their path. The possibility of their own choices may be purloined away by the social pressure of the group that the pastor represents. The protective function, therefore, of the pastor as a parent often has to be applied to the congregation as well as to people who are not Christians. The pastor should always stand *between* his family and his church both as a protector from many well-meaning " authorities " on child guidance and as a mediator of the more desirable graces of the Christian fellowship.

A third meaning of the requirement of effective parenthood that is laid upon a candidate for the ministry is embodied in the instruction to Timothy: " If a man does not know how to manage his own household, how can he care for God's church? " (I Tim. 3:5). The word translated " care for " is used only one other time in the New Testament. In Luke 10:34-35 the word describes the way the good Samaritan treated the wounded man whom he found. Actually, then, it means in this context that the pastor cares for the church with a *healing carefulness.* The minister cares in the same manner for his children, supplying their economic and bodily needs as well as their spiritual ones. In another place, Timothy is instructed: " If any one does not provide for his relatives, and especially for his own family, he has disowned the faith and is worse than an unbeliever" (I Tim. 5:8).

This is not to say that a pastor is to let luxury and extravagance determine his ministry. It is to say, however, that real question may be raised as to the sincerity of a candidate for the ministry who uses his Christian calling as an excuse to neglect the basic physical and emotional needs of his children. If a man neglects his own children's needs for affectionate tenderness, spiritual instruction, and economic security, he will have no basis for a genuinely pastoral care of the flock of God.

Not necessarily

An acid test of the fitness of a minister for his work is whether he is such a parent that his children can look up to him and want to be like him and his Lord. This test reveals the connection between family maladjustment and the use of religion as an escapism from what would otherwise be an impossible home situation. The face-to-face ministry of a pastor to his people calls for the skills and patience of a successful parent. By and large, people react in most subsequent groups in much the same way they learned to react to their mothers and fathers, brothers and sisters.[4] They carry these established patterns with them into the rest of life. In the church, more often than not, the other members of the family are present also. This requirement of successful parenthood, then, is as old as the New Testament and as contemporary as some of the most recent research in psychology.

Sane, Sensible, of a Sound Mind

The mental health of a man who aspired to the office of an overseer of souls was of concern to the early churches. Jesus himself was vitally concerned with people being " clothed and in . . . [their] right mind." He gave himself to the healing of those who were demented and stimulated the compassion of

[4] S. R. Slavson, ed., *The Practice of Group Therapy* (International Universities Press, Inc., 1948), pp. 219 ff.

his disciples then and now to bring the therapeutic power of the Christian gospel to bear upon life situations. But when he had healed such persons, though they "begged that . . . [they] might be with him, . . . he sent . . . [them] away, saying, 'Return to your home, and declare how much God has done for you'" (Luke 8:38 f.). He did not choose them for the places of heaviest responsibility. Their best witness was as well persons in their home community, now that they were healed.

The epistles to Timothy and Titus both use the same term, which may be translated variously as "sane," "sensible," or "of a sound mind," "self-controlled," "sober-minded." Those words from which the term is derived, and those words to which it is related, refer unmistakably to the emotional stability of the candidate for the ministry. The writer specifies the several different ways by which the mental health of a candidate is to be judged.

First, he must be a person whose moral sensitivity has not been dulled and gapped by the use of alcohol. He cannot be a person who "spends his time sitting by a bottle." The lowered threshold of moral sensitivity, the shaken loss of physical precision, and the aching emptiness of unresolved anxieties characteristic of the person who solves his problems with alcohol are all counterindications of his fitness for the ministry to other people. He stands in need of a physician himself. But a minister who himself becomes the victim of alcohol addiction is no moral failure beyond repair. The same resources of healing available to the Christian who is not a minister are open to him also.

With such help available through pastoral counseling, psychotherapy, and the effective participation in Alcoholics Anonymous, the minister may himself turn and strengthen others. The ideal of sobriety is not equivalent to Christian redemption, although it may seem so to a person who is in the grip of alcohol or drug addiction, or even more so to members of his family. Rather, if any man is overtaken in this fault, he should be cared for with gentleness and responsible realism, whether he

is an ordained minister or not. No double standard can exist
here without doing away with the Protestant principle of the
priesthood of the believer.

Secondly, a pastor must also have control of his desire for
money. He cannot be a person who is avaricious for gain and
whose simplicity of devotion to the care of the flock is adulter-
ated by the worship of accumulated money. He cannot serve
two masters, God and mammon. He cannot bypass as of secondary importance the primary concerns of human need and
the edification of the mental and spiritual lives of his people
in order to achieve his own financial ends.

Thirdly, the pastor must have control of his desire for power.
His prestige-seeking impulse must not be so out of proportion
to his other spiritual hungers that he feels that he must "lord
it over" his flock and squelch anyone who dares compete with
him or oppose him. He cannot push his own needs for independence of his people so far that he does not recognize his
dependence upon them for that reasonable degree of approval
that makes for mental health and social usefulness. He cannot
succeed in such a manner that he causes one of his "little ones"
to fail.

Fourthly, most emphasis, however, is placed upon the degree
of mastery a man has over his temper. Paul says that a man
should be a "master of himself." This implies that he has great
strength and power of spirit, but he knows how to express his
aggressions in a positive and healthy manner. He is not "arro-
gant" and self-pleasing, inclined to orgies of bad temper in
which he delivers himself over to his own meanness of spirit.
He is not "violent but gentle," not "quarrelsome" and continually searching out something over which to start a fight. He
may be described also as a "noncombatant" in the fights that
those around him choose to start. In a word, the pastor does
not label his own lack of self-control as his "prophetic ministry," but is keenly conscious of the fact that he "prophesies in
part."

The absence of these negative factors does not attest to the
mental health of a person unless certain positive values live in

their place. Therefore the writer specifies that a pastor needs to have a well-balanced sense of moderation, rather than to be given to extremisms. His sense of fairness and his appreciation of fitting behavior appropriate to each occasion reflect the precision of his self-control. Paul calls this "being just," or "rendering to every man his due because of his own uprightness." Matthew Arnold most aptly described this fine mental balance as "sweet reasonableness." The mentally healthy person is the one who has a reasonable degree of insight into his own weaknesses and has learned to turn them to the best advantage. He has the capacity for bearing a reasonable amount of frustration of his own desires, for sensing other people's privations before deploring his own, and for accepting responsibility for his own thoughts, decisions, and actions.

The New Testament writers tend to interpret mental stability in terms of self-control. This is something very different from repression as described by the psychologists, which, as Sigmund Freud has said, lies "simply in the function of rejecting or keeping something out of consciousness." Repression consists of an unawareness that one even has inordinate aggressions, in which case the person may feign humility in such a way that it angers all those around him. But self-control consists of the frank recognition of one's hungers and impulses and the acceptance of the personal responsibility for their management.[5]

Mission boards have realized the importance of the requirement of a high degree of emotional stability for appointees to foreign service, and have enlisted the aid of personality tests and psychiatric examinations of the candidates. More recently, some denominations, especially the Episcopalian and Presbyterian, have begun specific programs for the strengthening of the mental health of candidates for their parish ministry. Much effort is being made to guide those persons who have "severe personality disturbances which may cause difficulty to themselves and embarrassment to the church" into other vocations

[5] Sigmund Freud, "Repression" (1915), *Collected Papers*, Vol. IV (Hogarth Press, Ltd., London, 1948), p. 86.

than the ministry.[6] Admissions committees in theological seminaries are gradually becoming aware of the necessity for psychological screening of applicants. The Educational Testing
Service, under the auspices of a grant from the Lilly Endowment, has, in the last five years, moved into the final stages of
validating a general "aptitude" test for theological students.
This aims to explore the motivation of the student, his conception of the ministry, and much of his interpersonal competence
to do the things a minister is expected to do. Individual denominations have much more personalized and intensive testing programs for candidates for the ministry. Theological
schools have paid considerable attention to health records,
psychological tests for emotional adequacy, and letters of recommendation concerning the capacity of the candidates for
degrees to function as effective and healthy persons. However,
these emphases in most schools with which the author is acquainted are balanced by attention to basic abilities such as
the capacity for concept mastery, the use of the English language, and the degree of intelligence of a given man. These
tests and measurements are more of a basis for guidance and
counseling than for inclusion and exclusion of men. The objective and spirit of theological schools is to participate with the
man in defining his real strengths, encouraging him to use what
would otherwise be weaknesses to the best advantage, and
formulating what the providential as well as the charismatic
call of God is in his life. This in itself is a major achievement
of the last twelve years in the pastoral care and counseling of
theological students.

These steps toward promoting a high standard of mental
health for candidates for the ministry are heartening. Yet there
is a real need for younger ministers to conduct a voluntary
search for guidance. A young minister preparing for this noble
task should systematically set about the business of removing
emotional weights that so easily beset him and render him in-

[6] Clifford E. Davis, *Counseling the Candidate, Psychological Techniques in Recruiting Church Leadership* (Board of Christian Education
of The Presbyterian Church in the U.S.A., 1949), p. 4.

effective or positively harmful in his personal ministry to people. The most natural way of accomplishing this is to turn to older ministers and theological professors who have devoted their lives not only to their own active ministry but also to the careful training of other ministers. Another way is to serve an " apprenticeship " alongside spiritually healthy ministers from whom one can learn. Then, too, the growing facilities for the clinical training of theological students provide controlled conditions whereby a prospective minister can face the hidden anxieties in his own personality as he ministers to large numbers of institutionalized people.

If a prospective minister discovers that he is using more energy fighting his inner conflicts than he is in doing the work of the Lord, if he senses that his personal relationships to his family and his associates are such that they prevent him from being an " able minister of the New Testament," he should feel no embarrassment about searching out a qualified Christian physician who can render him whatever therapy is needed. A good majority of personality handicaps *can be overcome*, given a spirit of teachableness on the part of the afflicted person. The minister-to-be should not expect to solve all his personal problems *before* he attempts to deal with those of others. This is a fantasy in itself. He will do well to have dealt adequately with his major handicaps by the time he starts his active and full-time ministry.

Since 1951 several significant contributions have been made to the understanding of the mental health of the minister. Wesley Shrader, in an article in the August 20, 1956, issue of *Life* magazine, wrote an article asserting that more and more ministers were " breaking down " under the unrealistic expectations of themselves and their churches. In 1958, the Lilly Endowment sponsored a conference on " Motivation for the Ministry " under the leadership of Samuel Southard, and privately published extensive findings of a team of experts as to their estimates of the relation between men's reasons for entering the ministry and their effectiveness, satisfaction, and productivity as ministers. In the meantime, Niebuhr, Williams, and

Gustafson, in their study on *The Advancement of Theological Education,* analyzed the various categories of theological students in terms of their reasons for coming to a theological seminary.[7] An unevenly valuable set of papers were brought together in 1961 under the editorship of this author in which were published the most significant and informed opinions of persons who spend much of their time in instruction and in the care and counseling of ministers.[8] This literature points to one ancient piece of wisdom to remember in all statements about the ideal qualifications of ministers. Ministers are men and not God. They have illnesses, too. The presence of illness is not necessarily a disqualification for the ministry. On the contrary, illnesses have to be distinguished from one another. Is the illness a way of life for the minister, or is it a gate to a new life for him? Illness may be the sum total of the failure of an inadequate, poorly grounded way of existence. It may be the "opening" for the reconstruction of a more realistic, solidly grounded way of life. Men like Frederick W. Robertson, H. Wheeler Robinson, Harry Emerson Fosdick, and Anton Boisen are examples of ministers who, with far less medical and pastoral help than is available to the average minister today, found their way to a powerful witness for Jesus Christ. With the comfort with which they themselves had been comforted of God, they in turn became a comfort to others. This kind of disclaimer has to be entered in discussions of mental health among ministers. Otherwise, the canons of mental health will become a new legalism whereby the minister, by his own efforts struggles for some imagined perfection. This, like all other legalisms, destroys his own sense of need for grace and renders him helpless to exercise grace in relation to those who seek his help.

Churches seeking pastors and lay leaders, such as deacons, elders, vestrymen, stewards, are most in need of education along the line of choosing men who are spiritually healthy. The size of a man and the sound of his voice are not adequate

[7] Niebuhr, Williams, and Gustafson, *The Advancement of Theological Education* (Harper & Brothers, 1957), pp. 146 ff.

[8] Wayne E. Oates, ed., *The Minister's Own Mental Health.*

standards for judging this. The New Testament, as has been seen in this context, speaks with definiteness and accuracy on the things to look for in a minister's personal stability. The churches are under obligation to "try every spirit" to see whether it is of God, because there are many false prophets gone out into the world. The true prophet needs all the fiber of personality he can muster to stand the test of the pastoral relationship. False prophets often find their ways most easily into the affections of their people by reason of their "standing head and shoulders above the rest," their speaking "in the tongues of men and of angels," or their compulsive zeal that "scours land and sea." Only when the churches demand something better will ministers be chosen who are capable of bringing health as well as goodness, soundness of mind as well as strength of zeal, and wholesomeness of direction as well as intentness of purpose to the life of the body of Christ.

Must Have a Firm Hold on the Sure Word

The emotional stability of a minister has a great deal to do with the quality of his beliefs and largely determines the manner in which he seeks to impart these beliefs to others. Therefore the New Testament writer insists that the minister have a firm hold on the sure word of the gospel. He must have a sense of certainty about the truths he teaches and the Person whom he represents.

The pastor must be competent to give his people a sense of certainty about their life in relationship to God, because, as Paul has said: "If the trumpet give an uncertain sound, who shall prepare himself to the battle?" (I Cor. 14:8). Two evident reasons support placing such a demand upon the pastor: First, people depend upon their pastor for confidence, security, and certainty, amid suspicion, insecurity, and doubt. As Goethe appealed, so do they: "Give me your convictions; I need them. Keep your doubts; I have enough of my own." Secondly, every congregation has a legitimate need for authority in its minister. He must be able to speak as one having authority from his own personal experience with Christ, from the thoroughness of his knowledge of the record of revelation, from the firsthandness of his own understanding of human nature, and from the intimacy of his own acquaintance with grief and pain. Such an authority meets a group's needs, whereas the traditions of the scribes leave them thirsty.

A Healthy Teacher

The minister is expected not only to have a firm hold on his beliefs as a Christian but to have laid hold of a healthy quality of teaching. He needs to be a mature man in Christ who is no longer " tossed to and fro and carried about with every wind of doctrine, by the cunning of men, by their craftiness in deceitful wiles " (Eph. 4:14). He is to have a firm hold on the sure word that is taught in order that he may give instruction " in the health-giving doctrine." New Testament writers were aware of the fact that many congregations of people do not want a man of stability. They prefer the unstable pastors: " Having itching ears they will accumulate for themselves teachers to suit their own likings, and will turn away from listening to the truth and wander into myths " (II Tim. 4:3-4). Creative teaching is the church's most effective means of producing spiritually healthy people. It plays the same part in the life of those who are whole that healing plays in the life of those who have need of a physician. This gives a vital significance to the original meaning of " orthodoxy." From the point of view of the pastoral epistles, orthodoxy is that kind of teaching which creates wholeness of life in an individual's relationships to himself and to his fellows by reason of his firmer hold upon the reality of God in Christ. From the point of view of the individual, the soundness of a teaching may be determined by its influence upon the forces of spiritual growth within the life. From the point of view of the group life of the church, the soundness of a teaching may be determined by whether or not it contributes to the " edification of the church." If a teaching confirms childish irresponsibility in an individual, and justifies that person in remaining just as he is with no need for teachableness and no confession of the need for growth, it can be justly called unsound. If a teaching or a practice divorces a group of people from a Christlike spirit and alienates them from one another and the larger community of Christians, genuine questions may be raised as to its soundness.

Yet, according to the more recent studies of Blizzard, less than one twentieth of the minister's time is spent in actual teaching relationships, as such. The ministry of pastoral care has, however, taken on new diversity and strength in the last ten years through more attention to the importance of small-group and teaching ministries of the pastor. The student-centered teaching emphases of Carl Rogers, the spiritual renewal of the churches through small groups as stressed by John Casteel, and the reappraisal of the teaching ministry of the church by James D. Smart and Jesse Ziegler have impinged heavily upon the practice of pastoral care. The dramatic therapeutic success of the disciplined groups of the Alcoholics Anonymous suggests that a part of the lost radiance of the churches has been the power of a small learning group to change human life. The more recent reassertion of the priesthood of all believers and the ministry of the laity by Hendrik Kraemer, Elton Trueblood, and Tom Allen has tended to redefine the role and function of the clergyman as a teacher of the laity, as one who equips the fellowship of believers for the work of ministry. This, furthermore, shifts pastoral care from a sacramental mold in which the ministry is a confessional-type care of an individual in isolation from the community. The more recent pastoral care follows instead an instructional pattern in which the pastoral care is done in the context of a caring fellowship. Here the minister does not operate under a seal of the confessional as much as he works within the context of a covenant of responsible communication. He may *need* to talk with other responsible persons about the individual with whom he is working. He covenants with the individual, however, not to do so without his full knowledge and consent. The relation of the members of the community to each other, in turn, becomes the "content" of the pastor's instructional approach to both the individual and the community in the light of Christian truth.

An Apt Teacher

The New Testament writers expect of pastors, not only that they be sure of their teaching and that the quality of their teaching be sound, but that they be capable of making these teachings come alive to their people. The pastor must be "an apt teacher."

The aptitude of a minister for his task is one sure evidence of God's intention in his life, because God does not call a person to do something without reference to his own creative gifts to that person in the first place. Colloquially, the word "apt" has a curious double meaning. It is often used to mean "likely to come to pass." In this context, the question could be asked concerning a candidate for the ministry: "Is this person likely to function with success in the role to which we are setting him apart?" Then, again, the word "apt" is often used to mean "capable, or possessing the ability" to do a task, in this case, to teach. Much research needs to be done and clear instruction given by already active pastors as to the specific skills necessary for competent action as a minister. The Spirit of God always takes the form of the vessel that it fills, and the specific form that the sense of mission takes in an individual's life is largely determined by his basic intelligence and his vocational aptitudes.

This matter has been left to chance and to the competitive struggle for existence among the churches and among ministers. A natural law of selection works in weeding out incompetent men, but it works apart from the loving intelligence of Christian people and is often a cruel thing in its operation. Because of prayerless and careless vocational choices and irresponsible spiritual guidance on the part of pastors who counsel young people about entering the ministry there have been bitter disappointments in wasted human lives. The sight of a thirty-year-old man who has spent half of his life in school preparing for the ministry and finally ekes out a living selling encyclopedias would frighten his earlier spiritual guides. Many are called into the ministry without a full knowledge of its demands. The blight of disappointment sets in when they, by their own word, conclude that they will never be capable of doing the work of a pastor.

Wise counsel suggests that spiritual appeals for life dedications to Christian work should be made in such a way as to allow room for the processes of time, growth, and spiritual instruction to fit the intentions of the consecrated person to the realistic objectives that he is actually capable of achieving. The rigorous requirements of the ministry as *both* profession and calling should be made clear to him. Some on-the-job observation of the minister at work in preaching, teaching, caring, leading, worship, organizing, and administering will demonstrate the realities of the ministry to a prospective candidate. This would involve a deepened and broadened understanding of "the glory of God in the Christian calling." It would also involve a step-by-step path of preparation and decision rather than a one-leap approach. Some sensitive spirits find their place in the world in a moment, in a twinkling of an eye, but they are the rare ones rather than the customary ones. To make a wholesale, detailed, specific dedication which one finds out later he has neither the ability nor opportunity to realize may actually do a person harm. To move under the sealed orders of one's Lord may call for equally as much faith and reward one with equally as much adventure.

Working Not by Constraint but Willingly

The standard that is set forth in I Peter for a minister is that he be spontaneously happy in his work. This is one sure test of the call of God to a work: the degree of peace and satisfaction one has in doing the work. The shepherd is enjoined in I Peter 5:2-4 to do his work not out of a dull sense of necessity and morbid compulsion but of his own free will and desire.

This cuts across the grain of much conviction that men must have "fought the call" to be a minister, and that they would be doing something else if they had had their own choice in the matter.

Then too, the shepherd is encouraged to maintain a sense of spiritual anticipation and eagerness in his work. He does not look upon his work as a "professional service rendered" for which the congregation "owes" him his pay. There is a vast difference between the shepherd and the hireling. The one enters into a creative fellowship with the Chief Shepherd. The other is counting the hours until payday and wondering whether those who came in later than he did are getting as much pay as he is. The one has a sense of mission and the other has a job.

However, let us face ruefully a hard fact about ourselves as Christian pastors. We tend to hide slovenly work and a lack of spiritual discipline under a proud claim of being free of "professionalism." At the same time, we are uneasy and feel inferior in the presence of men of other professions such as medicine and teaching who are subject to distinct professional requirements and disciplines for their tasks. Since 1951, creative work has been done by Hiltner, Cogan, Goode, and others on the reappraisal of the meaning of "profession." Hiltner points out that a professional person does his work on the basis of principle rather than merely upon the accumulation of unexamined skills. Cogan says that a profession serves the vital needs of man and is built upon the ethical imperatives of service to man.[9] Goode points out that a profession is governed by both legal and ethical codes which have been clearly written. The ethical codes exercise a heavier power over a genuine professional than do legal codes.[10] This author has discussed in detail the problem of defining the ministry as profession in

[9] Morris L. Cogan, "The Problem of Defining a Profession," *The Annals of the American Academy of Political and Social Science*, Jan., 1955, pp. 105–117.

[10] "Encroachment, Charlatanism, and the Emerging Profession," *American Sociological Review*, Vol. 25, No. 6 (Dec. 1960), pp. 902–933.

his more recent work, *Protestant Pastoral Counseling*.[11] The ministry is hurting today for a more specific definition of its ethical code. On the basis of this, ministers need a deeper sense of commitment to the welfare of one another as ministers. This is never more crucial than when ministers themselves prey upon one another in open and hidden conflicts and competition.

The neotraditional understanding of the minister as professionally trained, dedicated, and disciplined in his identity has done much to rescue the meaning of "professional" from unsavory connotations of "money-getting." The reverse side of the coin of the professionally paid religious worker is that the minister is responsible for doing the things for which he receives money. He must be a good steward of his time. Side issues cannot be allowed to pull him from the main center of his working day. For example, the pastor who does not learn to limit the demands upon him that interfere with his solid preparation for teaching and preaching will soon jeopardize his opportunities to perform central functions. This is one sturdy reason for thorough clinical pastoral education. Here, the pastor learns to measure his time and strength according to the real needs of parishioners instead of according to his own need for approval. He handles his time and his energy in a disciplined and purposive way, i.e., as a professional and not as an amateur. Thus he does more effective pastoral care and counseling and conserves his time for other tasks as well. In these senses, the "aptness" of a pastor as a teacher and shepherd portrays him as one who knows what he is doing. He does not do a "hammer and hatchet" kind of patchwork. He does a genuinely professional work. He professes faith in Jesus Christ. He commits himself to fellowship and discipleship with Christ. He removes the option of being either known or not known as a Christian from his decisions. He sets himself to the commission of caring for people. His responsibility for them as persons is an ethical imperative. As such, he is "professional" in the

[11] Wayne E. Oates, *Protestant Pastoral Counseling* (The Westminster Press, 1962), pp. 156 ff.

highest sense of the word. He makes all who are " professional " in the lowest sense of the word uncomfortable in his presence. He is an *apt* teacher and shepherd.

The absence of such discipline and commitment underlies the servile attitude of a hireling. Naturally following this comes an increasing necessity to " lord it over " the flock. Then there is no spontaneous joy in a pastor's work. When there is a fleecing attitude on the pastor's part, the people soon begin to rebel against him. Then he becomes anxious, irritable, and unhappy, because no dictator can be otherwise. The love of power, no less than the love of money, is the root of the evil of crass commercialism in the ministry. Such a minister is always afraid lest his authority be questioned, challenged, defied, or betrayed. He has to depend upon a " gestapo " that he cannot trust to enforce his commands. A happy pastor, though, is the one who depends upon his affectionate ties with his people for the force of his leadership. He depends, not upon the love of power, but upon the power of love for the achievement of results — not as " domineering over " those in his charge but as an example to the flock.

The pastor's love, however, is not sufficient. That cannot be his crown of glory. Rather, the consummate requirement of the pastor is that he depend devotedly upon the Chief Shepherd for his own spiritual sustenance and live in the buoyant expectation of the Shepherd's continual manifestation of himself. Paul calls this being " holy " and " a lover of goodness." These terms of endearment of the life of a pastor lay the emphasis upon his consecration and devotion, without which all other qualifications are in vain and usually are consumed in their own vanity. Søren Kierkegaard has called this " purity of heart," by which he means the power " to will one thing, and that is Christ."

The pastor cannot haggle with halfheartedness, partializing of desires, reservations of mind. Having brought all mixed emotions and ambivalent feelings to consciousness, he has brought them to a positive conclusion. The multiplicity of selves that cast a vote in the congress of this man's destiny must have cast their " Yes! " in favor of the noble task of the pastor. Then the man is ready for his work as a good minister of Jesus Christ, capable of standing, and having endured all, of remaining. He can say with Walter Rauschenbusch: " I have found a task apart from which nothing I have ever learned or done is foreign."

" Who Is Sufficient for These Things? "

The apostle Paul disavowed the identity of one of the " peddlers of God's word." He rejected what we today call " phoniness " in order to be a man " of sincerity, as commissioned by God, in the sight of God " to speak in Christ. The fragrance of the knowledge of God in Christ was an aroma of life to those who participated in redemption, but a fragrance of death to those who willfully remained estranged from God. The basic qualifications of the Christian pastor set forth here were developed through the experience of the early church in implementing this sense of commission of which the apostle Paul had earlier spoken. When the apostle Paul compared himself with the claims of the gospel of Christ, he asked: " Who is sufficient for these things? " When anyone of the contemporary ministry compares himself with these ideals, he feels a contrast rather than a comparison. As one student commented: " Even in the New Testament, you can draw out some less than exemplary illustrations of pastoral care." Other students have asked: " Who, then, can be a minister of Jesus Christ if these are the qualifications? " Thus we are confronted with the ambiguity between a Biblical statement of ideal expectations and life as it is. Humanly we realize that these ideals produce tension in and of themselves in the effort simply to approximate, much less achieve, them. The genuineness of the conflict that such ideals create in the best of ministers cannot be ignored.

Furthermore, these ideals can be taken as legalistic maxims. Taken apart from the grace of Jesus Christ and the power of the Holy Spirit, these maxims give those who imagine they have achieved them a basis for pride, rejection of others, and a means of punishment of others. Therefore, these ideals should instead be light and guidance to every minister in his continual confession of sin and search for forgiveness, grace, and mercy. Then his ministry becomes a pageant of gratitude on the part of one who, as Paul and John Bunyan both said of themselves, is the chief of sinners. The fellowship of believers is not a company of perfect people. It is a communion of sinners who accept one another. They have covenanted together to bear one another's burdens and so fulfill the law of Christ. As such, the minister is the chief of sinners who offers sacrifices not only for the people's sins but for his own as well.

Demands upon the minister are stressed in this chapter. These demands cannot be allowed to obscure the succor and support offered him by his community of faith and by the God and Father of the Lord Jesus Christ. The ease with which sources of strength are obscured in the average community makes it all the more imperative that ministers, as spiritually called and professionally trained men, learn how to sustain one another in times of stress and frailty. Small groups of ministers can do much for one another in this way. Reuel Howe, at the Institute for Advanced Pastoral Studies in Bloomfield Hills, Michigan, has demonstrated how such groups may be a part of the continuing theological education of the minister. A willingness to accept one's humanity and frailty without denying the validity of the ideals of the Christian ministry set forth in the pastoral epistles is a paradoxical tension inherent in the nature of the ministry. To do this with inner sincerity and in fellowship with other ministers both clarifies the minister's identity and rests his integrity in the awesome goodness of God.

Chapter IV

The Identity and Integrity
of the Pastor

This chapter was entitled "The Total Task of the Pastor" in the first edition. The shift of the title represents a changed emphasis. The minister is justified by his faith relationship to God in Christ, to himself, and to his faith community and not by the tasks he performs. This is a shift from a task-oriented, work-centered meaning of the existence of the Christian pastor to an identity-centered and *being*-centered integrity of the pastor. With clarity of identity and integrity of being, the Christian pastor does and does not do many things. *What* he does is not determined by the other-direction of the most recent demand laid upon him. His functions are determined by his inner sense of identity and integrity or lack of it. The major thrust of the Christian pastor's dialogue in prayer with God, in conversation with himself and his family, and in interaction with his faith community of the church is, then, the clarification of his identity and the focus of the integrity of his "person-hood" under God. From this he draws his guidance as to the nature of his task. By means of this he resolves conflicting expectations of himself by others.

The average pastor is on a quest for a unified perspective of his calling under God that issues in a joyous participation with the people whom he serves. If he is to do his work well, refreshing strength must be afforded him from a coherent vision of his identity. Instead, the Christian pastor is often confused in his identity. He seeks to find his way between the divided

How about temptations →

camp of the contradictory social demands and personal ambitions that beset him, knowing neither who he is nor where he is going. A vision of his identity both challenged Jesus to lay down his life and at the same time gave him satisfaction that "the world knew not of." The vision must have been renewed daily in our Lord Jesus Christ through his worship in intimate communion with the Father, through his powerful interchanges with the expectations of his disciples, and through his responses to the shepherdless multitudes who sought his ministry. As undershepherds of the Good Shepherd, it can hardly be different for the Christian pastor who is an authentic person in his own right under God, not just a walking job description.

In 1956, a pessimistic note was struck by H. Richard Niebuhr. He said that "the contemporary church is confused about the nature of the ministry. Neither ministers nor the schools that nurture them are guided today by a clear-cut, generally accepted concept of the office of the ministry, although such an idea may be emerging." [1] Niebuhr spoke of the ministry as "the perplexed profession." He averred that the emerging new, clear-cut, generally accepted conception of the ministry was that of *a pastoral director*. In this sense, when a pastor cares for people, he does so as the spiritual overseer of a church; he administers a community that has as its purpose the increase of the love of God and neighbor among men; and the church is the minister and the minister its servant, directing it in its caring ministry.

The work of Samuel Blizzard in an indirect way further refined the more or less general hypothesis of Niebuhr. He consulted six hundred active Protestant ministers as to their perception of their identity as ministers. They were asked to describe, from three different vantage points, their own self-image concerning whom they considered themselves to be. First, they were asked what they thought was *most important* in their calling; second, they were asked in what identity they considered themselves *most effective;* and, third, they were asked in which identity they were happiest and from which

[1] H. Richard Niebuhr, *The Purpose of the Church and Its Ministry.*

they received the *most enjoyment.* The following ranking of
the six functional identities of the minister was found:

IMPORTANCE	EFFECTIVENESS	ENJOYMENT
1. Preacher	1. Preacher	1. Pastor
2. Pastor	2. Pastor	2. Preacher
3. Priest	3. Teacher	3. Teacher
4. Teacher	4. Priest	4. Priest
5. Organizer	5. Administrator	5. Organizer
6. Administrator	6. Organizer	6. Administrator

Considerable internal contradiction prevailed in these ministers' self-images. They felt that preaching was their most important function and that they were most effective at preaching. But they received more satisfaction from their work as a
pastor, which they ranked next in importance and in personal
effectiveness. Thus they probably allowed less time for preparation of sermons, and neglected that which they, for one reason
or another, felt more important than pastoral care. On the
other hand, their sense of effectiveness as pastors was less than
that as preachers. This indicates that pastors need more knowledge and skill in pastoral care in order to do this more effectively in less time. Ranking fourth in importance and third in
effectiveness and enjoyment was the work of teaching. The
pastor's identity as a man of prayer and worship was third in
importance but fourth in effectiveness and enjoyment. At the
very bottom of the scale in importance, effectiveness, and enjoyment were organizing and administering the life of the
church. Thus the function of pastoral direction, which Niebuhr
chose as the emerging new conception of the minister, has less
theological meaning or inner identity in the minister's self-
image. The internal integrity of the identity of the pastor is
perplexed, confused, and frustrated, according to Blizzard's
initial findings.[2]

Blizzard sought some objective basis for measuring the actual
decisions of the same group of ministers regarding what their
identity is in fact and function as well as in their idealizations.

[2] Samuel Blizzard, " The Minister's Dilemma," *The Christian Century,*
April 25, 1956.

He asked these ministers to analyze their use of time, as ministers, on ordinary working days. The use of time is one candid criterion of a person's internal sense of identity. In the same article cited with reference to the previous data, Blizzard published the following information on the ministers' use of their time. He combined the priest-preacher categories because of their close affiliation in the preparation and participation phases of the minister's work.

The minister's workday: Rural: 9 hours, 17 minutes.
Urban: 10 hours, 32 minutes.

Administrator	8/20
Pastor	5/20
Priest Preacher	4/20
Organizing	2/20
Teacher	1/20

Average time per day spent in sermon preparation: 34 minutes (rural), 38 minutes (urban).

Stenographic tasks: 1 hour, 4 minutes.

Blizzard's study reveals that the particular roles that the ministers in their own self-concepts value least, feel least effective in performing, and receive the least satisfaction from, i.e., administration and organizing, occupy exactly half of their time. Their identity as a pastor comes more nearly to having the same place in their output of time that it does in their personal values, taking one fourth (five twentieths) of their time. The priestly, preaching, and teaching functions of the pastor consume the other fourth of their time. Teaching, as such, was the most neglected dimension of the pastor's identity, receiving only one twentieth of their time. Stenographic tasks occupied more time than did the teaching ministry of the pastors.

Blizzard was careful to note in his studies that these impressions were derived from the ministers themselves, not from their parishioners. Charles Y. Glock and Philip Roos of the University of California studied twelve Lutheran congregations in order to get the parishioners' view of how their ministers

spent their time, and what kinds of performance on the part of
the minister received the greatest and least approval from the
congregation.[3] Their study was based on 2,729 questionnaires
received from a sample of the membership of twelve churches.
The persons were asked what two kinds of work they thought
their pastor spent the most time on, and what two kinds of
work he spent the least time on. The following table represents
their replies:

PARISHIONERS' RANKING* OF TIME
SPENT ON EIGHT ACTIVITIES
BY MINISTERS IN TWELVE
LUTHERAN CONGREGATIONS

Activity	Most time				Least time				Mean rank
	1	2	3	4	5	6	7	8	
Sermon preparation	8	2	2	–	–	–	–	–	1.5
Work for church at large	2	5	3	1	–	1	–	–	2.6
Attending church meetings	2	2	5	2	1	–	–	–	2.8
Office work	–	–	–	5	2	2	3	–	5.2
Giving people advice	–	–	1	2	6	2	1	–	5.0
Visiting nonmembers	–	1	1	1	1	5	3	–	5.4
Visiting members	–	2	–	1	2	2	5	–	5.4
His own recreation	–	–	–	–	–	–	–	12	8.0

* Ranks were based on scores for each activity computed by sub-
tracting the number of "least" responses from the number of
"most" responses and dividing by the total number of responses,
"n." "Don't know" responses, which ranged from 27 to 52 percent of the parishioners in the twelve congregations, were omitted
in the computation of this table.

Glock and Roos concluded that parishioners formed their
opinions on the basis of visibility, i.e., the importance of an activity was determined by the number of members who directly
saw the minister in action at this particular kind of work. As a

[3] Charles Y. Glock and Philip Roos, "Parishioners' Views of How
Ministers Spend Their Time," *Review of Religious Research,* Spring,
1961, pp. 170–175.

result, they felt that he spent most of his time at (1) sermon preparation, (2) work for the church at large, (3) attending church meetings, and (4) office work, in that order. They felt that he spent the least amount of his time in (1) his own recreation, (2) visitation of members, (3) visitation of nonmembers, and (4) giving advice and counsel to individuals, in that order. Glock and Roos compared this information with Blizzard's studies. They concluded that the wide margins of difference between ministers' self-images and actual reports of time use, on the one hand, and the parishioners' perceptions of these same things, on the other, reflect a serious failure of communication on the part of the church and its ministry to interpret to its membership "just what the ministerial role entails in practice."

Although Glock and Roos do not say so, the main avenue of communication between the leadership and the membership of the church, namely, effective teaching, occupies only one twentieth of the pastor's time. From these data the hypothesis can be drawn that the failure of communication may lie in the devaluation of a teaching ministry for the pastor himself on the part of both the pastor and his congregation. If he were involved in more give-and-take discussion with small groups of his church, possibly the level of communication could be effectually improved. Apart from some such face-to-face encounter in which minister and people can communicate on a common ground with two-way interchange, the hypothesis of Glock and Roos will hold unchanged: "The image of a profession will be largely informed by what is visible in the professional activity."

Glock and Roos then asked additional questions of the parishioners as to their evaluations of what their minister ought to be doing with his time. They were asked whether they felt that their pastor spent too much, too little, or about the right amount of time on each of eight functions. The study revealed that the majority of the parishioners were uncritical of their ministers. The following table represents the opinions of those who did express an evaluation:

INDEX OF PARISHIONER APPROVAL OF EIGHT
MINISTERIAL ACTIVITIES ACCORDING TO
PARISHIONER CONCEPTIONS OF TIME
SPENT ON THEM

Activity	Approval score * for parishioners who perceive their ministers as spending:		
	Most of their time on an activity	Least of their time on an activity	Neither most nor least of their time on an activity
Sermon preparation	.65	.05	.80
Work for church at large	.25	.55	.70
Attending church meetings	.45	.50	.55
Office work	.00	.85	.65
Giving people advice	.60	.10	.80
Visiting nonmembers	.80	.10	.65
Visiting members	.85	.00	.65

* Scores should not be interpreted as representing proportion of parishioners approving an activity. In fact, a majority of parishioners were uncritical of their minister. [" His own recreation " omitted by the authors of this article.]

Two activities — visiting members and nonmembers — were most approved by the members. Although the members perceived their ministers as spending most of their time on sermon preparation, they believed this to be of only moderate importance. It is heartening to see that these members considered attending church meetings and doing office work as minimal or insignificant in their approval of their minister. When we compare these parishioner expectations with Blizzard's estimates of what ministers themselves consider to be most important, they are almost identical. The preaching and pastoral functions take precedence in the minds of both the pastor and the parishioner. A positive conclusion can be drawn from these two studies: The minister should delegate some of the clerical tasks, and reject the compulsion to attend *all* the meetings both in and out of the church. In turn, he should concentrate the time saved in this way upon a more effective teaching ministry of his own. Thus, he would create a situation in which the basic truths of the Christian faith could be communicated in depth and detail. Some of the failures of communication between him and his congregation could thus be overcome. At the same time, he would have natural group situations for developing lay ministers for preventing and remedying some of the problems that consume his energies in individual counseling work.

When such a conclusion is drawn, however, the defenses of the average minister begin to mobilize. He perceives himself predominantly as a preacher. He thinks of himself as most effective here, and, next to his pastoral work, actually enjoys the pulpit ministry most. In his education and in the church at large, he has both been taught and encouraged to think of his ministry of teaching as something any willing housewife can do. He feels, therefore, unfaithful to his call to prophesy if he does not strictly define his ministry to groups in the formal preaching situation.

These data suggest several pertinent ideas concerning the diffusion of the minister's identity. The administration takes far more time than the minister feels is important, uses him most effectively, or provides him with the most meaning and satisfaction. Niebuhr's attempt to enrich this focus of the minister's identity with new meaning is a valuable step in the right direction. The minister himself, however, must reappraise his identity as an "overseer" of a particular congregation. He is a shepherd and cannot divorce his pastoral ministry, in which he does get such real satisfaction, from his creative oversight of the fellowship of believers as a community.

Again, the minister himself apparently should reassert and

reactivate his own identity as a teacher. James D. Smart says that "very widely the task of the minister is conceived as primarily that of preacher and pastor. If he carries any educational responsibility, that is something added which does not properly belong to his office. He does it only because his church cannot afford an educational director or because he cannot find laymen who will accept the full responsibility." [4] It might be added that if he is fortunate enough to have the additional servies of an educational director, the duties of this person are largely administrative and involve all too little actual teaching.

However, if the *pastoral* instruction of the Christian shepherd were reactivated, he could equip many lay persons to be pastors to one another. An effective perception of himself as a teacher enables the pastor to develop an appropriate atmosphere for many of the things he preaches from the pulpit. Two-way communication in teaching groups creates a healthy dialogue between the person in the pew and the message being preached. Jesse Ziegler, in his small but perceptive volume, points out ways in which a minister may do this through the implementation of what is known about the psychology of personality. [5]

But a mistaken sense of prophecy pervades much of the contemporary minister's conception of himself as a preacher. He directly identifies himself with Old and New Testament prophets and apostles in their forthrightness of utterance. However, he neglects to note that the situation in which the prophets and apostles preached was an open, informal one. Rarely did they preach under the highly formal circumstances of the typical Sunday morning audience of today. They could be interrupted, asked questions, and disagreed with by their hearers. The conditions of prophetic and apostolic preaching were much more akin to the two-way group teaching situations of today. The

[4] James D. Smart, *The Teaching Ministry of the Church* (The Westminster Press, 1954), p. 12.

[5] Jesse Ziegler, *Psychology and the Teaching Church* (Abingdon Press, 1962).

pastor of today has neglected these opportunities and ruled them out of his working day to such an extent that only one twentieth of his time is spent in this way. As a result, he attempts to prophesy in a preaching situation in which response, retort, and resonance are improbable if not impossible. The members of his audience have no way of expressing their feelings except by compliments or by personal hostility, withdrawal from attendance at church, and/or suspicion-laden backbiting. These reactions must, then, be dealt with through personal diplomacy. This consumes the time of the pastor and leaves him with the feeling that he dare not speak his mind fully in the pulpit. The end result is insipid preaching and bored listeners who endure silently while the pastor has his say. This is one major source of what Glock and Roos call " the failure of the church and its ministry to communicate."

The point of the argument here, then, is that the minister's identity can be integrated most effectively around his role as teacher. As teacher, the minister, according to Blizzard's findings, spends the least time and is less likely to perceive himself as doing something important, as being effective, or as being genuinely secure and happy. Teaching is a situation in which the pastor does not do all the talking, as in preaching, or most of the listening, as in counseling. Rather, teaching is a communication " halfway house " between preaching and counseling, providing background for and entrée into either preaching or counseling. Yet in Blizzard's additional findings, he discovered that only one in twenty-five ministers perceived themselves as being an educator, an identity around which all the other dimensions of their calling were integrated. Let us see how pastoral care as practiced by the parish minister can be focused in his identity as a teacher; and also how his work as preacher and his work as leader of worship can be similarly focused in his function as a "teacher come from God"; and finally, how his identity as an administrator and organizer can be focused in his identity as a teacher.

Pastoral Teaching and the Caring Fellowship

The group life of the church as a teaching agency of the community is intimately related to the pastoral care and personal counseling that the pastor does. The pastor cannot relegate the teaching ministry of the church to assistants without doing violence to both his preaching and his pastoral relationship. The education that a congregation receives through the church school provides the background of understanding with which they hear a pastor preach. This education should serve as a front line of preventive defense against those conflicts which cause people to seek pastoral counseling. The reasons for this are not so evident and need clarification, however.

The pastor who takes his parishioners' personal problems seriously finds himself overwhelmed by the many individuals both within and without his congregation who seek help. He cannot possibly get to them all. He finds himself in need of getting persons with similar difficulties and needs together in groups in order that he may more adequately serve them in those needs which can be dealt with on a group level. Also, they need to know and learn from one another. A large measure of their distress is caused by their isolation and loneliness in suffering. For instance, many pastors have discovered that a wholesome group life cushions the shock of retirement for older people and keeps them from becoming ingrown in their later years. "Group work with, and pastoral care of, older people are complementary ways by which the church and pastor minister to those in later maturity. No pastor can make a choice between them. He must use both." [6] This could also be said of the other age groups and interest groups of the church.

Again, the teaching ministry of the church gives the pastor access to the families of the individuals who seek his counsel. The taproot of the unhappiness of the individuals with whom a pastor counsels is in their family relationships. A pastor spends great parts of each week in marriage and family counseling.

[6] Paul B. Maves and J. Lennart Cedarleaf, *Older People and the Church* (Abingdon-Cokesbury Press, 1949), p. 155.

To conduct such a program of pastoral care and personal counseling without an adequate curriculum in family life education, with which to prevent such difficulties and to do away with some of the need for counseling, is gross pastoral nearsightedness. The training of young people, not only in the dramatic story and ethical imperatives of the Bible, but also in the preparation for and participation in Christian marriage, is an indispensable part of the pastoral care and personal counseling of a pastor.

Furthermore, an adequate teaching ministry provides both an inlet and an outlet for pastoral care and personal counseling. For instance, from two contacts with a discussion group on the subject " Learning Spiritual Values in Family Living " a pastor received three requests from individuals attending the group for counsel concerning their family problems. One was an impending divorce situation, another a case in which a marriage had been consummated under false pretenses, and another a family in which the presence of both the man and the wife in their home was gradually stifling the growth of the children. Likewise, in this same group were several couples with whom the pastor had already counseled in premarital guidance, two of whom had invited the pastor to perform their wedding ceremony for them. The fact that instructional groups serve as an inlet through which people may come to a pastor for individual help and an outlet with which he can conserve the results of his personal counseling makes his own teaching ministry of primary concern to him. To neglect this center of his calling in the church or to relegate it to others without concern is to lose touch with one of the main soures of counseling opportunities.

Furthermore, the pastor is largely responsible for the selection and equipping of lay leadership in the teaching ministry of the church. At this point his counseling function and his work as an educator converge most meaningfully. Whatever methods the churches of various denominations have of recruiting lay workers in the educational life of the church, one need remains constant: *these persons should be emotionally healthy and carefully instructed in addition to being willing to serve.*

Religious work meets many inner needs of persons: relief from guilt, escape from home tensions and conflicts, relief from boredom, and other security needs. These needs, however, should be secondary to the welfare of the persons whom a Sunday school teacher seeks to guide. Quite often the parishioner who is most eager to gain or to retain a church office is the least competent to do the work.

Therefore, leaders should be chosen carefully and close attention should be given to the personal adequacy, emotional stability, and basic construction of persons who volunteer for a given task. This can be done tactfully through home visitation, personal counseling, and specialized groups taught by professionally skilled persons. One church in the acquaintance of this author consistently follows this practice, and the result has been a healthy church with a minimum of inner conflict and friction among its organizations.

Finally, the family life of parishioners and their group life in the church are psychologically and educationally separate facets of the same experience. The marital and parental happiness of the leaders of the church becomes a contagion for good or evil in the younger members who follow their patterns of living. Therefore, the pastor needs to work for the selection and training of leaders who have adequately succeeded as parents and as participating members of families. Such leaders can sponsor a strong curriculum in family life education. Healthy leadership and an adequate church school curriculum become bonds that tie the pastoral task and the educational work of a minister together in an inseparable union. The Christian pastor can bring new life and disciplined instruction into the whole life of the church if he takes the time he spends in attending meetings and doing clerical tasks for preparation for and leadership of " equipping sessions " in which he himself is the teacher.

However, one of the reasons pastors do not do this is that they are ill at ease in small groups. They want a crowd. They are defensive about groups in which they do not do all the talking but are open to being challenged by varieties of opinions. They are more secure in the lecture-sermon situation than in a workshop group. But the pastor can overcome these inhibitions. He can develop his skills and insights for small-group teaching ministries. When he does so, he has the instruments for releasing the powers of a congregational fellowship that the monotones of one-way preaching and the isolation of private counseling with individuals cannot touch.

Pastoral Teaching, the Preaching Ministry, and Pastoral Care

The vitality of the small-group ministry provides a fellowship of people who know one another. They are being taught by their pastor how to care for one another and for those on the outside of their fellowship. The atmosphere created by these two-way communication groups makes the preaching ministry of a pastor more than mere speechmaking. He becomes an articulator for the single-heartedness that the Holy Spirit has produced in the small groups. He has already dealt with heavily controversial subjects in situations where the listener could have his say. In the interaction between members of the group and between the group and the leader, definite understandings and new insights can be developed. The combined witness and wisdom of the group as a whole can become the basis for the development of sermons by the pastor. In turn, the sermons can be starters for new directions of thinking in the groups that the pastor teaches and leads. This gives the pastor more freedom in dealing with controversial subjects. It provides a medium for the expression of feeling and opinion that may be contrary to his own. Such teaching groups are in themselves preaching opportunities in the sense of dialogue as over against the monologue of formal pulpit situations of preaching. On the other hand, the individuals who listen to the formal pulpit sermon feel that they have had a part in " the making of the sermons."

The contemporary preacher often finds himself in a complaining mood because, for instance, " he cannot preach what he knows about the Bible" in the pulpit. He looks upon his technical training in the historical method of Biblical study, the literary approach to Biblical interpretation, and the results of modern scholarship concerning the Bible as something that he cannot communicate to lay people. He conveys just enough of his knowledge to make both his congregation and himself anxious, indecisive, and suspicious of one another. The pulpit situation provides him only twenty to thirty minutes a week in which to preach to the majority of his congregation. The lay-taught church school provides another thirty to forty minutes a week of instruction in the dramatic story and moral truths of the Bible, with all too little attention to the context and basis for Biblical interpretation.

Furthermore, as this author has indicated in his small volume entitled *The Bible and Pastoral Care,* many of the personal problems of family conflict, sexual temptation and deviation, hostility, and community distress presented to the pastor in personal counseling reflect distinct misinterpretations of the Bible at one or more significant turning points in the counseling relationship. These misinterpretations amount to gross superstition at times. They represent the failure of the teaching ministry of the church in the clear communication of the Word of God.

Thus the absence of an effective teaching ministry of the church and its pastor actually creates hindrances in preaching. On the other hand, some of the need for counseling grows out of the sheer ignorance and misinterpretation of the Scriptures. The falling away of young people from the church and from the stability of the Scriptures is just one of the many results of this lack of effective teaching. Therefore, the pastor who activates his identity as a teacher of small, face-to-face groups where he "leaps the gap" between his own education and that of his congregation in the Bible, theology, church history, Christian ethics, and pastoral care finds a coherent center for both his preaching and his pastoral care. He will find a fresh new kind of preaching in which he can be open, candid, and spontaneous with his people. He will cease to curse the darkness of his people about the Bible. He lights the candle of a teaching ministry. Even if at first he can get only two or three people to take the time to be with him, he has the leaven that may spread to the whole congregation.

More specific attention, however, must be given here to the interaction of formal preaching with the pastoral ministry to individuals and families. Historically, the renascence of concern with the intimate, personal ministry of a pastor to individuals in distress began with the emergence of a kind of preaching which Charles Kemp has rightly called "life-situation preaching." As early as the ministry of Horace Bushnell, there was a studied effort of ministers to begin with the human situation and derive the message of the pulpit from the dilemmas of their hearers. Bushnell preached such sermons as "Unconscious Influence" and "The Moral Use of Dark Things," which even now are used as models in homiletics classes. Later, Harry Emerson Fosdick became the main exponent of this kind of preaching and is said to have measured the effectiveness of his sermons by the number of persons who sought his personal guidance in the following week. Of course, this was not new with Fosdick, for Jonathan Edwards had himself done much of his most effective work with individuals who sought him out after his sermons. This indicates clearly that this approach to preaching does not necessarily presuppose a particular kind of theology.

Vital contrasts distinguish the preaching ministry from the pastoral task. Elaboration of each of these distinctives will add strength to this meaning. The preaching ministry is a public one; the pastor's access to the crowd is emphasized. But the pastoral task is ordinarily a private and personal ministry, and the relative anonymity of the service is emphasized. This difference is accentuated when a parishioner fears that what he has said to a minister in private may become topics and illustrations for his preaching in public. The pastor often discovers as he counsels with a parishioner that the person feels as though he were being singled out in certain statements made in a sermon.

Therefore, the pastor as a preacher-counselor does well to ask for the permission of a given individual before he refers to him or what he has said in a public address of any kind. When he does refer to the person, it is better to do so in a two-way communication group where the person himself or herself can respond if need be. But if the reference does happen to be in a formal, pulpit situation, then the pastor should do so only in such a way that the integrity and dignity of the person is enriched and not destroyed. For a pastor to hold individual persons up for ridicule, disdain, or as " horrible examples" should be strictly forbidden, *tabu, verboten, interdit*, i.e., unlawful in any language! The Bible and classical literature are replete with such bad examples. For a pastor to use acquaintances of his personal ministry in this way indicates laziness in preparation and ad-libbing in delivery. Therefore, before he makes any reference to individuals, he should observe the rules of advance preparation, ask for their permission, and do so in a way that will edify them and not ridicule them.

Furthermore, many people prefer to talk with a minister whom they do not see every Sunday and who does not know all their friends, rather than with their own pastor. This may be true even though these persons have no fear of or lack of confidence in their own pastor. The chaplain in the hospital observes this in remarks that patients make about their pastors. As one woman said: " I could never tell my pastor these things. He knows me too well. But I can tell them to a chaplain, because he is detached." The pastoral relationship, in its deeper reaches, requires a considerable degree of anonymity in order that the person may be aided in the difficulties that matter most to him.

This calls for extensive cooperation among ministers of the same community in referring persons who are too close to them to other pastors who can maintain a more detached and objective relationship. It also necessitates a close cooperation between the pastor and medical doctors who are skilled in counseling people. In larger communities, pastoral referral centers and pastoral counseling centers have been and will continue to be established. Specialized help of skilled psychologists of religion and pastoral counselors is slowly becoming a felt need in a few communities.

The second distinction between the pastoral and the preaching situations is the time element. Pastoral work is difficult to control in terms of the extent of time needed for individuals and of the number of persons who seek the pastor's help. The pastoral care and personal counseling ministry of a pastor can so encroach upon his time that he will have none left for anything else. This overloading in turn becomes a barrier to effective pastoral counseling. People will feel so guilty about taking the pastor's time that their qualms of conscience will prevent them from using wisely the time that he does give them. Conversely, the time element enters again when the pastor, pressed for the preparation of the sermon for Sunday, is interrupted by a person who needs immediate attention. The minister may have difficulty listening to the person's story. He may even be tempted to preach to the parishioner what little of the sermon he has prepared.

Again, the preaching-pastoral relationship proposes a paradox in the approach that a minister uses to meet the needs of the same people. As a preacher, he approaches their lives in terms of goals, ideals, objectives, and purposes for living in the Kingdom of God. But in pastoral care and personal counseling, the pastor approaches people not merely as one who is unswervingly loyal to the absolute ideals of Jesus but also as one who understands when people miss the mark of the ideals of Jesus. As a pastor, he has the wisdom of the serpents concerning the frailties of human nature, and an affectionate tenderness that will "lift up the fallen." This gentleness grows out of the forgiveness he has received for having missed the mark himself. Pastoral leadership casts its light in the arc of these two poles of influence: the devotion of a pastor to the absolute ideals of Jesus and the patience of a pastor with human imperfection. The preaching task is primarily that of challenging men with the distant and flickering but unquenchable lights of the City of God. The pastoral task is primarily that of being able to identify with people just as they are, "to sit where they sit," even in their "haunts of wretchedness" in the cities of men "where cross the crowded ways of life." The two functions are coalesced in the worship of God as the minister learns himself to participate with his congregation in the processes of growth in the covenant of the loving ideals of Jesus.

Enough of the distinctions between a minister's preaching function and his pastoral task have been named. However, some startling parallels between the two relationships ease the adjustment of these functions to each other. The similarities outweigh the difficulties.

The good preacher depends upon the same laws of personality as does the good pastor for the effectiveness of his work. The dynamics of preaching, teaching, and healing are much the same as far as the pastor's relationship is concerned. For instance, in pastoral care and personal counseling, the pastor must establish a "relationship of a trusted motive," before the person can be helped by him. He must be able to put himself in the place of the individual with whom he is counseling. In turn, that person must be able to identify with the pastor, i.e., to trust his motives, appreciate his way of life, and even desire to be like him. The establishment of this rapport takes time and patient relaxation of suspicions and defenses of all kinds.

This is equally true of the relationship of a preacher to a congregation. A bond of honor and shared feeling transmits the message of a preacher to a people. Some pastors can establish this more quickly than others, but the sense of togetherness must be there before the sermon becomes a reality to the hearers. The congregation tests the reality of a man's utterance without planning to do so, and the sermon becomes an "I–Thou" relationship, a personal encounter, as Farmer (following Martin Buber) has accurately said.[7]

Preaching as a personal encounter becomes the careful and devoted management of a growing understanding between a pastor and his congregation rather than merely an oratorical

[7] H. H. Farmer, *The Servant of the Word* (Charles Scribner's Sons, 1942), p. 56.

demonstration. The theological professor who has been a pastor and blended his mind with that of a congregation finds occasional preaching in first one pulpit and then another to a group of total strangers to be a tasteless experience in comparison. Pastoral care and personal counseling lend feeling and meaning to preaching. Preaching becomes the preparation for counseling.

As such, the preaching of a sermon becomes an inlet into counseling with individuals, an important source of precounseling contacts. Also, the ministry of comfort and reassurance, instruction and interpretation, can often be done more powerfully through preaching than through individual counseling, because it is done in the presence of the larger community of worshipers. Furthermore, the individual can more easily accept or reject a given interpretation when he is in a group or a crowd. On the other side of the pulpit, too, the pastor can give guidance that applies to " all mankind " and carefully avoid being too stringent on a given individual. Having done this, a pastor in private conference with parishioners can spend his time in listening to their side of the story. Such a reciprocal relationship between pastoral care and preaching will go far in alleviating the feeling that many lay people express when they object to not being allowed to answer the preacher back or to ask him a question. A listening pastor makes an understanding preacher.

The pastor who maintains a consistent counseling ministry will move in the direction of " life-situation preaching." By definition, life-situation preaching " begins with life situations and is aimed at them. . . . It starts where people live. Such preaching must, of necessity, have a close relationship to pastoral work." [8] In the previous edition of this book I called this " therapeutic preaching," but I find Kemp's term for this kind of preaching much more appropriate because the term " therapeutic " is, as Kemp says, too restrictive and tends to exclude

[8] Charles F. Kemp, *Life-Situation Preaching* (The Bethany Press, 1956), p. 16.

such aspects of life-situation preaching as instruction, interpretation, encouragement, and inspiration which must be included in a proper understanding of life-situation preaching. The characteristics of such preaching are fourfold: (1) the *interpretation* of human experience in the light of Biblical truth rather than the exhortation of people to the observance of certain moral precepts, as such; (2) the development of personal *insight into the motives of personal and group action* rather than the condemnation of this or that kind of behavior; (3) the *encouragement* of the congregation toward faith in God, in one another, and in themselves as means of gaining control over behavior that they themselves discover to be alien to the mind of Christ; (4) the growth of a *sense of comradeship with God in Christ* and the changing of personality through this " transforming friendship."

Contrary to some opinion, life-situation preaching may be thoroughly Biblical and even exegetical. However, the approach to the Bible itself is a life-situation approach. The studied effort of the exegesis is to reconstruct the " situation-that-was " at the time of the writing. The interpretation, however, is not simply paralleled with a similar contemporary situation-in-life. Instead the timeless elements of both situations are identified and become the outline of the sermon. The end result is a meditative interpretation of Scripture in the present tense. This was the intention in the writing of the book of sermons, *The Revelation of God in Human Suffering,* which I published in 1959 (The Westminster Press). Similarly, Charles Kemp has edited a book of life-situation sermons entitled *Pastoral Preaching* (The Bethany Press, 1963).

Of course, certain aspects of the life-situation approach are immediately identifiable as " the psychological approach " to homiletics. Such an approach implies a *conversational, eye-contact, extemporaneous delivery* rather than a more impersonal, formal, and oratorical delivery. It rules out histrionics and other appeals to the more superficial emotions that are united to the sense of touch, to sound, and to rhythm. It calls for a personal inventory, a confrontation of the self, and a re-ordering of the deep emotions of family love and hate, vocational intention, and the fundamental desires that drive human action.

The preacher, through the processes of sympathetic imagination, empties himself of his own frame of reference and takes upon himself the condition and cries of the people's inner lives. He hopefully seeks to articulate their prayers for them. In so doing, he is their spokesman before God as well as God's spokesman before them. In this kind of preaching prophetic and priestly functions are blended in one act of preaching. No artificial dichotomy separates these, for the prophet at one and the same time declares himself to be both a man of unclean lips and a man dwelling in the midst of a people of unclean lips. Therefore, he can sit where they sit. Naturally, life-situation preaching produces the relief from a sense of guilt and rest from tension through the resolution of conflict. It stands over against the type of preaching that creates unrest through the introduction of conflict into a complacent mind and the development of a sense of guilt in people who are "past feeling" a given moral or spiritual value. As such, a sermon based on life itself qualifies as an act of worship in itself. The people of God are refreshed on their way.

Worship: The Life's Blood of the Pastor

The relationship of a pastor to individuals, groups, and congregations undergoes a metamorphosis in the act of worship. Consciousness of his presence fades out and awareness of the real presence of God reaches its zenith. The quantitative differences of character between the pastor and those to whom he ministers become as nothing as the eternal qualitative difference between all men and God becomes more evident.

Worship, as Gaines S. Dobbins has said, is the "interruption of our daily routine" and of our involvement in the transitory things of life "to recognize the supreme worth of God, to praise him for his goodness, to meditate on his holiness, to renew devotion to his service" and to sever our idolatries.[9] The act of worship, therefore, has a wealth of connotations for the pastoral task of the minister.

Informal worship, where two or three are gathered together in the spontaneity of the shared knowledge of the presence of God, is the true atmosphere of the face-to-face relationship of a minister to an individual. The reverent care of living persons is a type of worship in its own right. This has been the primitive foundation of many religions, and, with all its limitations, is the extent of the worship of the vast majority of the people of the world. However, even in the Christian experience of worship, the reverence for God and the reverence for human personality are inseparable. The acute appeal of a suffering person is the medium of revelation most often promised by Jesus; "When did we see thee?" is the question of both true and insincere worshipers. "As you did it to one of the least of these my brethren, you did it to me." (Matt. 25:40.)

Although the face-to-face ministry of a pastor to individuals should be, and often is, an Emmaus-road form of prayer, it does not become such without personal discipline on the part of the pastor. The question regularly comes to a pastor: "To whom do you go when the worries of other people become too heavy for you?" The answer to this question in a pastor's private worship life is the beginning of his own response to "a serious call to a devout and holy life." As Thomas à Kempis said: "No man doth safely speak, but he that is willing to hold his peace. No man doth safely appear abroad, but he who can gladly abide at home, out of sight. No man can safely command others but he that hath learned willingly to obey." The transforming power of Jesus came through prayer and self-discipline, and the modern pastor cannot expect it to be otherwise with himself.

The pastor who considers his interpersonal work of caring for people as a form of prayer in itself finds personal resources that keep his confidence in people strong, prevent him from

[9] Gaines S. Dobbins, *The Church at Worship* (Broadman Press, 1963), p. 35.

losing patience with them, and undergird him with a steady calmness in the presence of acute pain and unhappiness. Without this sense of worship, the pastor becomes threadbare in the wear and tear of the emotional tension of his task. Fatigue sets in, irritability increases, aggressiveness and defensiveness are the next to follow. In order to allay his own sense of guilt, he then becomes overconcerned and overprotective toward those to whom he ministers. Consequently, he will spend more and more time with fewer and fewer people, and lose his perspective of even their needs.

Another connection between informal worship and pastoral work is apparent. The pastor's capacity to listen to people is dependent upon his reverence for them and his own teachableness. He cannot give such concern unless he has received it himself as an act of grace from God and those persons who nurtured him. The surplus of God's grace abounds to meet the needs of others. The Christian shepherd must necessarily be one whose " cup runneth over." Without this awesome sense of gratitude, without this sense of the abundance of the fullness of God in the satisfaction of his own needs, the pastor himself becomes demanding. He feels misunderstood and imposed upon. He feels like telling his own troubles to the person who is seeking his help. He becomes more talkative, and, with this, his capacity to listen has failed him. He becomes inattentive and insensitive to the subtle feelings of the person who seeks his help.

The third tie that binds worship to pastoral calling and counseling is the expectancy and need of people. The pastor who does not share in worship with those with whom he works soon begins to lose their respect. They begin to suspect his motives and to doubt his sincerity. A prayerless relationship between a pastor and his parishioners gradually relegates him either to the familiarity of all the rest of their social companions or to the atmosphere of an interviewer-client relationship. Both of these latter relationships have their intrinsic values, but they are peripheral to the central function of the minister as a representative of God.

Public worship, as indeed is true of private worship, likewise affords necessary resources for the conservation and multiplication of the pastoral effectiveness of a minister. One of the main distinctives of the role and function of the Christian pastor is that he is related to those whom he helps both individually and socially, both privately and publicly, both on horizontal planes of fellowship between man and man and on a vertical plane of communion between man and God. The place of public worship is where all these lines of influence and relationship meet.[10] Therefore, the minister has at his disposal the resources of the community of worship to meet the needs of the individual for worship and relief from isolation. The resources of the individual are at his disposal, also, to guide him toward the beautification of worship and the strengthening of the moral fiber of the community.

The chief end of worship is " to glorify God and to enjoy him forever." The church at worship is celebrating the joy of the resurrection of Jesus Christ. They are jubilant over the redemption of their lives from destruction, the steadfastness of their relationship to God, and the inseparableness of the fellowship they have in Jesus Christ.

The results of public worship are by-products of this fellowship. In these results, the fruits of teaching, preaching, and caring are multiplied. *Rest, the renewal of strength and energy through relaxation, is one of the shared objectives of both pastoral work and public worship.* The release from nervous tension and the discovery of new reserves of power for living through worship is a neglected emphasis in the activism of many Protestant churches. " Even the youths shall faint and be weary, and the young men shall utterly fall: but they that wait for the Lord shall renew their strength; they shall mount up with wings as eagles; they shall run, and not be weary; they shall walk, and not faint." (Isa. 40:30-31, ASV.) This need for rest prompted the institution of the Sabbath, sustains

---

[10] O. J. Hodges, " The Distinctive Role of the Minister in Psychotherapy," unpublished thesis, Southern Baptist Theological Seminary, 1948.

the continued practice of public worship, and vitally relates that practice to the caring ministry of the pastor.

The quest for community in a sense of the shared meaning of life with others is also a common venture that prompts people both to participate in public worship and to seek the understanding counsel of their pastor. The pastor is the chosen representative of that specific community. To converse with him personally is a private way of approaching that community. The relief from isolation through public worship with the people in Christ is the heart hunger of the worshiper's motive.

Sin and guilt isolate a person from those of his own community. They are accompanied by a longing for restoration " by those who are spiritual," for a sense of belonging again to the group whose approval is most important to the sinner, as well as for restoration to God who insists upon clean hands and a pure heart in those who " worship him in spirit and in truth."

The private confession of sin has very little meaning apart from the corporate worship between imperfect people and the God and Father of the Lord Jesus Christ. These persons in turn are people of unclean lips also, and the individual lives in the midst of a people of unclean lips. All sin is shared guilt as well as an individual responsibility before God. Corporate worship is God's remedy for corporate sin. Here a person realizes that he is not alone in his sinfulness nor in his dependence upon the forgiveness of God. " All we like sheep have gone astray; we have turned every one to his own way " (Isa. 53:6) is an accurate description of the path toward isolation, self-centeredness, and loneliness in a person who is burdened with sin. The ingathering of corporate worship leads to the unification of persons who have a common experience of the forgiving grace of God. The outgoing of the worshiping community is a witness of the joy of fellowship. This witness is the most convincing form of evangelical outreach. " That which was from the beginning, which we have heard, which we have seen with our eyes, which we have looked upon and touched with our hands, concerning the word of life . . . that which we have seen and heard we proclaim also to you, so that you may have fellowship with us; and our fellowship is with the Father and with his Son Jesus Christ." (I John 1:1, 3.)

Thus the values of personal insight and the beginning of a lasting community are created, conserved, and then multiplied in public worship. The radiation of gratitude and self-acceptance lays the foundations upon which Christian worshipers can agree as to common goals and objectives for concerted Christian action. At this point, the work of a pastor, in the secret places of personal counseling to change people's attitudes privately, becomes manifest in public work and social action as these individuals set about righting glaring social wrongs in the community.

The Pastor's Integrity as a Spiritual Overseer

The center of the pastor's integrity rests in his own faith in God and his identity as "a teacher come from God." The circumference of his identity is the body of Christ with which he lives in worshipful fellowship. This parish of his is not an "administrative fiction," but as George Bernanos called "the face of his parish," the church is "a living cell in the everlasting church." In his perspective of himself as a "spiritual overseer," the pastor finds the integrity to sustain himself in his identity as "a teacher come from God." Some ministers who read this description will feel that it is not in keeping with the realistic problems of time and quantities of work with which the average pastor must grapple. Such a concept of pastoral work in the context of the identity and integrity of the minister, however, implies radical departures in the underlying philosophy of the oversight of the church.

American churches have been schematized according to two secular patterns of administration: (1) mass production in business, which depends primarily upon volume rather than discipline of quality for profit, and (2) promotional advertising techniques, which depend upon the depersonalized mediums of publicity, correspondence, telephone, and bulletins

*Mass pro-
duction &
administration*

for results. Churches and denominations have more or less
unconsciously fallen into these same patterns by insisting upon
the largest congregations possible and relying upon the
cleverest techniques of propaganda possible for the recruit-
ment of members. All this moves preaching and the sacraments
to the center of the church life. It insulates the pastor from
personal contact with people, making of him an executive and
administrator of a corporation rather than a shepherd of a
flock.

The end result of this has been that the participation of the
individual church member has decreased in direct proportion
to the increase in the size of the congregation. He accepts less
and less personal responsibility for participation in the Kingdom of God. He shifts more and more of it to paid workers.
He gives less and less money to the causes of the church, and
the paid workers must depend more and more upon small
gifts from larger and larger numbers of people. The early
churches were in a reversed position. They were exclusive
rather than inclusive in their membership. They emphasized
personal discipline rather than promotional values. They ex-
erted influence and gave gifts all out of proportion to their
numbers and wealth, because they " first . . . gave themselves."

Consequently, the position taken here is that numbers,
whether large or small, are not the criterion for effective church
life, pastoral ministry, and Christian outreach. In the first
edition of this book, I emphasized the small church, as opposed
to the large church, as a solution to the problem of adequate
pastoral care. Since that time I have profited from the reactions of readers and from further scrutiny of the problems involved in both small and large churches. I have drawn new
conclusions and revised my hypotheses. The mere fact of
largeness does not predestine a church and its minister to
carelessness in the oversight of the flock. In fact, the church
may have by reason of its larger numbers a wider variety of
services, potential leadership, and professionally trained ministers to perform the work of ministry.

Such a church, however, must have a conception of the ministry as a group effort in which the pastor is not a soloist, assisted and accompanied by others. Rather, he is a more experienced person with more seniority and historical wisdom in the given parish. At the same time he functions as a quarterback of a working team who stay in close and unbroken communication with each other. The whole issue of the March, 1963, number of *Pastoral Psychology*, under the guest editorship of Russell J. Becker, is devoted to the analysis of "The Ministry as a Team." Robert A. Edgar reports on a ten-year experiment of the Glenview Community Church. A multiple ministry of four pastors served on an equal basis in this church — equal in status, salary, preaching, etc. The experiment was a gratifying success in terms of what they learned together about human nature and the interaction of ministers with each other. "The experiment ended abruptly when the four ministers were unable to work out their differences at one point," says Edgar. The reasons for this were listed: No two, much less four, ministers are equal! Decisive action should be taken by one member of the team, especially in time of crisis. The decision as to who does this should be based upon experience, seniority, and historical wisdom of the person so designated, and determined by the congregation itself. Plenty of theological reason underlies the importance of taking into account both diversity of talents and proneness to self-regard, pride, and hidden motives in ministers themselves and the importance of realizing that no one member of the team is free but each is bound to Jesus Christ to act in behalf of the church as a whole and not for himself alone. More positively, Edgar recommends that ministers who work together on a large church staff build a covenant of communication with each other and "carve out of a busy ministerial schedule" time for "sharing their faith and theology in freedom, acceptance, and trust, so that their relationship with Christ and each other is deepened." [11] Such an approach has possibilities for transmuting the organization

[11] Robert A. Edgar, "A Ten-Year Experiment," *Pastoral Psychology*, Vol. 14, No. 132 (March, 1963), pp. 25 ff.

of a large church into an organism of fellowship of the staff members with one another with concern for people other than themselves, either individually or corporately.

On the other hand, the mere fact of *smallness* in numbers is not a guarantee of effective pastoral care and personal concern on the part of members for one another, much less for those on the outside. Many small churches expect only that the minister be the "preacher" in the strict sense of the word. They will assume that they must handle their personal problems with no regard either for the church or for the minister. The exceptions to this would be socially acceptable problems such as acute physical illness, death, and bereavement. Then too, a small church can be a mere extension of two or three families and their employees, tenants, or servants. As such, the patriarchs and/or matriarchs of these families exercise the overseeing functions. The pastor serves only in the strictest formal sense as an "overseer of the flock," responsible primarily for preaching at formal services, officiating at funerals, and occasionally performing a wedding ceremony. The family "ingroup" may both exclude by silence anyone who is "outside," and almost automatically "rank" those who are on the "inside." A small church, therefore, can become a colony of hell much more easily than it can become a colony of heaven in which the church is a self-transcending fellowship, disciplined by obedience to God. Lewis J. Sherrill has said that in a spiritual community every other dimension of the community — cultural, family, personal — is transcended in that "God is present in this community; . . . the Spirit of God is forthgoing into, and present in, every relationship within the community." [12]

Therefore, the conclusions and hypotheses that have been reached here are simply stated: whether the church is large or small numerically, it should be a *disciplined church*. By "disciplined" I mean an *instructed, committed, self-aware, self-transcending, and self-forgetting church.*

These five dimensions of the disciplined church all center

[12] Lewis J. Sherrill, *The Gift of Power* (The Macmillan Company, 1955), p. 50.

upon the first one, *instruction.* The minister and the church place primary value upon *openness and teachability* as a prerequisite for membership in the church. Granted that the person has either been brought up in the church or comes new to the church seeking membership as an adult, the point of discipline at which to begin is his willingness to enter upon a thorough program of instruction and guidance as to the meaning and direction of his own history, calling, and destiny as a Christian. This calls for what Findley Edge rightly identifies as a "period of waiting" for persons professing their faith in Christ or even for those who wish to shift from one church to another. The length of the period of waiting should vary from individual to individual, but a certain minimum time should be maintained. A representative group of persons who have already been so taught and disciplined should practice pastoral oversight along with the pastor. They should determine whether the individual gives "indication that he has a growing understanding of the mission to which he has been called by God," and whether he gives "concrete and observable evidence that he has accepted and is fulfilling this ministry in the world." [13]

Samuel Southard has related the task of pastoral care to the work of evangelism and the disciplined instruction. He interprets the evangelistic outreach of the ministry in terms of the principle of "pastoral patience" whereby ministers move with the prospective Christian through a cumulative process of reflection, decision, and self-exploration prior to any public commitment or presentation for admission to the church. In addition, he evaluates the pastoral care of new converts through the use of Sunday school classes, inquirers classes, person-centered groups, and individual counseling and visitation. [14]

In the second place, the disciplined church is a *committed* fellowship. Commitment involves an explicit and definite covenant of faith based upon the knowledge of the Biblical account

[13] Findley B. Edge, *A Quest for Vitality in Religion* (Broadman Press, 1963), p. 212.
[14] Samuel Southard, *Pastoral Evangelism,* pp. 105–130.

of the revelation of God in Jesus Christ, the witness of the church throughout Christian history, the bond of ethics that holds Christians together with one another and makes their witness distinctive among others, and the kinds of responsibilities that Christians have for caring for distressed and broken persons about them. For example, when the Christian fellowship participates in the joyful celebration of a wedding, this is an act of worship and commitment of two persons to each other and also to the church. They disavow their previous sins and commit themselves to Jesus Christ as Lord of the home they are about to establish. When they become Christians, this is not just in order to keep the marriage together in the same social group, but it is a commitment to the fellowship of faith that will sustain them in the same way of life in Jesus Christ as Lord. When, by whatever means a church does so, the fellowship baptizes a person, this is done with explicit knowledge, previously arrived at by the individual and observed by the fellowship of believers, of the meaning of the Christian faith. The church should be an instrument of confrontation for prospective marital partners, new parents, and new Christians. These people should be confronted as to what they know of the Christian faith and whether they are genuinely committed to what they know. The church is a " company of the committed," as Elton Trueblood has eloquently said.

In the third place, the disciplined church is the *self-aware* fellowship. Members do not worship in isolation from each other. They are aware of the nature of their relationships to each other. For example, students in theological seminary classes often attend them as " courses to be passed," " requirements to be met," and "notes to be taken." They are often rudely awakened to the fact that a professor expects them to become aware of the other members of the class around them, to become acquainted with them, and actually to learn from them. Only slowly do they take hold of the awareness that they have a responsibility to one another in the learning process. In turn, members of their churches are similarly individualistic

in their relation to the church and its minister. Church members are startled to become aware of the church as a powerful,
interacting field of varied and exciting human relationships.
The disciplined church has, as Fritz Kunkel used to call it, a
"we-consciousness" in Christ and in each other. I saw this
most vividly when I thanked a widow for her ministry to an
unwed mother in New York City, a girl about whom my wife
and I had been concerned and to whom we committed ourselves to minister. This widow has provided a room in her
apartment for the girl. When I thanked her, she said: " Oh, I
haven't done anything. You see, I am a member of Riverside
Church!" She saw herself as a part of the living organism of
Riverside. She saw what was done as the ministry of her
church. This self-awareness of a group and its members is
what Anton Boisen has called "the group whose approval one
considers most worthwhile." The church that is disciplined is
the one that has made its approval that which its members
consider most worthwhile among men.

Again, the disciplined church is the *self-transcending* church.
This is not just a mutual admiration society. The community
judges itself not by itself but transcends itself in the worship of
God. It is not religiously shy about mentioning God. On the
contrary, the transcendent light of the Father beams brightly
upon this fellowship and the members are aware of both the
light of God's love and the shadow they cast when that light
falls upon them as a people of God and as individuals within
the we-conscious group. The petty idolatries of family, causes,
programs, pressure groups, trivial ambitions, etc., are brought
into serious confrontation with the Lordship of Christ. This is
the heart of the meaning of worship.

The disciplined church comes to the pinpoint of the caring
ministry in its *self-forgetfulness*. The church has to lose its life
if it is to keep it. The pastor who represents the church becomes weary, for example, of "badgering" people into coming
to church, being more active in the church, giving more money
to the church, etc. He must discover deeper and richer reasons
for visitation than these, for example. If he does not, visitation

will be to him a chore to which he goes "like a quarry slave" and from which he returns as if "scourged to a dungeon." Sooner or later he forsakes visitation of this kind as sheer boredom. Conversely, the perception of the church as an organization which is in the world to be ministered unto provides most of the excuses for those who are opposed, indifferent, and suspicious toward the church. They are completely disarmed when the church and its ministry forgets itself, ceases to devise ready-made answers for criticisms, and becomes genuinely interested in the persons themselves for their own sakes.

The discipline of the church to the outsider, then, becomes the intention to build a durable, trustworthy relationship to him and his family as persons, quite apart from whether they attend all the meetings, listen to all the sermons, or give money. The church must in this way seek first the Kingdom of God and his righteousness, and all these other things will be added to them by God. To be self-forgetful in this way requires an act of faith on the part of the church itself, for faith is not just an individual matter. Groups of people have a corporate faith, too. It must be something rooted in God, and not in the human desire to get prospective members in the community before some other denomination — or, God forbid, before some other church of our own denomination — does.

One may rightly ask: Where has this call to instruction, commitment, self-awareness as a people of God, self-transcendence, and self-forgetfulness been tried recently? Gordon Cosby returned from World War II, in which he had served as a paratroop chaplain. In the unrelenting stress of battle, he saw even active church members torn away from their spiritual resources. After the war, he returned to Washington, D.C., and established the Church of the Saviour. The fellowship of this group extends to people of all races, denominations, and creeds or creedlessness. The requirements for membership are stringent. A person must have completed satisfactorily an extensive program of instruction in Biblical studies, church history, the study of great devotional literature, the arts of caring for distressed people, etc., before he is considered for membership in the church. Members are pledged to tithing and to specific tasks in the service of the church. Each member belongs to a small group dedicated to vital Christian outreach. The whole exciting story of this church has been written by one of the original members of the staff of the church. With anecdote, specific program descriptions, and her own gift of the Holy Spirit, Elizabeth O'Connor challenges most of our major presuppositions about church life and the Christian life in her book, *Call to Commitment* (Harper & Row, Publishers, Inc., 1963). When one reads this story, he will be convinced that one positive example of a disciplined church outweighs all the negative evidence.

Finally, these conclusions all imply that the church must have an aggressive missionary strategy for its own community. New churches must be formed in order to localize and personalize the ministry of both the pastor and the churches themselves. Individual churches cannot live on a competitive basis in relation to one another, therefore, but must devise plans for a cooperative missionary strategy in which the total life of the community as a whole is the primary concern of each group. This implies a cooperative rather than an organic relationship, in order that the autonomy of each face-to-face group may be conserved. At the same time the effectiveness of the social outreach of the whole Christian community can be increased.

Part Two

Pastoral Methods

Conditioning Influences
on Pastoral Methods

Ever since David rejected Saul's armor and chose to use his own slingshot, shepherds have been faced with the necessity of devising ways of working that are best adapted to their own personalities and the conditions under which they must function. Some methods of pastoral care, such as the minister's use of creative listening, are applicable to more situations than others. But no single technique or ideology is applicable to *all* the situations with which a minister has to deal.

Every relationship of a pastor to people is determined by many unspoken factors that tend unconsciously to be taken for granted by both the pastor and the person in need. But the success or failure of the relationship depends upon the pastor's ability to observe these influences and to take advantage of them as he chooses his methods of procedure. He should not remain unaware of them and in turn have his ministry determined by them. They certainly condition what he does. But careful inspection and conscious analysis of these factors prevent them from determining the outcome of the pastor's ministry.

The Christian Equation

The religious situation of the person who comes to the pastor exerts a primary shaping influence upon the methods that the pastor uses in his pastoral procedure. This is not to say that the basic problems of Christians are materially different from those of non-Christians. Rather, it is to say that the spiritual resources available for the solution of such difficulties are different. The person who is committed to God in Christ, who accepts as dependable and true the precepts of the Bible, and who has access to the friendship of the church is vastly richer than the person who does not have these bases of security.

Furthermore, this is not to say that the Christian pastor should have one stereotyped approach that he uses with non-Christians and one other approach that he uses with members of his own flock — making him a total of two procedures. Rather, it is to say that in non-Christians a pastor confronts not only the necessity of discovering the person's more mundane difficulty but also that of introducing him to Jesus Christ and the practice of his way. As we have seen earlier in the discussion of the principle of " linkage," the most trivial and mundane issue may be either causally or symbolically linked to the person's total quest for redemption. In the case of a person who has Christian training and experience, the pastor may draw upon that, although he may face the necessity of correcting misinformation concerning Christian experience.

In both instances, however, the basic problem may be the same. For instance, a thirty-year-old woman says that she can no longer get any joy and security out of her prayer life and feels that she may have backslid. Another woman of approximately the same age says that she has tried everything in order to find happiness with her husband, and she has decided that the reason her home is not happy is that she is not a Christian and does not have a safe place on the inside of her heart. Both women, when careful exploration of their difficulties is made, are found to be suffering from a sense of sin over marital infidelities. In the case of the Christian, however, the practice of Christian life is being hindered, whereas in the case of the non-Christian the beginning of Christian experience is being sought. Likewise, both women express deep feelings of insecurity in their family as well as their religious relationships by reason of the fact that both of them were neglected as children by their fathers and as adults by their husbands. They were the children of inadequate fathers and are the wives of incompetent husbands. In both instances the basic difficulties are very similar, but the pastoral approach is quite different in each case because the religious attitudes of the persons involved give a different structure to the basic difficulty.

The Factor of Initiative

Another conditioning effect upon pastoral technique is whether the person comes to the pastor of his own accord or had to be approached by the pastor. Most pastors have had members of a person's family say to them, " I want you to go talk to my husband, my wife, my brother, my son, my daughter." Quite often this request comes just before or just after a church gathering when little time is available. This is an opportunity to make a later appointment with the person who makes the request. At this time the minister may say, " We can get a better picture of the situation then." Such an interview will often reveal the deeper motives the person has for wanting a minister to see the relative. It will cut down the possibilities of the minister's becoming, in the midst of a family quarrel, a shield in the hands of one member and a target for another member of the family.

Many people come to the pastor because of the insistence of someone whose approval they want very badly. For instance, a young girl may call for an appointment to talk over some premarital difficulties she is having with her boyfriend. Upon arrival she says that she was reluctant to come herself, but her fiancé " twisted " her arm to get her to come to see the pastor. The responsibility for shifting the consultation into one in which she herself wishes to participate rests upon the pastor. It may be that if she learns to make her own choices rather than let someone else do so, she will have gone a long way toward preparing for a more stable marriage.

Ideally constructed, however, are those situations in which a person comes voluntarily, and not out of constraint, to his pastor about his own problems and not about someone else's difficulty. Such a person has already spiritually prepared himself for the pastor's work. Even here, nevertheless, the minister must be sensitive to the person who is a chronic "counsel seeker," with the habit of going to first one person and then another without following through with his relationship to any of them. In listening to a person, the pastor will note the other pastors, teachers, doctors, psychiatrists, etc., to whom the person has been with his problems. If such information is not reflected by the person's own discussion, a pastor can tactfully ask for it at an opportune moment. A standard question on a first interview is: "To whom else have you been able to talk about this?" If the person is not a member of a pastor's own congregation, a minister would do well to discover how it came to pass that this person chose to come to him. Such measures do much on the first interview to define one's relationship and to indicate the particular approach the pastor should follow and the technique he should use. He can evaluate the kinds of guidance the person has already received and profit by the work of others who have ministered to the person.

The Social Role of the Pastor

Gardner Murphy suggests that the social task or function carried out by an individual in a community is shaped by the social role that the community assigns to him by virtue of the confidence it has in him as a person. This social role is made up, in our society, of the age status, the marital-sexual status, the educational background, and the unique and individual features of the person who is called upon to perform a given task. All these combine to give a person his concept of himself and to give him the status in the community that makes it possible for him to do his task more effectively. In a word, the pastor's concept of himself and the part that he is assigned in the drama of interpersonal relationships in his community largely conditions the techniques with which he functions as a pastor.[1]

The pastor's age has an important bearing upon his methodology. The more nearly he is the same age of the person whom he seeks to help, the more of a " fellowship " approach he uses and the less social distance he has in the relationship. If he is much younger — or even if he is youthful only in appearance — older persons may tend to mother him or father him, although this does not always happen. If he is middle-aged or elderly, young persons more readily express feelings of a filial nature. Inexperience enters to judge the young man and too much age causes some people to feel that the elderly man will not understand. The importance of the age relationship of a pastor to his parishioner is suggested in the advice of Paul to Timothy: " Do not rebuke an older man but exhort him as you would a father; treat younger men like brothers, older women like mothers, younger women like sisters, in all purity " (I Tim. 5:1-2). The fact that the pastor *is* the pastor often erases the age distinction in people's minds. Also, people who are uneducated will often look to even a young pastor as an authority if he is both considerate of them and thoroughly trained. His training offsets the age factor.

Then, too, the marital status of a pastor conditions his approach and method. Especially is this true in family counseling situations. A married pastor visiting a woman patient in a hospital finds her a great deal more at ease in speaking of the effect that her recent operation may have on her childbearing ability than would a single minister. Likewise, a married pastor who is also a parent would find more ease in this situation than would the pastor who has no children. Furthermore, single persons seem to feel more secure in giving confidences to a married minister. In such instances, women feel more secure because the married minister is not a potential husband. It seems that the pastoral situation calls either for a married

[1] Gardner Murphy, *Personality: A Biosocial Approach to Origins and Structure* (Harper & Brothers, 1947), pp. 784 ff.

man — with children, if possible — in the case of Protestant ministers, or for a celibate, as in the case of Catholic priests.

The New Testament calls for another trait, which subtly affects a pastor's methods. It requires that he be " given to hospitality." Another way of saying this is that the pastor is a " lover of strangers." The pastor's effectiveness as a counselor hinges upon his ability to put those people at ease who are strangers to him and also to identify himself with people whose experience is quite often poles apart from his own. People of different standards, family background, social standing, education, and personal tastes from his own nevertheless find it easy to identify with him. They feel that he loves them and welcomes them into his confidence. Such a pastor finds that all manner of people come to him with all manner of requests.

Of course, whether or not people turn to a pastor is inspired by the personal magnetism of the man himself. All that has been said on the subject of the personal qualifications of the Christian shepherd is applicable here. The writers of the New Testament did not list such standards in order to be legalistic; they were searching for men to whom " the flock of God" could turn for personal counsel and spiritual edification. They were looking for the most spiritually healthy men they could find to be " physicians of the soul," men who did not themselves stand in need of a physician, and whose very shadow would have a healing effect.

The Time Element

The time element conditions everything a pastor does. Face-to-face pastoral care of individuals is one of the most important things he does, but it is only one of the numberless things he has to do. The administrative responsibility of a complex organization, the social demands of his community life, and the constant pressure of his preaching ministry draw upon his time. Likewise, in church bodies that have a congregational form of church government the pastor has heavy responsibilities on governing boards of trustees and commissions. Special committees often take weeks of his time.

The result of these pressures has been that responsible pastors tend to fret under four great frustrations: (1) they do not have time to study, (2) they do not have time for their own families, (3) they do not have time for a face-to-face ministry to their people, and (4) they do not have time for the cultivation of their inner spirits before God. The pastor becomes an isolated, lonely, tired individual who is cut off from the fulfillment of the four basic functions in society that offer him personal satisfaction in fulfilling his call to service.

Therefore, the minister must take intelligent measures as to the use of his time. He needs to decide for himself what is important in the ministry and leave other things to persons who consider them important. Chang Ch'ao says, " Only those who take leisurely what the people of the world are busy about can be busy about what the people of the world are leisurely about."

The average minister loses a great deal of motion in his work because he does not *plan* the use of his time. One way he may use his time wisely is to keep an appointment book and to deal with his parishioners' more serious personal problems at a later time than when people first present them, except for those cases of acute emergencies. For instance, a thirty-nine-year-old woman comes saying that her sixteen-year-old daughter has fallen in love with a twenty-six-year-old divorced man and plans to be married three months from now. The minister has preached three times and conducted a funeral that day. It is now eight forty-five in the evening. It would be wise to spend a little time with this person to demonstrate genuine concern and to stabilize her anxiety. Then the pastor can make an appointment for one day during the week to attempt to deal at length with the situation.

Another timesaving device is to break a personal conference into two or three discussions of forty-five minutes each rather than to spend three hours with a person all at once. Especially is this true when the situation is a chronic trouble of long standing and will hold for another week or two. Ministers in pastors' conferences often tell of having talked until three or four o'clock in the morning with people who come to them. Rarely does an interview of over an hour and a half in length accomplish anything constructive that was not achieved in the first hour. When the pastor breaks the interview into two or three conferences, he is worth three or four times as much to the person as if he used the time all at once. The "fallowing" of the mind of the person enriches his understanding of himself. Often he will come to many of the same conclusions of his own accord that the pastor would have to tell him in only one interview. This is not to say, however, that there will not be times when only one conference will be possible — such as those times when a pastor is the conference speaker at a religious assembly, and many other such occasions. Therefore, he must be continually studying ways and means of making one interview count for the most. The problems of time management have been discussed at length in the volume, *An Introduction to Pastoral Counseling,* edited by Wayne E. Oates (Broadman Press, 1959).

The amount of available time a minister has at his disposal in dealing with a person conditions but does not determine the techniques of counseling he uses in a given situation, the extent to which he can help the person himself, and the possible necessity of calling upon some other skilled and devoted worker to minister to the person along with him.

The Social Setting

Another pressure on pastoral practice is the social setting within which a man functions as a Christian shepherd. Some social situations within which Christian ministers operate are controlled and some are uncontrolled. For instance, a chaplain in the Army, in addition to being a minister, is an officer. He is not financially dependent on the personnel who come to him for counsel, but rather their future can be changed by his intervention. The pastor of a congregation is dependent upon the persons with whom he counsels for his living and for his status as a minister. Another comparison is similar: a chaplain in a state hospital is not in danger of slander if some woman patient, in transferring feelings to him, imagines that she has fallen in love with him or accuses him of having made immodest sexual advances toward her, or if some man patient accuses him of a homosexual attack. But if a pastor in a small community has one such accusation occur, his community position may be threatened. Even in the open community the length of time a pastor has been in a community will affect the way in which a community accepts and answers such charges. The Army and the hospital are controlled social settings, whereas a church community is an uncontrolled social setting.

Then, again, Christian ministers function in authoritarian social settings and permissive environments. A chaplain in a prison or a delinquency reform school quite often represents the mind of the law to a prisoner or an adolescent child. A minister who teaches in a church-related school has mixed roles of authority and permissiveness that often stalemate each other. The man who goes as pastor to a church where his predecessor was a " dictator of the people " inherits an authoritarian setting, and his people expect him also to tell them what to do so they can tell him where to go — too!

Again, it makes a vast difference whether the social setting of a pastor's counseling ministry is rural or urban. Many ministers work in a rural setting, i.e., in towns and villages of less than 2,500 population or in the open country. The rural minister spends much of his time in face-to-face relationships. Nevertheless, these are so informal, privacy is so difficult to achieve, and gossip and idle speculation are so active that he finds himself pressed in his attempts to deal with his people's intimate and personal problems. The literature on pastoral care and personal counseling helps him very little because few of the authors seem to have been in his situation. But some profound personality changes have been effected as a pastor sat with a fellow Christian on a woodpile after an " all-day preaching and dinner on the ground " or as he sat fishing with one of the country doctors.

The rural minister also has fewer community agencies upon which to call and fewer competent specialists in the field of medicine with whom to work. This writer was lecturing to a group of rural ministers who told him that there was not a psychiatrist within a two-hundred-mile radius. Much that would be turned over to other professional workers in a city must be carried along by the rural minister as best he can. The available resources for referral determine largely the pastoral techniques of a minister. A city pastor, in talking with a young mother of two children, finds that she cannot talk for crying about her hungry children at home whose father is mentally unbalanced and incompetent to support them. This pastor's situation is different from that of a rural pastor. The city pastor calls the family service organization, which his church helps to support, and gets supervised economic assistance for the family and psychiatric help for the father. In the meantime he comforts the mother through his ministry of prayer. Some of the other church women care for the children while the mother visits the husband in the hospital. The minister keeps in touch with the doctor as to how the church can serve the husband. Both the husband and the psychiatrist are members of the minister's church.

The rural minister would be able to accomplish many of the same results, but his procedure would be very difficult and different. In the first place, he could not call a family service organization because there might be no phone and no community chest. In the second place, he could not call a psychiatrist since there might be none within two hundred miles. He must turn to the state hospital, and increasingly, since 1951, state hospital care has been improved. The minister also turns to the neighbors, and in loving tenderness the men gather in the patient's crop and the women see to it that the family is fed. The pastor in the meantime, along with one of his lay leaders, takes the mother and father to a nearby city to a great clinic where treatment for the father is available.

The Age Level

The age level of those who come to a pastor does not merely condition, it determines his method of dealing with them. A child below the age of ten usually presents his fears and worries in the form of action and behavior rather than verbal descriptions. He "acts out" his troubles. Of course, this is no monopoly of little children but is also characteristic of immature adults. But little children usually embody their problems in the stories they tell and the games they play. Extremely old people will quite often need companionship and reassurance in a bereavement whereas a twenty-eight-year-old man whose wife dies suddenly needs an additional and different type of ministry involving extensive counseling. The developmental process of aging needs careful study by a minister as he seeks to adapt the eternal truth of the gospel to the changing situations of little children, young lovers, young parents, middle-aged people, retiring and declining people, and senile folk. *Emotional Problems of Living*, by O. S. English and G. H. J. Pearson (W. W. Norton & Company, Inc., 1955), is a readable book which describes the growth of personality. Since 1951 when *The Christian Pastor* was first published, *Emotional Problems of Living* has been thoroughly revised and made even more useful to the pastor as well as the physician. It can be used effectively as the basis for doctor-minister discussion groups that now are being developed over the country through the work of Granger Westberg of the University of Chicago and Richard K. Young and Albert Meiburg of the North Carolina Baptist Hospital in Winston-Salem, North Carolina. Also, since 1951, the readable and useful concepts of Harry Stack Sullivan, especially with reference to the hitherto unmentioned needs of preadolescents in what he calls the "chumship stage," have been made available.[2] Furthermore, the application of the developmental principle to the learning process by Robert J. Havighurst with his concepts of the "teachable moment" as being at the point of "developmental tasks" provides a common meeting ground of

[2] Harry Stack Sullivan, *The Interpersonal Theory of Psychiatry.*

conversation between ministers and public-school teachers in a community.[3] And, as has been mentioned previously in this volume, the work of Erik Erikson has begun to exert a remarkably creative influence upon ministers, doctors, and teachers in the understanding of the age factor in human experience. With the increase of the aged population of our country, growing attention is being given to the total life involvements of later maturity.

Level of Intelligence

Pastors usually have no specific way of knowing the basic level of intelligence of their people. Close attention to muscular skills and coordination, extent and use of vocabulary, extent of education, the repetition of grades at any point along the way, and reasons for dropping out of school helps the pastor to make a rough guess. Suffice it to say that the lower the level of intelligence, the less good use can be made of verbal discussions and the more nearly one has to treat a person as he would a child.

The point at which extreme cases of low intelligence come to the attention of a pastor is in his home visitation. For instance, a pastor heard of a rural family of three children in which the second child was, as they put it, " afflicted." A brief home visit was made during which the child screamed and beat his mother in the face, jumped up in the pastor's lap and tried to bite him, and also caused his brothers and sisters considerable discomfort. Finally the children ran out to play, at which time the mother expressed her great distress over the " afflicted " child. She asked for her pastor's guidance and the way was made clear for the pastor to say: " You feel that the child, however much you love him, is getting in the way of the other children's normal growth? Have you ever thought of placing him in an institution? " This question led easily to the referral of the mother to a nearby child-guidance clinic where she found institutional care for the child.

[3] Robert J. Havighurst, *Human Development and Education.*

The father of another feebleminded child presented this problem on a fishing trip with his pastor: " I was a mighty mean man before I became a Christian. Do you feel like God may have given this dull child to me to punish me for my sins? " The pastor countered with a question: " How do you think that would make the child feel toward God? "

One discussion of pastoral techniques has preoccupied the thinking of some pastors almost to the point of obsession since 1951. This concerns the wisdom of the use of the " nondirective " method of counseling. This will be discussed in detail in a subsequent chapter but it is pertinent at this point to say that the nondirective method of counseling was devised by clinical psychologists. They are more expert than any other profession in assessing intelligence. Implicit within their training is the tradition and the skill to adapt the techniques of counseling to the basic intelligence of the counselee. However, when ministers attempt to use these methods of nondirectiveness, they do not have commensurate equipment for assessing the basic intelligence of the counselee. It is only fair to say that the verbal ability of a person is related to his intelligence, his capacity for abstract concepts, etc. Therefore, *any* form of counseling is shaped by the ability of the counselee and the counselor to talk. Low intelligence of the counselee would be a direct index as to how directive or nondirective a counseling pastor can be. To become a slave to any one method would cut the pastor off from some meaningful relationships to handicapped persons that could be sustained by other methods. And the primary commitment of a pastor is not to be directive or nondirective, but to sustain a durable relationship to people in all stations of life.

The Family Situation

Such an illustration indicates that the family situation of a person is an all-important determinant of a pastor's method of dealing with him. It is a fact that "the individual tends to relive his primary family group experience in any group to which he belongs." For instance, in the academic atmosphere the major professor may become a parent substitute, the associate professor a rival brother, and the student in conflict with both of them may turn to the college pastor for arbitration of disputes much as he did to his mother as a child. This concept is aptly portrayed in Wittenberg's book, *So You Want to Help People* (Association Press, 1947), and his later volumes, *The Art of Group Discipline* (Association Press, 1951), and *On Call for Youth* (Association Press, 1955). The dynamic factors in pastoral situations thus arise from a habit-formed pattern of family relationships, and this in turn conditions the technique to be used in relation to individuals.

Three lively areas of interest have developed since 1951 concerning the relevance of the family situation for the principles and procedures of pastoral care. The first concern has come from the psychotherapeutic principle of " the transference relationship" in human life generally as well as psychotherapy specifically. Karl Menninger states this well as that situation in which " the therapist becomes various someones — a husband, wife, mother, brother, sister, father, grandmother, etc. — in the fantasies and unconscious formulations of the psychoanalytic patient." [4] Menninger points out later in the volume how doctors — and we might add, pastors — are likely to assume that they represent one person to their patient or parishioner when in fact they represent someone else. For example, a pastor may interpret himself as representing the person's father figure, when in fact he represents the mother whom the person expects to protect him from the consequences of his acts! But the therapist has controlled circumstances under which deliberately to develop and *work through these* distortions of his *real* relationship. Contrary to this, the pastor in the environment of the church, at the same time that he recognizes these distortions, works deliberately at having a realistic, honest, and person-to-person relationship with the person as an adult in reality, not fantasy. In other words, he encourages his counselees to be

[4] Karl Menninger, *Theory of Psychoanalytic Technique*, p. 77.

adults, and does not attempt to "treat" them as sick persons. He calls upon the physicians for this function that is more appropriate to their identity.

A second area of interest has developed concerning the shaping effect of the family situation on pastoral methodology. This is the emergence of marriage counseling as an interdisciplinary profession in its own right. The American Association of Marriage Counselors, of which David Mace is Executive Director, includes ministers as one of the several professions doing marriage counseling in a disciplined and formal sense. The Merrill-Palmer Institute in Detroit, under the direction of Aaron L. Rutledge, the Marriage Council of Philadelphia, under the direction of Emily Hartshorne Mudd, and other agencies offer intensive training to pastors alongside social workers, doctors, lawyers, and teachers. Nearly a hundred counseling services conducted by ministers have been established in this country. The literature in this area of the pastoral care of families has become extensive. Clark Vincent gathered the best of the journal material in his volume, *Readings in Marriage Counseling*. Skidmore, Garrett, and Skidmore produced an interdisciplinary volume entitled *Marriage Consulting* (Harper & Brothers, 1956). J. C. Wynn wrote a helpful volume on *The Pastoral Ministry to Families* (The Westminster Press, 1957). Charles Stewart wrote more specifically on *The Pastor as a Marriage Counselor* (Abingdon Press, 1961).

The third emphasis relevant to the family situation as a focus for pastoral care and as a conditioner of methodology is the current emphasis on "family therapy." C. F. Midelfort and Nathan W. Ackerman, both of whom are psychiatrists, have quite independently of each other established treatment procedures that involve the whole family in the treatment of any one member of the family who is considered sick.[5] The concept of the covenant household as a whole underlies these proce-

[5] See C. F. Midelfort, *The Family in Psychotherapy* (McGraw-Hill Book Company, Inc., 1957); Nathan W. Ackerman, *The Psychodynamics of Family Life* (Basic Books, Inc., Publishers, 1958).

dures. The Biblical discussion of "the church in thy house" controverts the hyperindividualism of dealing with individuals in total isolation from their family milieu.

The Cultural Pattern

Another conditioning factor in the use of pastoral techniques is the cultural pattern of the various people with whom the pastor works. What is very funny and would increase friendship and rapport in one culture would be the occasion of a fight in another culture. The pattern of social inferiority, hypersensitivity to criticism, and embarrassment over family background characteristic of the Southern cotton mill student who goes off to college determines even the exact phraseology of a pastor's interview with him. A person from an upper social level quite often would be conscience-stricken over having done a thing to which a person from a lower social level would not give a second thought, and vice versa.[6] Especially is this true of social practices that are sanctioned or tabooed by the community in which a pastor works. The minister needs enough social insight to locate the dangers that caused the taboos, and enough social feeling to walk circumspectly among his people. For example, Milton Lewis Mason in a study of social status characteristics and pastoral care in a semirural community found that recreational habits were approved or disapproved on almost exact scales with the social class identity of the persons consulted. Also, expectations of the pastor taking initiative toward the parishioners in visitation were much higher in the lower classes than in the upper classes. Similarly, the degree of covertness and shame about alcoholism, divorce, and marriage conflicts varied from social class to social class.[7]

[6] This is one of the valuable conclusions reached by Kinsey in the survey of sexual behavior of the human male in America. Also, J. S. Plant, *Personality and the Cultural Pattern* (Commonwealth Fund, 1937), and Liston Pope, *Millhands and Preachers* (Yale University Press, 1942), give detailed analyses of this factor.

[7] Milton Lewis Mason, "Social Status Characteristics and Pastoral Care," unpublished doctoral dissertation, Southern Baptist Theological Seminary, 1951.

Accordingly, the degree of prestige of a minister varies from one cultural group to another. In his work in the Elgin State Hospital in Illinois and the Kentucky State Hospital in Kentucky, this writer discovered that, as a minister, his role as " the preacher " was accepted and even respected with awe by the Kentucky patients, whereas the second-generation Europeans at Elgin hardly distinguished him from any other type of worker. The cultural pattern of the person with whom the pastor counsels determines the level on which he can be approached and the method that the pastor uses. Therefore, one's pastoral role is conditioned by his whereabouts, and the pastor must be as versatile in his approaches to different cultural groups as was Paul in dealing with people of such vast cultural differences as existed between the Galatians and the Corinthians. Seward Hiltner in his book *The Christian Shepherd* discusses the necessity for getting inside a parishioner's frame of reference as to " what he assumes, believes, and has experienced in reference to the class structure of our society." The stringencies of the yearning for acceptance and fear of rejection, the tacit feelings of right and wrong, and the openness or closedness of opportunities for fulfillment or service are the substance of Hiltner's treatment of " Shepherding and the Class Structure."

Physical and Mental Health

A minister is required by the nature of his calling to visit the sick. Much of his time will be spent in the company of physically and mentally ill people. Dealing with such persons calls for a radical shift of method from that of dealing with people who are physically sound, fully clothed, and in their right mind.

This requires that the Christian pastor be a close ally of the medical experts who also minister to his people. Many of the problems that people present to a minister have an organic cause, and the minister often does a service when he tactfully suggests a complete physical checkup. Fortunate indeed is the pastor if the physician to whom he refers a person is a doctor who has had psychiatric training in his medical education, and who will treat the patient's religious concerns as an integral part of his adult life and not merely as a vestigial remnant from his childhood. Only the younger physicians have had such training, as a general rule, but it is necessary if a doctor is to have a total view of the patient as a person.

Furthermore, the minister himself needs enough psychiatric information to be able to detect incipient mental disorders and to know when to seek medical help in his ministry to his people.[8] This is not to say that he is to usurp the function of a doctor, nor is it to say that he will forsake the simplicities of the "language of Zion" for the technical terms of another field of study. It does mean, however, that he needs the capacity and proper information with which to "try the spirits" that take hold of his people, to see "whether they are of God" or not. The responsibility of a minister is not to diagnose the patient's problem but to evaluate his functioning in order to determine whether the person is sick or well, whether he needs a physician or not. This is not so difficult as it seems. The basic functions of sleeping, eating, working, and communicating with those who are meaningful to a person — husband, wife, children, work associates — either are operating at a minimal level or not. When any one or more of these basic functions is not operating, the pastor can safely assume that the person is either sick or getting sick rapidly.

The pastor can ordinarily suspect deep-seated mental pathologies when the person who comes to him is deluded with exceptionally *grandiose, unrealistic,* and *detailed* plans for his own redemption or destruction of the world. An example is a twenty-seven-year-old girl who went to the Wednesday prayer service and made a dedication of her life to Christian service.

---

[8] Clinical pastoral training in a mental hospital is designed to give this kind of equipment to the pastor. Firsthand experience under supervision has no substitute. However, reading such books as follow will help considerably:

Harry Stack Sullivan, *The Interpersonal Theory of Psychiatry;* Wayne E. Oates, *Religious Factors in Mental Illness* (Association Press, 1955); Viktor Frankl, *The Doctor and the Soul;* Arthur P. Noyes, *Modern Clinical Psychiatry,* 4th ed. (W. B. Saunders Company, 1953).

Afterward she told her pastor that the Holy Spirit was driving her to ask *everyone* if he were a Christian. Consequently, she did not sleep, eat, or rest for over a week; rather, at all hours of the night she would go to the homes of people whom she did not know and ask them if they were Christians. Her pastor quickly discerned the situation, and helped the family to secure psychiatric aid. The girl was hospitalized, restored to her mental balance, and returned to her work as a librarian within ten weeks. The careful attention and devotion of her pastor enabled him to detect her condition early, and the good results were partially due to the pastor's soundness of judgment and decisive action and largely due to the early medical care she received.

Again, a person may become deluded with overwrought *feelings of persecution,* as did a woman who felt that her God was trying to make her leave her husband and children to become a prophetess who would marry the savior of the world. Anyone who sought to help her was a "frustrator of the grace of God."

Then, too, the person who is profoundly and unexplainably *depressed* may be suspected of being mentally ill. This means that the person's melancholia is unreasonable or is concerned with some triviality. An example is the case of a man who wept profusely and continually over having caught the wrong bus when he went to work. Often deep depressions come to the pastor's attention in those persons who are convinced that the "Holy Spirit has left them," and that they have committed "the unpardonable sin." They are usually quite vague and abstract as to specific things they have done. Depressed persons may be agitated and hand-wringing, perplexed and confused, stuporous and unable to talk at all, or philosophical and questioning. No amount of reassurance comforts them, and no reasoning convinces them that God cares and is able to forgive them.

A pastor who reflects upon it can readily see that among these various types of depressed persons, no one approach is applicable to all situations. As Dr. E. E. Landis, chief of the

Norton Psychiatric Service, has said, "A person can use a listening cathartic approach in relation to some depressed people and he may precipitate a suicide!" Such is one of the dangers of a minister's attempting to deal with psychiatric patients without the help of a specialist, and in an uncontrolled environment. One of the easiest ways of answering one's own questions concerning the mental health of a person is to determine whether or not the person is dangerous to himself and to other people. The threat of suicide or homicide, and disturbance of the peace of others by becoming a public nuisance, and the loss of the capacity for supporting one's self are some of the social results of mental illness that indicate institutional care for the person. This is ordinarily a complicated legal procedure, varying from state to state, with which a pastor should acquaint himself thoroughly. The family of a person should accept responsibility for instituting such procedure, and a pastor should *never* assume this responsibility himself.

These are the more obvious symptoms of mental illness; the more subtle ones take closer and more skilled attention. The first place where such illnesses manifest themselves is in *disturbances of the family and work routine of a person.* He may cease to eat, stay up all night for no apparent cause, leave his work without explanation, or fail to remember when he is on duty. An example is the man who quit his work in an automobile plant, went back to the community in which he had grown up and had left many years before, registered in the hotel, but would not go to his parents' home. He did not eat, sleep, or leave the room and barricaded the door against all visitors.

Then, again, *unusual changes in personal grooming* suggest mental illness. A beautiful and dainty woman who has in the past been known for her immaculateness of appearance comes to her pastor's study. He observes fresh food stains on her blouse, disheveled hair, misplaced lipstick, and dirty fingernails. Likewise, *misplaced remarks and acts,* inappropriate emotions and behavior suggest mental illness. For instance, a young mother meets her pastor on Monday morning and accuses him of having tried to kill her children. Such behavior calls for an exceptional kind of pastoral method. Therefore, a pastor would do well to gauge a person's relative degree of mental competence as an important determinant of all his counseling methods.

Finally, the forerunner of an open mental break is the observable increase in the *degree of compulsion* with which a person lives and does his deeds. When in the major portion of a person's life he is compelled to do things apart from his own choice and against his own better judgment — by constraint and not willingly — he is in the danger zone of mental safety.

These conditioning factors — the Christian equation, the personal desire for help, the social role of the pastor, the time element, the social setting, the age level, the intelligence level, the family situation, the cultural pattern, and physical and mental health — are unspoken but powerful conditioning influences in every situation in which a pastor works. His ability to observe silently these facts and to gauge his own methods according to what he sees and senses largely determines his success or failure as a pastor. In no sense does an unfavorable condition at any one of these ten points relieve the pastor of all responsibility for the spiritual care of the person at hand. The responsibility may be all the heavier. The person is still " one for whom Christ died." The method, however, whereby the pastor tends this person from the flock of God is modified considerably by these factors.

Chapter VI

The Levels of Pastoral Care

The Christian pastor cares for people on many different levels of relationship. At one and the same time, he may be the personal friend, next-door neighbor, pastor-preacher, pastor-counselor, and golf or fishing companion of the person to whom he ministers. Furthermore, he does not, unless he is a pastor in an unusually large city, spend much time with people whom he never sees again after he has finished a series of three or four interviews. He is related to the same persons over a period of years, during which his relationship moves from one level to another and back again, depending upon the variety of crises endured.

These are the facts that make it unwise for pastors to carry over *in toto* the office techniques of professional counselors of any kind, or of dubbing their work as "pastoral psychiatry," to use Bonnell's phrase. It is true that hospital chaplains, professors of pastoral psychology in seminaries, a few "specialist" pastors such as John Sutherland Bonnell and Norman Vincent Peale, and other persons have a good deal of very formal counseling to do. Some exceptionally large churches have placed clinically trained pastors on their staffs to do nothing but such formal counseling of people who are referred to them. Since 1951, churches, associations of churches, and councils of churches have developed counseling services in which exceptionally well trained ministers have a full-time responsibility as counselor. Every pastor needs to know what to do when he is called upon for "deeper level" pastoral counseling which might be characterized as one of the "nonmedical forms of psychotherapy." But specialized and controlled situations are the exception rather than the rule in the pastorate. Therefore, the average minister cannot depend on the methods of a specialist unless he has the necessary training for such work and similarly controlled conditions under which to work.

One basic principle, however, operates in the work of both the pastor and the specialist. One of the major problems underlying both parishioner and patient problems is the individual's inability to establish and maintain durable relationships to significant people. Whether it is a doctor suggesting longer-term, multiple-interview psychotherapy, a pastor initiating a formal, multiple-interview kind of counseling, or the same pastor seeking to get this person to be a faithful, regular churchgoer, the issue tends to stand or fall on the individual's ability and willingness to link a covenant with a significant person and carry through with it on a sustained basis over a period of time.

The pastor, therefore, does his best to study and to evaluate the specific level on which he does have access to personal encounter with people to whom he is related in a helpful way. On what basis *is* this person able to sustain a durable relationship? On that level the pastor can begin work where he finds himself. He must be flexible enough to adapt himself to a person on *that level of relationship at which he can best serve him.* When the pastor does this, he discovers several different levels on which an individual reacts to him as another human being to whom he can reveal himself. He will also find different levels of the individual's personal insight into his own problems and willingness to do something about them before God. In this respect, the pastor has more than one kind of relationship on which to meet people on different levels of formality, informality, and combined formal and informal relationships. His major work is keeping the relationship clarified and unconfused in both his and the parishioner's mind.

These areas of action may be called *the levels of pastoral care.* Another way of describing them would be to call these levels *types of pastoral care*. Preference is given to calling them levels for two reasons. First, these levels tend to appear in any given relationship of pastoral care in the order in which they are to be described in the following pages. Therefore, the character of a relationship may change perceptibly within the scope of a single hour or from one conference to another with the same person. Secondly, the depth psychologists have been sufficiently convincing that a pastor needs to learn from them. A knowledge of the deeper layers of personality reveals that the most important forces that determine behavior are quite often unconscious to the clear level of awareness of a person. In the pastoral relationship, as it grows with time and acquaintance, " deep calleth unto deep," and " in the hidden part " people are made to know wisdom. Thus the pastoral bond is more than a mere " telling " of things by one person to another. It is the provocation of wisdom through an especial relationship. This is essentially a Hebrew concept in which a distinction is drawn between the Hebrew word that means " to tell " in the sense that one would be taught from reading a book, and another word that means " to cause to know," in the sense in which one is taught by immediate, firsthand experience. It is something of what the men of the Samaritan village meant when they said, " It is no longer because of your words that we believe, for we have heard for ourselves, and we know that this is indeed the Savior of the world " (John 4:42).

Furthermore, one might use the working model of personality that is used by what has come to be known as " phenomenological psychology." Here we would say that these " levels of pastoral care " represent the different contexts or "frames of reference " in which a pastor encounters his fellow human beings. At one time the field of relationships focuses most meaningfully in these varying identities of the minister — as a friend, comforter, priestly confessor, teacher, and counselor. These are different foci for the caring identity of the pastor in the light of the parishioner's frame of reference.[1] However, the sym-

[1] See Donald Snygg and Arthur Combs, *Individual Behavior* (Harper & Brothers, 1949).

bolism of " levels " of pastoral care still presents to this author
the most effective basis for describing the vitality of pastoral
relationships, although the phenomenological approach yields
what Seward Hiltner calls a " perspective " of human relationships too important to be ignored, depreciated, or left unused
as a way of thinking. Recently Orlo Strunk has given a brief
but authentic description of this interpretation of man's spiritual pilgrimage in his book *Religion: A Pscyhological Interpretation.*

Christian experience, when seen from the vantage point of
levels of feeling relationships, moves from hearsay *about* Christ
to the level of personal acquaintance *with* Christ and personal
dependence *upon* Christ, to the level of learning *from* Christ,
to the level of confession *to* Christ, to the level of healing *by*
Christ, to the level of reconciliation *with* Christ, and finally
achieves spiritual usefulness on the level of comradeship *alongside* Christ to witness *for* Christ.

The minister, as an " ambassador for Christ " by his own
spiritual maturity, must at least be on his way to comradeship
with and witnessing for Christ. As he does this and people seek
his personal counsel by reason of his accurate representation of
Christ, he works " on behalf of Christ." Then, he works in accord with the example of Christ and the nature of Christian
experience on *five different levels of pastoral care* of people in
terms of their movement toward spiritual maturity. These levels are: the level of friendship, the level of comfort, the level of
confession, the level of teaching, the level of counseling and
psychotherapy. On every level he is a witness to the good
news of the grace of God in Christ. His ultimate objective is
the development of a co-worker in the Kingdom of God.

The Level of Friendship

The Protestant pastor most aptly comes to his people in the
role of a friend. The term " brother," which many church people use for their minister, reflects the democratic friendship
they have for one who is " first among equals." The pastor min-

gles as a friend and neighbor with the people whom he serves. He goes to wedding gatherings, all-day meetings, young people's social gatherings, and many kinds of men's social clubs. However, as we have seen earlier, his people do not expect this of him as often as he thinks. His being "given to hospitality" is an asset to him. It is soon sensed if he is hard to get to know and does not mingle well with people.

On social occasions, timid, isolated, and withdrawn persons can come to know their minister. Their confidence in him can be established so that they will later say, "It was at the 4-H cattle show when you stopped and said hello that I decided that if I ever got courage to tell this to anybody, you would be the kind of person I could talk with." This establishment of rapport is the gracious making of oneself accessible to people, rather than the compulsive falling over oneself to "win friends and influence people." This latter attitude springs more from the fear of not being approved by others than it does from an easy sense of affection for people for their own sakes. Through his ministry of casual friendship, the pastor avoids the fate of being seen as *only* a man of crises. Pastors who during World War II delivered telegrams advising their members that a relative had been killed or was missing in action know how the minister can be a sign of bad news. If he participates in the simple joys of life, he offsets this perspective.

The ministry of friendship is the indispensable necessity for all other deeper levels of pastoral work. It is the seedbed of any fruitful service to people. Furthermore, a great majority of the real help that comes to people in crises is through persons whom they would term "just a good friend" and not through professional people or "full-time Christian workers." Some of the most effective pastoral care in churches has been done by lay persons who have had rich experience as parents and who are masters at the simple business of making, meriting, and keeping friends, i.e., they are "given to hospitality." Someone has called this "back fence" counseling. Ways of teaching this rudiment of the Christian life should be devised through the teaching ministry of the pastor.

However, the establishment of a friendly confidence with a person who comes for help needs to be objective and unencumbered by too much reference to mutual acquaintances and to the personal life of the pastor. For instance, a pastor was visited by a member of a nearby church. When he made a friendly reference to the pastor of that church, the woman became somewhat restless. The pastor, sensing her uneasiness, found it necessary to say: " But, of course, you know that when people come to me for a special kind of personal help I do not talk over their problems in any way with anyone else except at their request or with their permission. Also, let me ask that if you choose to talk with others about our conference, you will let me know."

The ministry of friendship and example is the extent of a pastor's ministry to many people. It is the main necessity in his relationship to people of other denominations. In hospital visitation a minister finds this " social approach " of a " hello visit " with Catholic and Jewish patients and with persons who are the responsibility of another Protestant minister most valuable. Likewise, the ministry of friendship to small children is exceptionally rewarding. Pastors give little children an example, a hero with whom to identify, and a friendship that lends security. Especially is this true in instances in which the home has been broken by death or separation of parents.

Whereas the objective, considerate management of a personal friendship is one of the least artificial and most effective means at the pastor's disposal of changing human character, naturally it has severe limitations. Many pastors complain that their people think of them as a hail-fellow-well-met, but seem to avoid situations in which a private, serious conversation about the deeper issues of life can be discussed. An example of this is the rural pastor who is always greeted by a large gathering of neighbors when he goes to take a meal at the home of his parishioners. The host and hostess feel the need for their neighbors' presence in " entertaining " the preacher. Whereas this may turn out to be an excellent opportunity for an informal kind of *group* guidance, it does not allow much room for a personal conference with an individual or for developing an intimate acquaintance with a family group.

Again, the pastor may find himself socially identified with his people in such a way that the amount of social distance necessary for them to reach out for his care and help will be lost. Familiarity need not breed contempt, but it does represent a loss of effectiveness in a pastor's leadership when he becomes just " another one of the boys " and his " separateness " as a man of God is completely obscured by his " togetherness " with the people of the community. The pastor needs enough detachment that when people do come to him they will feel that they have been somewhere when they get back.

This suggests the most outstanding limitation of the social level of a pastor's ministry: there are some things a person can tell only to a stranger. As one person said in conference with a pastor in a neighboring community: " I would not dare tell these things to my own pastor because he knows all the people I do. I have no doubt that he would never tell a soul. I have confidence in him, but I feel that I must talk to someone who is not so close to me." Certainly a pastor needs to be able to entertain strangers.

But in spite of such limitation, the pastor's friendly access to people in the natural setting of their homes is his greatest opportunity for careful observation of their personal needs and for a saltlike influence on their behavior.

The Level of Comfort

The pastor at his best, like Jesus, is thought of as " a man of sorrows, and acquainted with grief." Under inevitable hardships, people turn to their pastor for spiritual fortification, emotional support, and affectionate companionship. Here the Christian shepherd goes with his people into the " valley of the shadow of death," stands beside them in the testing times of great tragedies such as economic failures, intolerable losses of self-respect, and terrors of such calamities as war, flood, pestilence, and economic depression. People of every walk of life traditionally give the minister this task in life, and expect him to fulfill a ministry of encouragement and comfort. " If he is not available when people are in trouble," said one layman, " a minister need not be on hand any other time."

The different situations in which a ministry of comfort is needed are legion. *Bereaved persons* most often are in need of the supporting help of a minister. *Those who are facing death* lean heavily upon their pastors and draw upon the sources of spiritual strength that he has to offer and that he represents. Likewise, the minister's approach to *persons with long-term chronic illnesses,* such as tuberculosis, the more serious kinds of arthritis, and the many afflictions of old age, is usually one of companionate encouragement. A supportive ministry is also a necessity in the case of *persons who are permanently handicapped,* such as blind persons, persons who have lost a limb, or those who have been paralyzed. Such losses are much like the loss of a loved person by death, and the process of mourning over the loss through which these persons go, in adjusting to their plight, is much the same process as that through which a bereaved person goes. Closely akin to bereavement is the plight of parents of *deformed or mentally deficient children,* who continually need fortification of spirit. In the same grouping of difficulties in which a supportive ministry of comfort is indicated are *those persons who suffer from acute physical pain,* which often is so intense that pain-killing drugs seem to be of little avail. The pain itself is aggravated by the straining tension with which the excited person fights to bear the suffering. The first step in relief is relaxation, which quite often comes through the efforts of a well-poised minister who does not waver in the presence of trouble and is relatively serene in the presence of fear. This is one reason why clinical pastoral education should be considered an indispensable part of every minister's education. He learns under supervision and under " combat conditions " what it is like to see people in acute pain, facing death, and losing the persons who are important to them. In 1945–1951, when the first edition of this book was written, there were very few facilities for such training. But now the facilities are abundant, the supervision is more experienced and better trained. Therefore there is no excuse for a minister to be without training.

Furthermore, *mentally depressed persons,* whose reasons for being depressed lie unrecognized in the unconscious, need a supportive ministry of comfort. Rational attempts at analyzing their troubles and giving them a ready-made solution quite often meet with failure, which in turn depresses such persons all the more. Most often they are in need of a medical doctor as well as a minister, although they quite regularly go to the minister first. The possibility of suicide in such cases is rather high, and caution should be taken at every move.

Another group of persons who vitally need the ministry of comfort that a pastor can afford are the *disappointed lovers* of his parish. A smile flits across most people's minds when such persons are mentioned, but a pastor cannot afford to let humor be his only treatment for persons who have been seriously hurt in a love affair. Efforts at patching up such situations usually are less valuable and more dangerous than a ministry of comfort and supportive encouragement of the person who expresses such a grief to his pastor.

More specifically, the " how " of a pastor's ministry of comfort consists of the oldest methods of personal influence that exist: *suggestion, catharsis,* and *reassurance.* These methods have been criticized by persons who have often seen them used to exploit rather than to bless human life. Nevertheless, even the worst use of an instrument does not justify the condemnation of the instrument itself, but only of the ends toward which it is used.

The minister often underestimates the tremendous power of *suggestion,* which his presence itself carries even in the lives of those who actively despise the way of life in which he walks. Paul expressed it accurately when he said that "we are the aroma of Christ to God among those who are being saved and among those who are perishing. . . . Who is sufficient for these things?" (II Cor. 2:15-16). The pastor's presence itself is a spiritual fortification as he comes alongside people in time of stress and sits where they sit as a reminder of the presence of God.

The knowledge of this fact should relieve the minister of the compulsive necessity to " say something " on every occasion, because there are many times when silence itself is a means of prayer during those " groanings which cannot be uttered." Especially within the fellowship of the household of the Christian faith, among those who share a common loyalty to a living Christ, " there is no speech nor language, without these their voice is heard " (Ps. 19:3, marginal reading). Job aptly railed at his comforters: " Ye are all physicians of no value. Oh that ye would altogether hold your peace! And it would be your wisdom " (Job 13:4-5). The minister today who has not learned the disciplined and re-creative use of silence as a means of spiritual communication draws similar reactions from those whom he seeks to comfort with windy speeches and worn stereotyped " answers " to human suffering, and he is simply relieving his own anxiety by talking.

Not only is the minister's presence a spiritual fortification to his people, but his capacity to listen to their griefs affords a *catharsis* of the spirit for them. Catharsis is something more here than confession: it is a sharing of difficulty in which the weight of pain, grief, and disappointment is actually lightened. As Bacon has said, the sharing of a trouble cuts it in half, but the sharing of a joy doubles its strength. The observant minister finds that his people's expressions of deep feelings in times of bereavement afford him an unexcelled opportunity to cooperate with the Spirit of God in the growth of the soul through grief crises. He knows that at the earlier stages the bereaved person quite often *cannot* talk about the loved one but that at a later stage he wants to talk and by then his friends are hesitant to let him talk about his loss.

Such a catharsis also restores the perspective of the person and helps him to lay hold of the positive forces working in his behalf. Likewise, it gives him access to the pastor and the community resources, which the pastor represents. And in many instances the pastor's actual supportive ministry will depend more upon the way Christian fellowship groups can "prop up" a dependent brother or support a "wounded comrade" than upon the pastor's minute analysis of an unchangeable situation.

Much of the pastor's time, also, will be given over to reassuring his people. *Reassurance* is a primary method of comfort, and is a necessary part of the pastoral ministry. A pastor says to a young college student who has an intolerable sense of inferiority because of the cultural backwardness of his family: "You are going to do an acceptable year of college work. I know you are, because your high school principal told me that you have good intelligence, and I have seen that you are willing to work." This is reassurance, and the pastor may find himself saying it more than once. A reassuring letter, written in the pastor's own hand, will be read again and again. A pastor may say to a forty-one-year-old woman who has just recently given birth to a child and feels that she is not "a fit mother" for him: "You have told me why you feel that you cannot go through with this. You have also told me that you would die if you had to give the baby up. You *can* carry through if you really *want* to do so; I believe in you. I want to encourage you in your struggle to be a responsible parent." This is reassurance, and the woman may need to talk with the pastor again and again and receive such encouragement. The ministry of reassurance involves the basic problem of low morale and the necessity for continued impartation of hope to the person. Sometimes the person's hope hangs by the thread of the concern of the pastor himself. If he can ward off the isolation by building a community of concerned people around the person, they and he together become a bridge over the abyss of despair.

Naturally, the use of reassurance incurs many problems. First of all, the pastor should be careful that this encouragement of people is in keeping with the facts of their own situation. Idle words said just to make someone feel good are an offense to the person. Idle encouragement given as a palliative does more harm than good. But a hardheaded optimism that nevertheless faces the facts makes of a minister one who imparts hope and doggedly searches for fresh alternatives. A careless reassurance, on the other hand, can cause a person to feel that his pastor is minimizing his troubles and does not understand at all. Quite often this breaks the relationship completely, and the person searches for help elsewhere.

Again, ministers readily become trite, impersonal, and vague in the reassurances they give people. Their encouragement is not based on attention to the personal problem of the individual to whom they are talking, consideration of the way in which the person will hear what they say, nor care for the essential well-being of the person and those other people to whom he is related. Therefore, ministers are likely to say the same things to everyone regardless of the specific nature of his trouble. For instance, a minister was talking to one of his most substantial contributors during an illness that called for hospitalization. At the age of forty-three this man was suffering from hypertension, arteriosclerosis, and a reactive depression. He was on the verge of a divorce from his wife for having carried on a clandestine love affair for ten years, and his business was facing failure. Not knowing these facts at all, his pastor visited him for about eight minutes, at the conclusion of which he said: " You are going through the deep waters. I have had all the troubles you are going through, and I can say to you from experience that if you will just put your trust in the Bible, you will come through."

Such an approach at best missed the mark of the man's life situation. This is not to say that the pastor's words were insincere; it is to say, however, that they were shots at random rather than being carefully aimed at the man's situation itself.

The resource of prayer is especially helpful in the ministry of comfort. The pastor brings the assurances of the power of God through prayer. Prayer therefore should be handled as carefully as any other powerful explosive would be handled. Several guides should be followed to determine the use of prayer in any given situation:

The *appropriateness* of the atmosphere is one guide. To

bring formal prayer into an atmosphere of frivolity or empty gossip often is to do violence to the nature of prayer.

Again, _brevity_ is a guide to the use of formal prayer. This means that every word must count and that words should be chosen to fit the need of the person to whom the pastor is ministering. This rules out the trite, worn-out phrases that are used not only by liturgical ministers but also by persons who decry "form prayer." Spontaneity in prayer is to be desired, but this is not to say that the language of prayer is not a thing that can be learned. The best-written prayers are found in the Bible, and the language of the Bible is the language of prayer. The pastor does well to carry great sections of the Bible in his memory for use in his prayers. (Ps. 1; 15; 23; 37; 46; 51; 79:8-9; 90; 91; 103; 139; Isa. 40:28-31; Matt., ch. 6; John, ch. 14; Rom., ch. 8; I Cor., ch. 13; II Cor. 4:15-18; Eph. 3:14-21; _et al._, are good examples of the "patience and comfort of the Scriptures.") Prayer should not always be formal. The pastor often finds himself ministering to persons in open wards in hospitals, in the crowded places of church corridors between church school and the worship hour, and in the marketplace as he and they go about their daily chores. A pastor can pray with the person what has been called "an open-eye prayer." Instead of bowing the head and closing the eyes, the pastor says to the person: "I want you to think of me as praying for you. When you do, remember that I will be praying that you will be strengthened with might to meet the challenge that every day gives you." Other words that are given to the pastor in that hour will be tailored to the very pressures the person is facing. But the basic point to remember is that this kind of prayer is informal and ordinarily unobserved by other people. Similarly, prayers can be written into the text of a letter; outstanding examples of this are the letters of the apostle Paul. For example, as I write these words, I can pray for you — my reader — that you will catch my meaning even when my words are confusing to you. In doing so, I would also pray that you as my reader would be given the wisdom to push my meanings and words aside and to let the Holy Spirit be your teacher.

Relaxation is another principle of prayer. For this reason, prayer should never be "used" merely as an excuse to end a conference with a person. Often prayer will be the point at which a person moves from a social level of conversation to the deeper levels of concern. For example, a pastor was visiting a rural family in which the mother was seriously ill. After a brief conversation, the mother asked, as her custom was, that he read a passage of the Bible to her. This he did and led a brief prayer for God's strength to be afforded the sick woman and for the love of her family to be a medicine in itself. After the prayer, the pastor did not hurry to say good-by. Rather, he paused in silence a long while. Then the mother told him of her fear that she was dying. Then the pastor had an opportunity to minister to her personally as a comforting strength in her last few weeks of life. He could not have done this had he himself been tense, in a hurry, and devoid of relaxation.

Finally, *prayer means more to a person if he voluntarily asks for it himself.* The pastor can do much to cause people to be at ease in asking for such a ministry. In many cases it is taken for granted that he will pray — such as in cases of acute illness, impending death, or recent death. But these are not the rule. The pastor can say, "There are many things a pastor can do for his people, and I wonder if there is anything that I can do for you?" The tone of voice inflects meaning, and the person may ask, as one woman did, "Well, I had never thought of that; what *are* the things ministers do for people?" Then the pastor had an opportunity to interpret his ministry of prayer to her. It was made easy for her to say she would like him to pray.

Likewise, the use of the Scriptures for purposes of reassurance, comfort, and support is especially valuable. Dr. John Sutherland Bonnell demonstrates this especially well in his books. The use of the concise, easily remembered verses of the Scriptures, especially the winnowed wisdom of Psalms and Proverbs, provides an undergirding for the minds of people. Their effect increases with repetition and multiplies when they are memorized. The pastor does well to leave a passage with a person for later reading. A pastor may with profit prepare a set of chosen Scriptures for people with different types of difficulties, as a sort of "spiritual prescription." An example of this is my own pamphlet, *Grace Sufficient* (Broadman Press, 1952), and the more extensive book, *The Bible in Pastoral Care*. It should be emphasized that reassurance, support, and comfort are not the only purposes, or even the major purposes, of the use of the Scripture. Interpretation, instruction, and historical wisdom take precedence over these purposes.

The Level of Confession

A pastor visited one of his parishioners at her home inasmuch as she was the victim of an incurable cancer. She was thirty-nine years of age, the mother of two grown children by her first husband, from whom she was divorced. At this time she was married to a second husband, who had also been divorced previously. On his first visit the pastor was received cordially, and the woman told him how good the Lord had been to her and how she had been given divine assurance that she would be healed. Then she asked the pastor to pray for her. His ministry was that of listening and prayer. Twice a week he visited the woman, and each time she protested almost too much that everything was all right between her and God. Finally, the necessity for skilled nursing help prompted the family to move her to the hospital.

At the hospital the pastor visited her regularly, and was met with the same overstated protestations of her assurances of God's care. The pastor listened with a sympathetic concern but without entering into the woman's conflicting feelings. One day, however, the woman said with great force that she was sure that she was a saved woman and that God was going to help her get well. Then the pastor ventured a remark: "Then *everything* is all right between you and God, is it?" In a startled fashion, the woman said: "Have you been talking to somebody? Do you know something that is not right between me and God?" The pastor said, "I know nothing about you except what you yourself have told me." Then the sick woman clutched at her pastor's hand and fearfully asked him to pray for her. He prayed that she might understand herself in the light of God's love and discover the peace of God that passes understanding. After a long silence he left.

Four days later he returned. The woman was very sick and close to death. When he entered the room, the woman sent all her relatives away in order that she might talk in private with her pastor. Then she said: "I have sins in my life that I must talk about before I die. I have confessed them to God many times and each time he has told me to confess them before men. You are God's minister and I must tell you." Then she proceeded to reveal a crushing load of guilts connected with a series of acts that involved her close relatives and friends over a period of twenty-three years. In great remorse she sought the assurance of God's forgiveness. Then the pastor brought to her the "patience and comfort of the Scriptures" that assured her of God's healing redemption in Christ.

This is an example of the confessional ministry such as every veteran minister could describe. This ministry has been institutionalized by the Catholics on a compulsory basis. In reaction, Protestants have neglected the importance of confessing their "faults one to another." This is one of the first functions of the Christian community. The restoration of those overtaken in faults is characteristic of Christians who have not become so sophisticated that they no longer feel the need for their own confession of sin.

But Protestant ministers who are near to the heart of God and sensitive to the feelings of their people still listen to the confessions of their people. A mother cries in bitter repentance for her mistakes in rearing her children. An otherwise respectable bank teller confesses a series of thefts for the first time to his pastor because he can no longer bear the guilt alone, nor tolerate the fear of being caught. A young man confesses the paternity of an unborn child and seeks the aid of his pastor in protecting the mother and child. A young white woman has suddenly fallen in love with a Negro classmate in a great university and knows that her Southern parents will not understand. A husband confesses his marital infidelity and seeks to find its causes and remedy. A defense worker caught by tuberculosis confesses his money madness, which caused him to work too many hours, too many days, and brought him to his bed.

The common characteristic of all these confessions is that they are all of a social nature involving many other people. But many confessions are more individualized, and the person condemns himself for the evil character of his private thought life. Or he or she may confess the practice of masturbation, as did one fourteen-year-old boy who felt that he was mentally affected by melancholia for having indulged in this practice.

Several facts need to be considered in the practice of a confessional ministry. First, isolation is the main effect of a known transgression. The person cannot face his community as he did before. He is "cut . . . off from the land of the living" and from the face of God. The confession is, therefore, more than a mere catharsis; it is also a socialization of an otherwise isolated experience. The person achieves a sense of togetherness with the people whose approval he considers most worthwhile, as well as with the eternal God. As Washington Gladden has said, the load of shame and remorse can be removed if the pastor "can draw forth the rankling secret, and convince the troubled soul, *first by his own forgiveness,* that the Infinite Love is able to save to the uttermost all who trust in him." [2]

Again, the pastor must be careful in his ministry of confession not to accept too quickly the stated problem or the confessed sin as the real one. This could be called the "A-ha reflex," in which a minister feels like saying, "Eureka!" when a person tells him of some foul deed. Especially is this true of confessions of sexual sins. These gross offenses are often merely the symptoms of deeper and more persistent ones. For instance, a young unmarried woman may confess the fact that she is with child, whereas her heaviest burden of guilt hovers around a burning hatred for her father, who is the chairman of the

[2] *The Christian Pastor and the Working Church,* p. 86. Italics author's.

official board of the church. Her act is an expression of her hatred of her father and an inadvertent way of bringing shame upon him.

Another hazard to avoid in the confessional ministry is that of taking the admission of a fault too lightly and reassuring the person to the point that he is made to feel guilty over having felt guilty. This is most common in one's ministry to children and adolescents. An adolescent boy or girl may be having all manner of difficulty over some seemingly insignificant habit. The pastor may pass the whole thing off lightly — even with humor — and miss the deep feelings the person has about his behavior. This applies not only to adolescents but also to adults. For instance, a thirty-five-year-old woman, upon being asked by her pastor if she had been to church recently, said, " No, I do not feel comfortable when I'm sitting in church." When pressed unduly for a reason, she said with great embarrassment, " I constantly fear that someone will hear my insides growl out loud." A touch of humor eased her tension. Then the pastor said: " I know that is not completely funny to you; I want you to know that I take it seriously. Would you like to talk with me more about these fears sometime? Maybe I can help you." This conversation led easily to another, and the woman confessed to feeling great remorse over having had an abortion performed several years before. Now she greatly desired children and could not have them. There was a direct connection between her fear of her " insides being noticed " in the church and her guilt over this deed.

Probably the point at which individuals most need the " disburdening " ministry of confession, as Calvin called it, is when they first enter the Christian community as adults. In some communions this will be when the young person takes his or her first Communion. In others it will be prior to his Baptism and after a public profession of faith. But the pastor should carefully create a private conference situation in which he can become acquainted with the person, learn something of his spiritual history, and let him confide prayerfully in the atmosphere of trust that develops.

Another point at which a confessional ministry is appropriate and often neglected is prior to marriage. Even though a couple plan to become one flesh in God, they still exist as individuals before God in their histories of sin. Some of these sins are quite independent of their chosen partner and should be confessed to God and to no man. The pastor can encourage these prayers of penitence, for if the person is left unassuaged by the forgiveness of God, it could tend to infect the marriage relationship with fear and compulsion.

The ministry of confession is closely related to medical psychotherapy, but *there is a vital difference.* The woman to whom reference has just been made was referred to her pastor by a psychiatrist. He stated the difference this way: " Here was a woman suffering from a sense of sin about wrong deeds she had actually committed. She needed forgiveness from God, and there was very little need of my trying to turn theologian. I referred her to her pastor. Now the people a psychiatrist can help are those who are *deluded* and *think* they have committed crimes of which they are innocent, or who are hearing voices telling them that the room is electrically wired in such a way as to cause them to murder."

The confessional ministry calls for different methods of approach according to the age of the person involved and the degree of " full-grownness " of the sins the person confesses. A child needs information and guidance in the presence of ignorance, temptation, and sin. An unwitting error cannot be treated in the same way a highhanded and premeditated crime is treated. Great care must be taken in distinguishing a temptation from a sin, because many people experience more guilt over the things they are tempted to do than they do over the sins they actually commit. Also, many people are afflicted with diseases that cause them to do things against their own good judgment, and they are powerless to control their actions. In such cases it is the minister's task to heal the volition and strengthen the person's sense of personal responsibility rather than to add to his loneliness and desperation by losing patience with him. Quite often such persons as epileptics, acute alcoholics, sex perverts, and psychopathic thieves and liars are in need of a physician as well as a minister. They are afflicted with diseases that express their symptoms in the moral behavior as well as in the psychosomatic disequilibrium of their personalities. The minister needs the compassion that Christ had for the demoniac when he starts to deal with these persons. Their communities have often consigned them to the tombs without the advantage of a funeral.

The Level of Teaching

The pastor as a personal counselor finds that some of his most effective teaching is done with individuals in a face-to-face ministry. Jesus most often appeared to his followers as a teacher. The matchless teachings that he left the world were ordinarily the outgrowth of his ministry to individuals who were drawn to him for help. The Christian shepherd functions as an instructor of the conscious minds, the moral intentions, and the undisciplined desires of his people. On the teaching level of his personal ministry, therefore, he must know not only the content of Christian teaching and practice but also the process whereby these become a part of the spiritual tissue of the personalities of his people.

When someone comes to a Christian pastor for guidance in a personal difficulty, he usually expects that pastor to be an interpreter of the mind of Christ, "a teacher come from God." The minister represents this reality to him. Furthermore, the minister is supposed to be an authority on the teachings of the Bible and Christian history. People come to him with thorny personal problems at the base of questions as to what the Bible teaches about divorce, remarriage, adultery, the unpardonable sin, money matters, profanity, war, and a hundred other things. The minister is expected to know the historical context of Christian experience and to be able to use this knowledge in a way that edifies and does not tear down the person.

The minister, in addition, is supposed to be an authority on the specific teachings and practices of his own church. Young engaged couples of different religious persuasions come asking him to explain the difference between the teaching and practices of Catholics and Protestants, for instance, and his knowledge and attitude will have a determinative effect upon their decision. If the pastor defines his role as a teacher, builds a democratic relationship of give-and-take, and provides the couple with factual information, he can exercise genuine shepherdly care for such a couple regardless of the outcome of their decision. Since 1951, James Pike, in his book *If You Marry Outside Your Faith* (Harper & Brothers, 1954), Algernon Black, in his pamphlet *If You Marry Outside Your Religion* (Public Affairs Series), and C. Stanley Lowell, in his book *Protestant-Catholic Marriage* (Broadman Press, 1962), have given pastors detailed guidance on this thorny problem. The minister also finds himself the interpreter of the social attitudes of his people all the way from such matters as personal amusements that are taboo to worldwide attitudes on race prejudice and war.

The Protestant minister as a teacher is caught between his stewardship of the absolute ideals of the teachings of Jesus on the one hand and the rigorism of special pressure groups in the church on the other hand. He bears a sensitive conscience in terms of his care for human persons who have failed to reach the ideals of Jesus Christ and his responsible instruction of the church in the Christian standards of human life. Edward LeRoy Long has done more serious and consecutive thinking on these dilemmas than many of us have. He has recorded this thinking in his two books, *Conscience and Compromise* (The Westminster Press, 1954) and *The Role of the Self in Conflict and Struggle* (The Westminster Press, 1963).

On the teaching level of pastoral ministry, the Christian shepherd finds a distinctive character of his work that sets him apart from professional counselors and necessitates a departure from their ideologies. This distinctive character, however, may bring him closer to the reality of people's problems, i.e., *the pastor represents both the individual's and the group's inter-*

ests, and he must combine individual and group counseling procedures. The person-minded minister knows that many of his personal counseling opportunities come as the result of questions he stimulated in group discussions. Conversely, he must confront the " reality principle " of his group connections and those of his counselees in all personal work with individuals.

But people come to their minister not only for guidance on specifically religious questions but also for information on the common ventures of everyday life. Parents who have not been able to have children want to know adoption procedures. Young people seek premarital instruction. High school graduates want to know about the college facilities available to them. Children of elderly parents want guidance concerning homes for aged people. Relatives of mentally ill persons want guidance concerning psychiatric help and legal procedures involved in institutionalization. Parents invariably want to talk over problems in child guidance with their pastor, seeking information about the simpler as well as the more complex problems in mental hygiene. The request for the recommendation of medical specialists in cases of physical illness is a very common appeal.

In all these instances and in countless others, the minister is expected to be a repository of information. As one young minister, after two years of pastoral work, said: " They came to me, but they did not ask me what I *thought*. They said, ' Pastor, do you *know* . . .? ' " Therefore, the minister should take heed to know his Bible, his church, and his community resources. These are his equipment.

The methods of instructional guidance are varied, but in every instance these approaches must be distinguished from long lectures of moralistic exhortations filled with such phrases as: " Don't you know . . .? " " I think you ought . . ." " Maybe you don't realize it, but . . ." *Instructional guidance is the impartation of the facts necessary for an individual to make a voluntary choice with intelligence. Recommending the use of good books is one of the most tactful methods* to be employed here. The pastor should take care to separate heavier volumes that he would use for his own instruction from those briefer, more plainly written books he would use for guiding other people. Likewise, he should not recommend literature before he himself has read it. Every pastor needs a loan shelf of books and pamphlets that he has bought with extra gifts of money that come to him from time to time. He will lose a few books this way, but they will be valuable even so. Suggestions for such materials have been made throughout this volume. A concise resource book was prepared by this author in 1957 entitled *Where to Go for Help.*

Supplying missing facts is another method of personal instruction. A pastor may be listening carefully to a mission volunteer who is making his educational plans, but he suddenly realizes that this man is already beyond the age limit for missionaries in the area in which he wants to serve. A member of the official board of the church may want to make a certain change in the financial policy of the church, and the pastor supplies the missing fact that the charter of the church expressly forbids it. This type of counseling is especially valuable to the religious counselor on college campuses and to people who teach in institutions of learning. " The rules " become the grooves on which much of their counseling progresses. Furthermore, outlining various alternatives and exploring these as to their possible implications, resources, and outcomes is another method of instructional counseling. This kind of pastoral care has the advantage of appealing to the responsible, healthy dimensions of the person. This in itself amounts to treating the person with integrity, respect, and dignity. This builds the kind of confidence necessary for any more complex and profound problems the person may wish to discuss.

Chapter VII

The Deeper Levels of Pastoral Care

The previous chapter, on "Levels of Pastoral Care," dealt with the traditional, *expected*, ministries of the pastor. However, neotraditional expectations have been focused upon a pastor by his parishioners. World War II, the Korean conflict, and the continuing cold war have imprinted the ministry of the military chaplain upon millions of civilians' expectations of the pastor. Less and less do they quietly expect the pastor to be a hail-fellow-well-met who "attends all the meetings." More and more they are expecting him to be a person who will converse in depth with them about the main meanings and excruciating meaninglessness of their lives. Consequently, this chapter is devoted to two kinds of conversations pastors tend to have with parishioners and nonparishioners alike, either when he visits them or when they visit him: *brief pastoral dialogues,* and *multiple-interview pastoral counseling.*

The Level of Brief Pastoral Dialogue

Pastoral care is essentially spiritual conversation. Two recent volumes on pastoral counseling, in different ways, emphasize spiritual conversation as the focus of pastoral care: Wayne E. Oates, *Protestant Pastoral Counseling,* and Eduard Thurneysen, *A Theology of Pastoral Care.* Brief pastoral dialogue, styled along the line of the Socratic dialectic, is the most easily used technique of approaching the personal problems of an

individual. This method is the commonsense approach to pastoral procedure that is most likely to do good and the least
likely to do harm. It is also a preparatory approach to any
longer-term counseling that needs to be done. The brief pastoral dialogue assumes that the help-seeking person is of average intelligence, fairly stable emotionally, and capable of talking freely about his situation with no unusual degree of mental
blocking. Further, this dialogue assumes a strong degree of
personal rapport between the individual and his pastor. It is
usually appropriate with people to whom the pastor has been
related over a period of time as a pastor and teacher. Ordinarily there is a permanent bond of identification between pastor
and the person at hand. These are rather sweeping prerequi-
sites for the use of such an approach. The psychologist or the
psychiatrist may ask whether or not there *are* any such people
living. But the pastor deals with such people every day of his
ministry, whereas these experts do not see them professionally.

The process of the brief personal dialogue is as follows:
First, the pastor simply listens to the parishioner who comes
to him in a time of decision and lays out a problem before him.
He asks an occasional question in order to fill in missing facts.
Here, in actuality, the pastor himself is the student, much as
Socrates was a "student" with the youth of Athens, learning
from the person at hand all the facts about the present situa-
tion confronting him. He is "leading the person out" (in the
Latin sense of the word "education").

Secondly, the pastor gives a factual summary, a sort of re-
capitulation or "read back" of what the person has told him.
He may initiate this by saying: "Now let me see whether or
not I have really understood what you have told me." Then,
upon finishing a concise statement of the situation at hand, he
may say: "Do I understand you properly? Have we left anything out?" Quite often the person will say, "Yes, I failed to
mention this . . ."; or, "No. I don't think you really understood
what I meant . . ."; or, "I didn't mean to leave this impres-
sion, but . . ."

Thirdly, the pastor asks the person to help him outline the alternative paths of action, and with the help of the parishioner explores the end results and methods of achieving those results in each one of the alternative paths of action. Usually this may be initiated by asking the question, " Now what are the things you *can* do in the situation?" After these alternatives are carefully enumerated, each one can be discussed freely in a give-and-take manner as to obstacles preventing their realization, ways and means of accomplishment, and unique advantages inherent in each choice. Often the condition of things calls for the pastor's adding another possibility for the consideration of the individual — a possibility that the person probably has not yet seen. Many times this " other possibility " may be a careful combination of the best advantages of the other alternatives. For instance, a young girl does not know whether to stay in school or to go to work in order that she and her fiancé can marry. Finally she decides to stay in school, lighten her class load, get a part-time job, and marry. Inasmuch as both of them have only one more year, she feels that they can " make it."

The fourth step is to appeal to the basic desire of the person. Often the pastor may ask, " If all things were equal, now, which of these alternatives do you really want to follow — deep down inside?" Quite often an amused light comes to the person's eye and he says, " Well, I guess I did not want your advice so much as I wanted sympathy for what I have already decided to do." But on frequent occasions the answer may be: " I guess that is my big problem: I don't know what I want to do. I want to have my cake and eat it too, and I am not able to choose one thing and carry through with it." The more intense this feeling is, the more likely it is that the person is suffering from some type of anxiety state. At any rate, the " big problem " is out in the open. The pastor is firmly established in the person's confidence, and now he may go into the deeper difficulties of the individual.

However, in the majority of the situations that confront a pastor, this brief pastoral dialogue produces a heightened degree of emotional maturity, whets the sense of personal responsibility, and leaves the decision-making capacity of the person free and inviolate. It lends itself to one-interview situations more readily, and is adaptable to the pressurized schedules of most pastors. The pastor must take two precautions in ending such a brief pastoral dialogue. First, he must be careful not to break the relationship by giving fixed advice. This is one of the main hazards of fixed advice: if the person cannot follow through with the recommendation, then he is hesitant to return to the pastor. Of course, in some relatively rare instances, the pastor may want this result. In the second place, the pastor should make some arrangement for follow-up of the conference. He should take great care not to forget about the person who has conversed with him about the main issues of his life.

The Level of Pastoral Counseling and Psychotherapy

Not all personal encounters yield themselves to the rational approach suggested in the discussion of the brief pastoral dialogue. The Christian shepherd confronts many people who are suffering from deep inner conflicts over which they have no control. They stand in need of a minister who has psychological foundations and knowledge of psychotherapeutic skills in his method as well as the healing power of God at his disposal. Such persons have come to the point where *they do not want to do what they want to do*. Their decision-making powers are deadlocked in a filibuster of *one* of their many selves in the congress of their souls. Unhappy people, they come to the pastor complaining that they cannot control their thoughts and actions. In the thought of Paul, they do not understand their own actions, for they do not the things they want, but do the very things they hate (Rom. 7:15).

Such persons are not "insane" in the sense that people are who suffer from gross delusions of grandeur and persecution and stand in need of institutionalization and protective care. Accordingly, they are not candidates for a psychiatrist ordinarily, and usually they are not wealthy enough to afford a psychoanalyst who specializes in their troubles. Rather, when they come to a pastor, they are usually people of limited means who are acutely unhappy and blocked out of the abundant life. Nevertheless, they may be conscientious church members and active in the affairs of the community. Their religion, however, seems to be conformed to the pattern of their unhappy way of life rather than a transforming power that renews their mind. Yet they hopefully look to their faith in God as a promise of redemption from their inner bondage to the legalism that they have mistaken for the Christian faith.

In order to deal effectively with the basic religious needs that these conflict-weary persons manifest, the pastor must be acquainted with the " heart's native language " of feelings as well as with the rational precepts of his theological formulations. As Nathaniel Hawthorne says:

> If he shows no intrusive egotism; . . . if he have the power, which must be born with him, to bring his mind into such an affinity with his patient's that this last shall unawares have spoken what he himself imagines himself only to have thought; if such revelations be received without tumult, and acknowledged not so often by an unuttered sympathy as by silence, and inarticulate breath, and here and there a word, to indicate that all is understood; if to these qualifications of a confidant be joined the advantages afforded by his recognized character as a physician; then, at some inevitable moment, will the soul of the sufferer be dissolved and flow in a dark but transparent stream, bringing all its mysteries unto the daylight.[1]

Such a " feeling for the feelings " of people, a careful clinical study of people's troubles, and an equally careful reexamination of the New Testament reveal a Christian explanation of the difficulties of people: idolatry in the sphere of values is the basic religious component in the malformations encountered in these particular psychological diseases. The person suffering from a neurotic way of life is a slave " to the elemental spirits

[1] *The Scarlet Letter* (Pocket Books, Inc.), p. 128.

of the universe . . . , in bondage to beings that by nature are no gods " (Gal. 4:3, 8).

Primarily he is possessed by the demand of one part of himself that the rest of himself bow down in its worship. As Plato said, this type of sin is " the rising up of a part of the soul over the whole." This individual is not a person, but many selves. He condemns himself roundly on every hand, giving the key to his plight when he says: " I could never forgive myself . . ." Thus it is seen clearly that he is an inordinate worshiper of fictitious goals in life, borrowed standards for his life, fantasies of what he thinks himself ideally to be. The viciousness of his idolatry lies in its self-destructiveness, its prating itself as humility, self-denial, self-rejection, and religious devotion. The person's desire to become a person in his own right overshoots the mark and he aspires to become God himself.

The only answer to his plight is that the eyes of his inner understanding be opened to his irresponsibility and his childish sense of omnipotence. His inner life must be opened to the ethically severe love of God. This convinces him that the root of his sins is in his self-enchantment, that God is consistent and can be depended upon to work within a person as he makes and carries out decisions, and that God is a rewarder of them that diligently seek after him. Such a picture is seen in the life of the man whom Jesus asked, before he healed him, " Wilt thou be made whole? " And the surest thing that a pastor can do for such a conflict-weary person who comes to him is to put him on his own before God, to give him all the loving confidence and intelligent affection that he has time and opportunity to give him.

But a theological orientation to the problems of neurotic people is inadequate unless it takes into account what is observably known about the processes of recovery from such states. The busy pastor needs a clear conception of *how* to go about " putting a person on his own before God and giving him all the intelligent affection that he has time and opportunity to give." Every responsible pastor knows that the neurotic personalities in his church not only are unhappy themselves, but cause unhappiness to others all out of proportion to their own number. Careful study of church splits and church failures will reveal that they are often initiated and perpetuated by chronically maladjusted people. Since the first edition of this book, such research has been done by Kenneth Pepper, who concluded that the insecurities and behavior problems of ministers themselves were at least as important as any other one factor in causing such splits and failures.[2] Therefore, the minister may be forced by circumstances to ask, " What am I going to do for and about the neurotic personalities in my church, including my own unrealism? "

In the first place, the minister needs to acquaint himself with the basic literature in the field of counseling and psychotherapy. Professor Carl Rogers, of the University of Chicago, has written the most often cited book in the field, *Counseling and Psychotherapy.* In this book he sets forth what he calls " nondirective " counseling. Shortly after the first edition of *The Christian Pastor* was published, Rogers published his second volume, *Client-Centered Therapy,* in which he shifted attention from the nondirective technique to a closer scrutiny of the attitudinal orientation of the counselor himself. The most important dimension of the attitude of the counselor is the element of *trust,* the capacity of the counselor to trust the counselee to deal responsibly with his own situation and with himself. This trust is contagious if it is real. If it is " phony," then the suspicion of the counselee is well grounded. In 1952, at a meeting of the American Association of Marriage Counselors, Carl Rogers gave a brief summary of his whole point of view, in which he then identified the counseling relationship as follows:

> Some of the theological students who have taken work with us in our courses in therapy have introduced me to Martin Buber, and I find his description of what he calls the " I-thou " relationship is the kind of relationship that I am seeking with

[2] Charles Kenneth Pepper, " The Dynamics of Intra-Church Tensions," unpublished Th.D. thesis, Southern Baptist Theological Seminary, November, 1953.

clients who come to me, not what he calls the "I-it" relationship; in other words, it is a relationship between two persons meeting at a deep and significant level, not between a person and a complex object.

Now, what attitudes in myself do I find rewarding to myself when I enter this relationship? This is something, certainly, which I put in a different way every year, trying to capture the essence of what is there in experience, when one has the feeling that therapy is really going on. As of today I like to think of it in terms of permitting, or providing, *safety and freedom*. Both of those terms have come to have a good deal of meaning to me. I sincerely want to make this relationship so safe that the client can relax, can let down his defenses, can begin to communicate with me, but, what is much more important, can begin to communicate with himself. I should like to be so sensitive to his total reactions that I can go with him, that I can accompany him into every nook and cranny of his experience, as an understanding companion who makes it genuinely safe to explore in regions that previously he has felt might be very, very dangerous.[3]

In the discussion period after this address, this author raised the question as to the applicability of Rogers' methods, etc., in the context of the pastor's identity and social structure:

OATES:
May I state a point, that it seems to me that here is a vital difference, not necessarily in ideology but in function, between the role of your clinic in Chicago, and the role of us out there, fifteen or twenty steps before they get to you, in such a way that a good deal of the diagnosis is already done when they get to you.

ROGERS:
I am not sure, Dr. Oates, what field you are even speaking of. What field are you speaking from?

OATES:
I work as a minister in an uncontrolled environment of the open community, and we are right out at the point that we

---

[3] Carl Rogers, "A Personal Formulation of Client-Centered Therapy," *Marriage and Family Living*, Vol. XIV, No. 4, November, 1952, pp. 342–343.

contact the individual when he first begins to feel distressed, and we do a great deal of the referring to the clinics.
ROGERS:
And that is the most fortunate time, but I am quite aware of the fact that the minister also has other obligations. Oftentimes he cannot, no matter how good a counselor he is, commit himself to the responsibility that might be involved in a longtime carrying of a very difficult case. I still feel the same attitudinal principles apply, but might not be practical in a given situation.

In 1956–1961, Seward Hiltner and Lowell G. Colston clinically contrasted the two different contexts of counseling — that of the clinical psychologist and that of the pastor. They published their findings in the book *The Context of Pastoral Counseling*. They used the term " context " for " what differentiates the pastor's counseling from that of other counselors." They concluded that " the attempt to understand and to articulate to ourselves the feelings people have about the whole context in which pastoral counseling takes place is not a nuisance but a vital instrument in the giving of help.[4]

The subtle conditioning factors discussed in the previous chapter are integral parts of the context. Also, the religious history and the characteristic modes of selfhood developed over the years of a person's life exercise reciprocal effect on counselor and counselee. One would agree with Rogers in his statement that "relatively little has been done to relate specific diagnoses with specific therapies." [5] Yet one also observes that some awareness of the importance of doing just this appears in Rogers' own statement that client-centered " counselors have been less successful with those individuals who are aggressively dependent, who insist that the counselor shall take responsibility for their care." [6]

For this reason and because of my own hypothesis that in the design of selfhood a particular counselee and a particular coun-

[4] Hiltner and Colston, *The Context of Pastoral Counseling*, p. 220.
[5] Carl Rogers, *Client-Centered Therapy*, p. 221.
[6] *Ibid.*, p. 189.

selor reciprocally shape the responsible covenant they form and the techniques that eventuate, I have in my own book, *Protestant Pastoral Counseling*, taken a definite position. That position, simply stated here and elaborated in that book, is: (1) The structure of the context in which a person seeks the pastor's help — informal or formal — may be or become confused, and must be continually defined, redefined, and clarified. (2) The methodology of the pastor is shaped by the patterns of self-confrontation that emerge in the relationship and that, in turn, must be sensitively appreciated, identified, and understood. (3) The religious history of the person is important to him when he seeks a pastor's counseling, and he should be given every opportunity to discuss it in detail. (4) The preponderant majority of pastoral counseling situations involve marriage conflict, which moves through a definable process of deterioration. This process shapes the procedures of the pastor and cannot be ignored.

These hypotheses were considerably influenced by specific counseling-experience studies of the author, but also by the additional help of the work of Harry S. Sullivan in his discussion of "Developmental Syndromes" in his *Conceptions of Modern Psychiatry*[7] and his discussion of the "Detailed Enquiry" in his book *The Psychiatric Interview*.[8] These hypotheses are sufficiently clear from extensive clinical application to be sure foundations for effective pastoral counseling. However, each one is open to continuing refinement by more sophisticated and detailed research design. New generations of pastoral counselors can no longer rely upon anecdotal and "hunch" approaches to methodology. But it is sustaining to find one's "hunches" validated from clinical studies.

However, without *supervised* application and research the pastor cannot appreciate or understand safely such literature as has been discussed and recommended here. In actuality, the

---

[7] Harry Stack Sullivan, *Conceptions of Modern Psychiatry* (William Alanson White Psychiatric Foundation, 1947).

[8] Harry Stack Sullivan, *The Psychiatric Interview* (W. W. Norton & Company, Inc., 1962), pp. 94–182.

only effective means of testing the hypotheses of the authors, which they describe in these books, is to engage in clinical pastoral education for ministers. A minister can get this training in his theological curriculum in many schools today. If a minister is already in a pastoral situation and cannot easily gain access to a training center during a summer, he should try to get a leave of absence or commute to the nearest center of training. The various resources for this type of training are described annually in the January issue of *Pastoral Psychology*. The training centers of the Institute of Pastoral Care and the Council for Clinical Training are published also in the *Journal of Pastoral Care*, the joint publication of these two agencies. Subscription to both these journals gives a pastor continuing theological education in pastoral care. In such a center of training, a minister becomes a part of the healing team — medical doctors, social workers, psychiatrists, nurses, and ministers are all helpfully related to the same persons in need. Furthermore, he is given close personal supervision in his individual work with people by a trained theological supervisor. Here "the living human documents of flesh and blood" become the textbooks for the minister. His gospel comes alive to him in the face-to-face ministry to people.

Some persons ask, "How far should a pastor go in 'deeper-level counseling'?" The answer is threefold: He should go as far as his training has equipped him to accept responsibility for the outcome of his treatment. He should go as far as the uncontrolled environment in which he works will permit him to accept responsibility for the person's life. And, finally, he should go as far as the limitations of his time and social role will permit him to give himself to the needs of the individual.

The counseling work of a minister is a dynamic and growing relationship. The pastor does well to think of himself as counseling in the creative processes of spiritual birth and maturation, and to think of the person before him as needing new life and spiritual maturity. This creative process moves naturally through five phases. The phases may take place quickly in one interview, but more often the relationship may extend over several or even a larger number of conferences. This allows time for growth and reflection, during which the person has to deal with his own problems alone.

The Preparatory Phase of Counseling

The more inexperienced pastor usually asks the question, "How is it that people come to their pastor for counseling help?" The veteran minister asks, "How can I get people who ask for help started off in an effective relationship for the best results in my counseling with them?" Others may ask, "How can I stimulate the need for counseling help in a person who does not yet feel either that he needs help or that I am the person to give it?" All these questions indicate the fact that there is a preparatory phase in most counseling relationships. In this phase the pastor does several things: He first discovers who needs his help, and establishes an initial contact with that person. If the person comes to him in an informal situation, he seeks to construct a more formal one in which time, privacy, and quietness can be achieved. If the person must be sought out by visitation or by cultivation of friendship, the pastor seeks to stimulate the sense of need for help and to shift the initiative in the relationship in such a way that the person "stretches forth his own hand" for help.

1. _Discovering persons in need and establishing an initial contact_. The pastor is one of the very few persons in modern society who is still expected to visit his people. In some communities even this expectation is losing its strength. But ordinarily, the pastor has a right to visit in the homes of his community, and this is his best means of discovering persons in need and of establishing an initial contact with them. Purposeful and patient home visitation reveals to the observant pastor, especially when he goes in times of crises, many of the quieter and more desperate needs of individuals and families. It establishes rapport that will be necessary to any future counseling. It gives a distinctly personal and nonprofessional touch to the pastor's interest in people. It offers him opportunities to see the individual in the context of the family and to sense the feelings

of other members of the family toward that person. Home
visitation presents the pastor with a *total pattern* of the way of
life of the person which only many hours of individual counseling would ultimately reveal.

Likewise, as has already been indicated in the discussion of
preaching and teaching, the pastor's public ministry affords
him "after meeting" conversations with persons who have
private matters they wish to discuss. This is the pastoral counselor's "outlet to the sea" of human suffering. Careful, insightful, and humanly tender preaching and teaching are avenues
of exchange of feeling between a pastor and the individual who
needs personal counseling.

Furthermore, the patient education of the leadership of the
church to guide persons in actual need to the pastor rewards
him with an abundance of initial contacts with such persons.
This is best illustrated by a negative example. A middle-aged
woman who had been married only about six years became
deeply depressed and took her life by self-poisoning. One of
her neighbors called the pastor immediately and asked that he
make his services available to the husband of the woman in
making plans for and conducting the funeral. In the telephone
conversation, she said, "I have known for some time that she
was thinking of doing such a thing, but I never believed she
would!" If the woman had been trained to do so, she could
have notified the pastor long *before* the tragedy. As it was, all
she knew to do was to call him for the funeral!

Probably the most Christlike method of establishing initial
contacts with persons in need is in what may be termed the
pastor's "marketplace ministry." As one reads the Gospels, he
finds only one example of a formal interview in the ministry of
Jesus, the conversation with Nicodemus. The rest of his conversations were beside wells, in people's homes, along the
roadside, and in or near places of worship. In the casual, informal contacts of everyday living with people — in the grocery
store, at the filling station, at the bank, at the garage, at social
gatherings of all kinds — the contemporary pastor also hears
the "uplifted voices" of human need. A young pastor tells this

story: He read in his morning paper that a man and woman, both members of his church, were seeking a divorce. That morning he stopped, as his custom was, to get some gasoline at the man's service station. He stood reading his paper inside the man's place of business. The proprietor was posting his books, while the attendant filled the pastor's gas tank. Everything was tensely quiet until the owner of the place looked up and snarled at the pastor: " Well, go on and say it. I know what you are going to say anyhow! " The pastor countered by saying: " I am not sure whether or not you feel that I am your friend. I don't want to say anything unless you feel that my friendship belongs to you."

The man was taken aback by this approach. Then he broke into a warm, anguished outpouring of his difficulties with his wife that had culminated in divorce proceedings. The pastor did not try to deal with it at that moment, but said: " I will take good care of your confidence in me. Do you think you and I could get together tonight, after your station closes, and talk this over? " An appointment was made, and the more formal kind of counseling relationship had been established.

2. *Making counseling appointments.* This latter step suggests one of the important essentials of the preparatory phase of counseling work: the pastor should be very effective in the use of an appointment system. Unless it is otherwise unavoidable, he should not attempt to deal with intimately personal problems of individuals in public places where other people can surmise and draw their own conclusions. He should make appointments either to visit the person at his own home or else to meet in the pastor's study. Such a simplified procedure will do much toward making his time more valuable to others and to himself. This is much wiser than setting arbitrary office hours for people to come to see the pastor if they need help on their personal problems. It is more personal, less of an affront to the autonomy of the people of the community, and therefore less likely to create unnecessary hostility. Furthermore, the identity of the pastor as a preacher, teacher, and overseer of the flock will not be obscured by arbitrarily set office hours which

" strike the pose " of a formal counseling ministry some people resent. But more important than this, such a plan does much toward " structuring " the relationship of the pastor to the individual in such a way that he can counsel with him without too many personal obstructions arising.

3. *Shifting the initiative onto the person needing help.* A pastor faces a difficult task in the preparatory phases of counseling in switching the initiative from himself as pastor to the person whom he is seeking to help. This is more easily illustrated than it is defined. For instance, a young woman called her pastor, asking for an appointment *for her husband* to come and talk with him about some marital problems in which they were involved. The pastor, in the preparatory phases of the counseling relationship, said: " I will be glad to talk with *him* as to a time that is convenient for both of us. Will you have him call me about it? " The purpose of the pastor was to shift the initiative in the search for help away from the wife and onto the husband.

Sometimes a pastor will recognize an acute need in a person in his community, but at the same time the person is hostile and resistant to any offer of help that comes his way. The pastor is confronted with the responsibility of lessening the hostility and uncovering a desire for his guidance. This is one of the most difficult relationships with which a pastor has to deal. For example, a pastor learned that one of the members of his church had made a vow that he would never return to church after seeing his father, the senior elder of the church, with " another woman sitting in my dead mother's place," as the man himself stated.

The pastor visited the home of the man regularly, inasmuch as the man was physically ill a good portion of the time. Little mention was ever made of the fact that he did not come to church, no reference was made to the fact that the pastor knew of the conflict between him and his father, nor to the fact of his father's remarriage. The pastor " waited him out " until the man himself felt secure enough in his affections to tell him about it without being asked. At this point, the man sought the pastor's guidance and became durably related to the pastor as a caring person. This relationship has lasted — at differing levels of intensity — over a period of sixteen years.

Another situation in pastoral care and personal counseling that calls for a switch of initiative is that of major moral offenses among persons in the congregation. These usually first come to the pastor's attention in rumors from different persons within the community. Whispers of embezzlement, shady business dealings, sexual promiscuity, sexual perversions, and any item of the catalog that each community compiles come to the ears of the minister as he moves about. Next, the person's place of authority and leadership in the church is questioned, and a rift in the unity of the congregation is in the making. In smaller congregations, the whole unsavory situation can come to a head in a clash of personalities in the open meetings of the church. The pastor's own leadership may become so involved that he may want to resign or be asked to resign.

Such a situation may best be handled in the rumor stage by a pastor who has a firm hand in dealing with people. The pastor may do as one reports in a case record:

PASTOR:
Wilhelm, I called and asked you to come by to see me for a reason. Before I tell you what I have on my mind, I want to say that my confidence in you as a person runs pretty deep and my affection for you is true and sure. Otherwise, I would not have been concerned about you. Then, too, I want to assure you that no one else knows that you are here and that all you say to me will be handled responsibly and with your full knowledge ahead of time.

You may justly tell me, when I say what I have on my mind, that I am sticking my nose into your business and have no right to do so. You will be right except in the fact that I would want you to do for me what I am trying to do for you, because I feel that you are my friend.

Now to come to the point, before you lose your patience in curiosity, let me say that I am not concerned about the truth or error of the reports that have come to me. They could be false and still do you harm. If they are false, I think

you are entitled to know that these things are being said. If
they are true, I think you are entitled to a sympathetic friend
with whom you can talk safely about your side of the
story. There are, as you well know, two sides to all such
things.

The word has come to me that you have been engaging
in sexual perversions with some of the young boys and girls
in our church. The exact situations are these: _____;
_____; _____; _____. I will not tell you who told me
all this, because I do not want to do all of you harm. But you
can imagine for yourself, and if this is not true, you can be
secure in knowing that they do not know that I am talking
to you either.

What do you think about all this?

WILHELM:

Well, for a good while I have wanted to talk with you about
this, but I never knew quite how to go about it. I have been
doing some of those things. Not all of them, though. I came
here a stranger and thought I had found a really Christian
crowd that didn't do those things. I got into it, though, and
found that they were not so different from myself. . . .

The conclusion of the whole history is too lengthy to report
in full, but this part of the record indicates that rapport was
established and that the preparatory phases of such counseling
can move from an authoritarian to a permissive relationship
between the counselor and the counselee. However, catching
in time an explosive interpersonal condition like this is not
always this easy. In later stages of deterioration the situation
may spread so far and so deep in the life of the church and
community that the pastor would be forced to distribute responsibility to members of his official board and to the members of other helping professions — medicine, the law, and
business persons. The pastor may have many difficulties in
dealing with such a problem in the next phases that are to be
discussed, but, at least if he is as fortunate as the pastor mentioned in the preceding record, he has "structured" his relationship in such a way that the initiative is with the counselee
more than it is with the pastor.

The Phase of Relaxation and Development of Trust

At the outset of this discussion of the process of counseling, the problem of the place and time of the counseling ministry needs to be considered. The initiative factor has already been discussed in connection with " making the contact." The pastor cannot be careless about the place at which he meets the person. Whether the counselee is a man or woman, in either instance the pastor communicates his identity as a caring pastor by the place where he suggests that they meet. It is highly preferable that the person come either to the pastor's study or to his home at a time when other persons are also in the church building or at home. This can usually be done and still allow discreet and unobserved privacy for the conversation. If this cannot be done, another time should be arranged when it will be possible. Responsible attention given to finding a place of discreet privacy, but with someone nearby, forestalls the pastor's being alone in a building with the person in the event that an emergency arises or in the event that his presence with the person would be for any reason misinterpreted either by the person with whom he is counseling or by other persons. For example, one pastor was alone in his study early one morning talking with a businessman about a personal problem, and the businessman had a heart attack. The pastor had great difficulty in handling this emergency alone.

The pastor, furthermore, should tactfully interpret the time situation to a person at the outset of a conversation. Thus, both he and the person will be more relaxed in the time they do have together. This avoids some of the stress and divided attention that may otherwise come at the end of the conversation. Usually an interview should be about an hour in length. It may be shortened to forty-five minutes or even to a half hour when the relationship has matured and strengthened. It may be lengthened a bit on the first interview or in the event that circumstances of distance in travel or length of time between the interviews necessitate this. Rarely should an interview continue over an hour and a half without a break. The pastoral counseling relationship does not really develop fully in less than three interviews. The amount of time the pastor, teacher, or administrator can give to one person usually begins to be strained when the more intensive phases of the relationship extend beyond a dozen interviews. However, effective pastoral counseling often comes in "rounds" of three to five interviews at a time, with months and even years elapsing between groupings of interviews. No careful research on the time factor, as such, in pastoral counseling is in existence, concerning that which a considerable number of pastors actually do. A study by Eugene Namache and Tilden H. Edwards revealed that the average amount of time spent in all counseling by two groups of ministers, one in Boston and one in San Francisco, was 3.5 hours per week.[9] Yet this study did not focus on the problems of the number of interviews with one person, the meaning-changes from interview to interview, and how this use of time relates to the rest of the functions of the minister, etc. Nor has detailed research been done on the place in which such counseling is done and the kinds of problems the placing of counseling interviews presents to pastors.

Most persons who are suffering from emotional handicaps are discouraged, tense, suspicious, and self-conscious. In the earliest phases of the pastor's relationship to such persons, he must put them at ease and disarm them of their personal mistrust of him. Likewise, he must establish some meeting point of feeling with the person and define clearly his own relationship to him. The success or failure of a counseling situation is often determined within the first half hour of the discussion. A "relationship of a trusted motive" must be established and the suspicions of the person relieved before progress can be made. Erik Erikson speaks of the element of trust as the foundational factor in human integrity and development. He says that in "adults the impairment of basic trust is expressed in a basic mistrust." He also perceives that the positive function of re-

[9] Eugene Namache and Tilden H. Edwards, "The Minister and His Counselee," *The Ministry and Mental Health,* Hans Hofmann, ed. (Association Press, 1960), p. 232.

ligion is to restore a sense of trust. "Whoever says he has religion must derive a faith from it which is transmitted to infants
in the form of basic trust." [10]

The pastor in this phase of any relationship, therefore, will
be sensitive to three trust-building and trust-interfering factors
in the experience of the person with whom he is conferring:

1. *The relief of nervous tension.* The person is often frightened at talking with a pastor and especially about his personal
life. Breathlessness may indicate either fear of the interview
situation or haste in making the appointment in time. Drawn
features may indicate sleeplessness, loss of appetite. Clenched
fists, sweaty palms, and twisted handkerchiefs may point
toward a burden of unrelieved anxiety. Rigid perching on the
edge of a chair, furtive movements of the body — all these and
many other signs are the tattered edges of a tense spirit showing themselves. A pastor must be alert and sensitive to the
degree of tension in a counselee at all times. By the composure
within himself, the unhurriedness of his manner, and the steady
certainty of his tone of voice he can communicate confidence
and peacefulness to the person. Often the pastor will purposely
avoid talking about significant and painful matters until the
person feels more at ease and under less tension. The person
must be relatively free from mental blocking that arises from
emotional tension before he can with profit discuss his difficulties. This process of relaxation, by whatever legitimate means
the pastor most aptly can use, is the first prerequisite of good
counseling. The small talk, superficial conversation about
places and relations, a brief prayer for peace and clarity of
vision, and direct suggestions such as: " Sit in this chair. I
think you will be able to relax more." " Why not pause a little
while and catch your breath? You've been running." " Lean
back in your chair and take it easy " — all these point toward
an easing of tension.

2. *The acceptance of personal antagonism.* The occasion
that brings many people with deep-seated emotional disturbances to a minister quite often is one of anger and resentment.

---

[10] Erik Erikson, *Identity and the Life Cycle,* pp. 56, 64–65.

As has already been mentioned (see Chapter V), a person may come to the pastor under pressure from someone else and resent both that other person and the pastor for putting him in such a position. But occasionally the point that stimulated the person's anger may be something the pastor himself has done that the person did not like.

Ordinarily the resentment is not a conscious one, but rather lies deeper than the person himself can sense. This is what Freud so accurately called " resistance." Deep wells of antagonism prevent the person from having a relaxed relationship to the pastor. The most common fear is that the minister will condemn the person if he makes himself known as he really is, or that the minister will betray him in some unknown way. But even more subtle are those antagonisms which cause persons unconsciously to misinterpret the words of the minister, to ascribe to him meanings that he did not reflect to them, and even to deny the truth of their own words that might be repeated back to them verbatim.

The minister also has the task of disarming his parishioner of any antagonism he may have had toward former ministers and may be unconsciously carrying over into his feelings toward the present pastor. The resentments that the person holds toward other people in the church also serve as inhibiting obstructions to a friendly relationship.

By careful definition of his own relationship with and an undivided attention toward the person, the minister can tactfully disarm the person of much of his resistance. Sometimes this may take a whole interview; with others a " meeting point of feeling " is never established. But no smoothness of ministry can be achieved until the thermostats of the person's heart have been opened by the warmth of friendship and sustained by the strength of a basic trust.

3. *Mutual acceptance of personal responsibility*. One hazard in the establishment of rapport is that the person will shirk his own personal responsibility for his difficulties and shift to a complete dependence upon the pastor for their solution. Whereas some people refuse to trust a minister at all, a great

many take the relationship of mutual trust as a parasitic opportunity "to pass the buck" of their troubles to the pastor. When he fails to measure up to their expectations, then he begins to get resistance from them. This is the genius of the client-centered principle of counseling: it leaves the responsibility for the solution of the problem with the person who has the problem. Client-centered counseling provides a permissive and warmly personal atmosphere in which a counselee can objectively work through his problems to a satisfactory solution of his own. Religiously stated, it is the careful observance of the principle of the autonomy of the individual personality before God. The counselor exercises a confident trust in the lawful working of the Holy Spirit "both to will and to work for his good pleasure" in the life of the person. Furthermore, the phenomenological principle of perceiving the person as he perceives himself, of getting the internal frame of reference, can be a religious discipline of self-emptying which in itself is "good news" to the stress-ridden counselee.

From the point of view of the pastor, he must take preventive measures in order that he may not become so encumbered with the difficulties of one person that he cannot minister to the many other people who come to him. It aids him in his own personal relaxation to get over the compulsive necessity to do something about every problem that is brought to him and to accept the realism of Paul's maxim, "Each man will have to bear his own load" (Gal. 6:5). The sense in which he is fulfilling the law of Christ by bearing the other person's load with him lies in his provision of a friendly presence of togetherness with the person. Thus the person is neither alone nor wrapped up in himself; he is sharing the reality of the Christian community.

These three problems — the degree of tension, the degree of personal antagonism, and the degree of personal responsibility — are the issues at stake in establishing rapport with the person who comes to the pastor with a more profound personality problem. At all stages of counseling, the degree of rapport may be strengthened or weakened in such a way as to help or hinder any further progress. No smoothness of ministry can be achieved at all, however, until the person has made room in his heart for the pastor through the warmth of friendship and the power of genuine trust.

The Phase of Listening and Exploration

Blending into the phase of relaxation and the development of trust is the period of " talking it out " in " an experience of emotional release, when the person uses the acceptance and permissiveness of the situation to pour out, or painfully to bring out, all the attitudes which surround his life problems. As he discovers that this is a situation in which it is safe to express real feelings, deeper and deeper attitudes are revealed, even those which have been previously repressed and which he has never dared admit even to himself." [11] The person socializes, often for the first time in his life, the thoughts and feelings that have hovered in the hinterlands of his consciousness, creating anxieties that he could not explain but could only feel and respond to with blind compulsion.

1. *The ministry of listening.* The pastor at this phase of the counseling situation depends almost entirely upon the ministry of listening. Much needs to be said at this point on the use of this powerful tool of pastoral work.

The easiest way to help people is to understand them. As Lin Yutang has said, " To understand is to forgive." The easiest way to understand people is to listen to them, to hear them out. Listening creatively is an art in itself. It calls into action those other nonverbal forms of communication which are dramatically more powerful than the use of words: eye expression, bodily responses of muscle and movement to meaning, and the effect of total silence. As Reik has said, " It is important that we recognize what speech conceals and what silence reveals." [12] Listening essentially means three things:

[11] Carl Rogers, *A Counseling Viewpoint* (Federal Council of Churches), pp. 13, 14.
[12] Theodor Reik, *Listening with the Third Ear* (Grove Press, 1956), p. 126.

a. It means *actually to hear what the person says*, to hear with an "evenly hovering attention." Pastors are most susceptible to letting their attention wander from the person to whom they are listening to any one of the thousand other things that they have to think about. Preoccupation with other things is like damp rot in the counseling ministry of a pastor. The shuffling of papers on the desk, the searching out of a letter from the pocket, the furtive glance at the watch — all these are subtle ways of telling a person that halfhearted attention is being given to what he says. Likewise, the pastor quite often misses the mark in his understanding of his people because he does not pay attention to seemingly insignificant details concerning their attitudes and feelings.

But it would be a mistake to assume, as Reik says again, that "all observation is purely conscious. Not until we have learned to appreciate the significance of unconscious observation, reacting to the faintest impressions with the sensitiveness of a sheet of tinfoil, shall we recognize the difficulty of transforming imponderabilia into ponderabilia." [13] In this sense, listening is a sort of "free-floating attention," which "makes note of everything equally."

b. Listening means *letting the person do the talking*. The pastor suffers the temptation to make comments and observations to the person with whom he is counseling, giving him freely his own understanding of the difficulties *as soon as he himself has seen them*. A careful restraint and an attentive listening instead often reveal that the person has already thought of these things himself. It is almost a miracle to hear a person say that which it seems impossible for him even to see, much less to articulate. The counselee who is genuinely trusted by the pastor to work faithfully at his problems will often take the words the pastor *would have* uttered right out of his thoughts.

In the sense of *letting* a person do the talking, listening is a passive process. Here the passive listening of the pastor lays hold of the "active power of silence," which "makes small talk transparent, and has a force that pulls the person forward,

[13] *Ibid.*, p. 142.

driving him into deeper layers of his experience than he had intended." Also, it calls upon the initiative of the pastor.

Of course, the use of silence, in the sense of letting the person do the talking himself, depends upon the degree of trust that is present between the pastor and the person at hand. Reik has pointed out that there are different kinds of silence:

> It is tempting to use the insight into the psychology of silence as a ladder that can be put aside as soon as we have descended to the depths. There are, of course, different kinds of silence; yes, there are even degrees of silence. We speak of a cold, oppressive, defiant, disapproving or condemning, as well as of a calming, approving, humble, excusing silence. The concept seems to unite opposite meanings, presenting itself with plus and minus signs. Compare, for instance, "silence gives consent" with the rejecting silence of a lady to a man who is forward or objectionable.
>
> Silence can be conceived of as an expression of quiet sympathy or intense hate. To be silent with a person may mean that we feel quite in agreement with him or that every possibility of agreement is excluded. Talkativeness as well as reticence appears as a character trait of the women whom men love. Lear disavows Cordelia, who loves and is silent, but Coriolanus returning to his wife tenderly calls her, "My gracious silence." The contrast between speaking and being silent was originally not as sharp as we might think. We are reminded of the characteristic of ancient languages (for instance, of the Egyptian) of forming words with antithetical meanings so that only a small change later indicated a differentiation of the opposites (compare, for instance, Latin *clamare* = to shout, *clam* = secretly; German *Stimme* = voice, *stumm* = mute). We have to assume that silence is primal and that speaking emerged from silence as life from the inorganic, from death. If we live here on "borrowed time," all our speaking is but a fleeting interruption of the eternal silence. We have to believe with the Gospel of John that in the beginning was the Word, but before that was the great silence. Carlyle, in *On Heroes and Hero-Worship,* says that speech is of time; silence is of eternity.[14]

[14] *Ibid.,* p. 124.

The silence of a physician of the soul "slowly changes its significance to the person with whom he is working." This writer was interviewing a thirty-year-old man who had always been passively dependent upon his pastors, college professors, and parents for the motivation of his behavior. The interviews consisted of many long and painful silences in between jerky, halting outbursts of insight into this infantile dependence upon others. On the fourth interview, the man said, "I have decided that I have been coming to talk with you just to get on the good side of you, just as I did with my pastor and my professors in college."

Then the writer said, "You feel that you have been pretty eager to have my approval?" Then a long, stringent silence ensued, at the beginning of which the writer felt a sense of impatience at the fact that the man would not talk any further. Then he remembered that silence could uncover what speech would hide, remained silent, and felt the impulse to pray silently in the man's behalf. During the meditative silence, the man arose from his seat and walked out of the room.

Two weeks later, the man sought another conference and told the writer this: "During that exceedingly talkative [laughing at his own humor] interview we had the last time we were together, I made up my mind that, in order to clear my own thinking, I would just have to break my dependence on you. I felt that the only way to do this was to come in and engage you in conversation and get up and walk out and leave you. But when I came, you just sat silent. *At first I felt that your silence was an unfriendly silence, but suddenly it changed and I felt it was a friendly silence. I had the feeling that if I did leave your office, you would understand.*"

Therefore, the use of a passive listening is predicated upon the "friendliness of the silence" of the pastor. This can best be approximated by facial assurances of understanding, and by creating the illusion of talking with such interjections as "Uh-huh," "Yes," "I see," "Did he?" Or it can be accomplished by repeating the trailing ends of sentences such as, "You say you went from home to work that morning." This is a continual flow of encouragement from the pastor to the person with whom he is counseling that stimulates the person's confidence to talk and makes it easier for him. If, however, the pastor is preoccupied with trying to formulate what he himself is going to say as soon as he finds an opening, he may find the opening sooner than he thinks. It is much more effective to follow the lead of the most emotion-laden response of the counselee and encourage him, by reflecting these feelings back to him, to explore them more thoroughly.

c. Listening, in the third place, means that the pastor *actually gets the person to talk*. In this sense, listening is an active experience on the part of the pastor. Here he takes some positive initiative. It is at this point that the pastoral counselor parts company with the earlier "nondirective" approach of Carl Rogers. Nevertheless, he maintains the basic attitudinal orientation that Rogers expressed much more adequately in his more recent books, *Client-Centered Therapy* (Houghton Mifflin Company, 1952) and *On Becoming a Person* (Houghton Mifflin Company, 1961). In the first instance, the pastor can take the initiative in the listening by following the lead of the person, and picking up the specific trailing end of the sentence that is spoken with the most feeling and strength of tone. This amounts to asking the person to talk a little bit more about the particular subject he is discussing, without using those words at all.

Again, active listening calls into action the right of a pastor to ask questions. Russell Dicks much earlier called this "directive listening" and says that what the "scalpel is to the surgeon, the question is to the pastoral counselor, and it is quite as dangerous. . . . The good pastor is one who knows what to ask and what not to ask, plus a feeling for timeliness." [15] The important thing for a pastor to remember is that he should not run ahead of the sense of trust that he has with the person. He should not ask a question that the person has not given him the spiritual privilege to ask. Then, for the sake of time and because of the informal nature of much pastoral counseling, the

[15] Russell Dicks, *Mental Hygiene,* October, 1948, p. 580.

pastor can, with safety for all concerned, encourage the person to talk by asking well-placed questions. Here he may fill out a gap of information, he may reflect a feeling, or he may even suggest an association by the way he asks a question.

These are the three significant meanings of the listening ministry — hearing what the person says, letting the person do the talking, and actively encouraging the person to talk. They should be borne in mind as the pastor enters upon the phase of counseling that has been called "listening and exploration." However, certain precautions as to the use of a passive or active listening approach need to be made. Such a method may cause the pastor to spend time that should be used more valuably by a person with greater skill who could give more concentrated attention to the person. An example of this would be the case of those persons who are so acutely depressed that they become more agitated and depressed as they talk more and more to their own confusion. An attempt on the part of the minister to explore their difficulties through a listening approach might even precipitate a suicide. This illustration points to the fact that a total dependence upon listening as a pastoral procedure, to the exclusion of basic knowledge and skillful evaluation of the different patterns of emotional reaction in people's lives, is dangerous. For example, Rogers notes that this approach is limited in dealing with passive-aggressive persons. In the more recent volume by this author, *Protestant Pastoral Counseling*, these patterns of self-structure are dealt with in detail.

2. *The achievement of insight.* The frank objective of the pastor in this second phase of the ministry of counseling is that the person with whom he is dealing will achieve insight into and develop personal control over his difficulties. This is done by indirection rather than by frontal assaults on the besetting difficulties of the individual. It comes to pass through the process of listening and exploration after this manner:

There is *a return of the repressed memories and present feelings* of the person. It is a mistake to think of these memories as

being *past* experiences. They live actively in the present existence of the individual, and he unconsciously considers them
as present realities rather than as things that are in the past.
As one hospital patient said upon having dreamed of her childhood, " All those people who have long been dead are now
alive again in my mind." These are buried memories, yes, but
they were buried alive, and, like Hamlet's father's uneasy
spirit, find their way back into the daily affairs of the person's
life. The ministry of attentive, careful, and considerate listening
provides the atmosphere in which these memories and present
feelings may return for the conscious consideration of the person himself and for later assimilation into his reasonable way of
life. The Gestalt psychologists, with uncanny insight, have
called these experiences and feelings " an unassimilated mass."

There is an *expression of ambivalent feelings* on the part of
the person. This means simply that the person has opposing
feelings about the same object of concern: he may say in one
context that he almost worships his father, and in another connection say that he has discovered recently that his father is
dismally wrong about many things. In the presence of the
contradictions, the pastor may be prone to say, " But I thought
you said you almost worshiped him! " This would give the
person a trapped feeling that might break rapport, and justly
so. Rogers wisely suggests that *simply to reflect these feelings
back to the person in a mirror fashion brings best results.*
Whereas people see through a glass darkly, and know only in
part, this is a way of moving them toward a completion of their
insight. As Carl Rogers says:

> Where the client is conflicted in his feelings, where both love
> and hostility, attraction and repulsion, or both sides of a
> difficult choice, are being expressed, it is particularly im-
> portant to recognize this clearly as an ambivalent attitude.
> Some of the sorts of recognition which may be given are
> exemplified in such statements as, " You feel you should go
> into commerce, but music is the thing you really like "; " In
> spite of your bitterness toward your father, you do like him ";

or, " You want to come for help, yet still at times you feel that
it is too difficult for you." [16]

This acceptance, clarification, and balancing of contradictory
needs in the person's life is one of the vital phases of the
achievement of insight. Especially is this true concerning people's feelings toward God. The tension between the need for
aggression and the need for passivity, the need for independence and the need for dependence, the need for individuality
and the need for social approval, the need for rebellion and the
need for authority, constantly calls for a sense of spiritual balance. The achievement of this balance in the lives of his people
is a frankly accepted objective of a good pastor. In reality,
these ambivalences are conflicts in the value structures of the
person's life coming to fresh focus in their perceptions. This
struggle is an ethical struggle of the self for consistency of
values.[17]

The *need for self-rejection and the need for self-acceptance*
constantly tend to stalemate each other. These opposing needs
usually appear in the context of the question that arises as to
whether the person at hand should express himself or deny
himself in his search for personal satisfaction. He may have in
mind his aggressive impulses and say that he feels very guilty
over losing his temper but that he cannot accept himself as a
" Mr. Milquetoast "! Or he may realize that he has freedom in
Christ to enjoy his sexual life but does not know what to do
with his freedom. Of course, all such instances again are illustrations of ambivalent feelings toward the self. They reflect a
fear of one's own emotions and a confusion as to one's purposes
in life.

Naturally, the problems of self-acceptance are basically of a
religious nature.[18] They suggest that the achievement of insight

[16] Carl Rogers, *Counseling and Psychotherapy* (Houghton Mifflin
Company, 1942), pp. 147, 148.
[17] See Prescott Lecky, *Self-Consistency* (Island Press Co-operative,
Inc., 1945).
[18] Robert H. Bonthius, *Christian Paths to Self-acceptance* (King's
Crown Press, 1948).

in the process of personal counseling may be superficial or profound, destructive or creative, temporary or permanent, depending upon the level of truly religious feeling it reaches. *The Christian pastor frankly accepts the fact that ethical values make a difference in the mental health of a person.* Discriminating judgment of such values reveals about four qualitatively different levels of insight:

a. On the *ascetic level of insight,* the individual refuses to accept the fact that he even has negative feelings of aggression, passionate feelings of a sexual nature, power drives of domination, acquisitive desires for possession, and self-destructive drives because of meaninglessness. He lives on the basis of complete repression and inner blindness to his humanity. In a word, he feels not only that he is without sin but that he is not tempted.

b. On the *fatalistic level of intellectual insight,* the individual is " sicklied o'er with the pale cast of thought," accepts intellectually that he has certain problems but finds more satisfaction in analyzing himself than in attempting any changes in his way of life. Quite often he will use the opportunity for an interview as a mirror before which he can preen his symptoms. It is as though he had a filmlike image of himself before him. His descriptions of his difficulties become means of satisfaction rather than an unhappiness to him. Again, such a person may subtly defy the counselor to solve his problems and, when the house is swept clean, he may return a few days later with " seven other " problems to take the place of the first one.

Or the person may take a fatalistic attitude of a stoic and become one whose " head is bloody but unbowed," engage in heroics of his determination, and resign himself to his fate. Stoicism is often mistaken for Christian faith by such a person.

c. On the *perverted level of Machiavellian insight,* the person sees his antisocial and asocial tendencies and rejoices in the new freedom of his insight. He takes his knowledge as an occasion to the flesh and sets about to make up for time he lost as an ascetic. He takes a delinquent turn, and the people around him pay the price for his newfound understanding of himself.

His insight is that of the perverted wisdom of the serpent. He takes advantage of society to get his own wishes, although he may use the appearance of socially acceptable standards to get his own way. This "acting out" of impulses may create havoc in the life of a church or a school.

d. On the *level of the Christian stewardship of insight,* which is the profoundest level of insight, the person comes to the conclusion that he is willing to give up immediate pleasures for more lasting and eternal satisfactions. He will use his impulses as "instruments of righteousness" unto life rather than as instruments of sin unto death. He interprets his own good in terms of the social feeling he has for other people. He uses his newfound freedom as a means to liberate and understand those about him. He alleviates their suffering even as his has been alleviated for him. This sounds the depths of Christian experience and lays hold of the need of the individual for community with other people who share in the fellowship of shared values, also. Here the individual has achieved insight not only into the nature of his own imperfections and lack of omnipotence. He also has entered into an acceptance of the imperfections and fallibilities of those about him. He has come to accept temporal reality in its proper relation to the Eternal.

The gift of such insight moves from "deep . . . unto deep" in the reality of the counseling situation. The pastor needs to be very careful not to accept the first statement of a problem as the real one, because it very rarely is. For instance, a young university student came on the first interview saying that he had begun to doubt "that God exists." Then on the third interview he said, "I have no doubt that God exists and that he is good, but I am beginning to see that my real trouble is that I am afraid my father and mother will not approve my marrying until I finish school." On the fourth interview he said, "I guess my main problem is that my mother has never wanted me to marry." On a later interview he stated, "I am going ahead with my plans to be married this summer, and I think I can help mother to take it."

The problem in this instance changed its form in the student's mind as the level of his insight deepened. Like Job, he did not begin to lay hold of the resources of strength until he sought help for those who were at one and the same time the closest to him and his greatest vexation.

The Phase of Reconstruction and Guidance

The pastor is concerned not only with helping persons with their inner conflicts. Their reconstruction of purposes requires his interest in and their guidance in a new way of life. The task of reorganization of personality is essentially a redemptive one, whereas the task of helping that person back his new commitments is one of growth and consecration. Therefore the pastor, in this fourth phase of his counseling ministry, is on hand when the person begins to formulate a plan of action in a new way of living. Consequently, his approach may change considerably in order that he may continue to sustain the new selfhood of the person.

Usually the pastor is most meaningful when he appeals to the sense of adventure and experimentation of the person with whom he is dealing at the time. Several opportunities present themselves at this stage of the relationship:

1. *The interpretation of the life situation.* He may want to give a brief interpretation of the basic causes of the trouble, or make a series of concrete suggestions. It is best that these avoid wordiness, be to the point, in simple language, and easily understood. *Usually, as in all phases of personal counseling, it is better to use the same words that the person himself uses and to lay hold of any figures of speech or ways of expression that the counselee himself has presented.* The writer is reminded of a member of one of his rural churches who once asked him " what to do when the plow hits a stump and a fellow swears before he can stop to save his life." Being in the midst of the preparation of a sermon on temptation, the writer went into a long, detailed, catacomblike explanation of how to stop swearing. The man listened with interest and attention, and when the pastor had finished he said, " Yes, but, pastor, by the time I remember all that, I've done gone and cussed! " A few words

would have been much easier to remember.

Several tested ways of interpretation are valuable: A pastor may interpret by the kind of questions he asks, the order in which he asks them, and the tone of voice in which he speaks. The interview that Jesus held with the woman at the well of Samaria is a case in point here. He interpreted her problem by asking her to go get her husband. Again, a pastor may interpret by giving a short summary of the relationship and the different turns the conversation has taken. Another method that Jesus used constantly was that of an appeal to the experience of other people, the use of a parable, or the use of a proverb. Sometimes the parables the persons themselves use are invaluable. One person said that his life was like a wagon full of barrels which they used to haul water from the river to the church baptistry: by the time the wagon got to the church, all the water that had been in the back barrel was in the front and vice versa. He averred that his family discord had so affected his work, and vice versa, that he could not tell which was which! This is a valuable " homemade parable " for use in interpretation.

But the best way that a pastor can interpret the life situation of a person to him is to encourage him to express frankly and objectively the personal responses of affection and antipathy that the person feels toward the pastor as a counselor. This was called "relationship" counseling by Jessie Taft and Otto Rank. An illustration of it is the young woman who, for several years, had moved from one denomination to another as she became attached to a different pastor. In bringing her difficulty to the pastor at this particular time, she finally came to the conclusion that she would unite with his church. He registered no surprise or undue elation. In the next interview the pastor was able to interpret tactfully what the changing of denominations had meant to her and to disentangle her church affiliation from too much dependence upon ministers. His interpretation of the relationship was the basis of counseling her.

2. *The brief pastoral dialogue.* The pastor may be asked by the person to whom he is ministering to confer with him on a specific plan of action with reference to marriage, parental re-

sponsibilities, educational plans, or vocational readjustments. Here he may resort to the use of the brief pastoral dialogue that was suggested earlier in this chapter.

3. *The introduction to Christian friends.* At the same time, he may take on the functions of a teacher-evangelist, seeking to relate the person to the church, to fellowship groups, and to other sources of spiritual undergirding. Also, he may feel that some member of his church or community, such as a doctor, a lawyer, a businessman and employer, or maybe one of the dependable women of the church, could be a meaningful friend to this person. Therefore, he may introduce him to one or more of these friends for specialized help.

4. *The selection of appropriate literature and Scripture passages.* At this stage of the counseling process, the pastor also may deem it advisable to refer the person to certain literature that will be specifically applicable to his reconstruction of his outlook on life. He may find that the person knows next to nothing about the Bible, and that he has the opportunity to cause the New and Old Testaments to come alive to the person in the light of his own life situation. By and large, the persons who come to a pastor are religious illiterates and stand in need of this sort of help. The pastor should be very careful not to hand the whole Bible to people and make some generalized and vague remark as to its healing power. He should carefully (ahead of time if possible) select the sections that give the clearest guidance to the person in terms of his educational background.

Whatever interpretation, instruction, or introduction to other people is given to the person, it should indicate a plain path of action. The person will need reassurance, spiritual support, and vital encouragement. The encouraging power of the pastor's own confidence in the person cannot be overestimated. The pastor, however, needs to use down-to-earth common sense in suggesting goals as he evolves plans along with the person. These goals need to be in keeping with the abilities of the person to achieve them. All these procedures are appropriate only after the pastor and the parishioner together have a

relaxed sense of certainty that they have arrived at the real
issues of the person's life situation. If the pastor has any doubt
at all that the person has not come to the core of the problem
with him, or if he is confused in his own mind as to what the
situation actually is, he should begin to angle for another interview. Reflection, maturation, and the opportunity for more conversation are the only things that can clarify the matter.

The Phase of Follow-up and Experimentation

Much effective counseling has gone to waste because of a
failure to follow up the progress of the persons with whom pastors have dealt. This is notoriously true of the counseling done
by pastors in evangelistic meetings, religious retreats, college
religious emphasis weeks, etc. In this final phase of personal
counseling, several issues are at stake:

1. *Overdependence.* The breaking of the continuity of regular interviews creates an emotional crisis in the life of the person in and of itself. The chances are that the person has become too dependent upon the counselor, and the interviews
have become something of a sedative to soothe his anxieties. He
may interpret the breaking of a series of formal interviews as a
personal rejection. At this point the pastor is made to feel more
keenly the powerful charges of affection that have been trans-
ferred to him by the person. One person said to his pastor,
"What will I do when you are too far away for me to find
you?" The pastor interpreted the relationship in this manner:
"You seem to wish that I were capable of being everywhere
and probably are assuming that I am all-powerful also, as far
as you are concerned. This is your attempt to deify me, but
only God can be God in your life. It is he who is all-present and
all-powerful, and you can talk with him any time. We call this
prayer, and I should like for you to try to develop that practice
in your life." The Christian pastor, in his ministry of "follow-
up," can do nothing more effective than "tutor" in the art of
prayer the people with whom he counsels. This can be done on
a group as well as an individual basis.

Another difficulty of an overdependent relationship between

a pastor and a parishioner at the point of follow-up is that the person will continue to bring each minor decision to the pastor for his opinion or in an attempt to sustain the former continuity. This is especially true of pastors or student counselors in a college setting. Adolescents draw a great deal of personal strength from being near a person with whom they can identify and like whom they would seek to become. They have an abundance of " free floating " anxiety that they allay in this way when they are away from home and those people who have naturally filled voids in their lives.

2. *Fear and hostility*. The failure to provide room for false starts and mistakes and relapses to old patterns of behavior by holding over the person's head a perfectionistic, " sure cure " goal to be achieved may cause the person to avoid the pastor in the event such things should happen. He feels that, if he makes one slip, he would not dare face the pastor who had such high hopes for him. He may come back later and say that he has " let the pastor down." In a real sense he has let his pastor displace God on this score also.

Another way of falling into the same error is by dominating the person's decision in such a way that the only means by which he can become a person in his own right is to rebel completely against the whole relationship with the pastor. In the context of a pastoral community, such rebellions can take vicious turns and do more damage than can be undone in a long while. Yet, a measure of real hostility — frankly and warmly accepted — may be a healthy sign of growth, even necessary for the continued autonomy of the individual. The calling of the pastor is to be a faithful servant, not to be liked or disliked!

3. *Gossip*. The gossip hazard also conditions the form that a " follow-up " ministry may take. The parishioner may become very uneasy as he gets more removed from the face-to-face relationship to the minister. Then he will become apprehensive lest the pastor be irresponsible in his references about the counselee to others. Out of sheer discomfort, he may move his church membership to another church. Or, in the pressure of a momentary crisis, he may seek out irresponsible persons in the

community and give an emotionally distorted version of some snatch of his conversation with the pastor. Jesus, in his pastoral ministry, was continually plagued by the results of such gossip. Little wonder that he charged people to go and tell no man of their interviews! A part of the covenant of communication involves the counselee's responsible commitment to confer with the pastor if and when he plans to discuss their conversation with others.

4. *Positive follow-up*. But more positively, the pastor may follow up his private conferences with people by visits in the home. He has this privilege and will often be invited into the homes of his newfound friends. He may be asked to perform the wedding ceremony of the young man or woman whom he counseled prior to the marriage. These same persons will occasionally invite him to conduct a dedication service in their new home, or when a baby is born to them. A young minister may ask him to preach his ordination sermon, or a young businessman may want him to speak at his civic club. Although he has numerous outside contacts such as these, the majority of persons with whom a pastor counsels will be members of his church. He will see them in church services, have them in discussion groups, and preach to them Sunday after Sunday. These contacts can enrich or impoverish the counseling ministry of the pastor, depending upon his appreciation of the dynamics of group life and his sensitivity to his people's feelings toward one another.

Quite often the minister will counsel with people whom he will not see again because they are not so closely knit with his own community. They may be people from another city who have been sent to him by some person who he has helped before and who has moved away. They may be the relatives of a member of his church and are hospitalized in the city where the pastor ministers. Or they may come to him from having read something he wrote, from having heard him over the radio or on television, or from having seen him in a religious assembly. As one " person-minded " minister wrote: " I sometimes wonder how it is the word gets around about one, if he is competent to help others when they need him. But I am learning daily how much it does get around. I count it a privilege to counsel with those who come, although I am constantly amazed at my total inadequacy — but by leaning hard on the counsel of the Holy Spirit, the friend and I work out in our thinking helpful avenues through many and varied problems."

This seems to define the feeling of a minister who is concerned with the inner peace of his people: he feels competent and full of confidence in his ministry, yet he senses his inadequacy as he confronts the magnitude of human suffering. When he discovers his own perennial source of dependence in the Holy Spirit and a sense of community with the person in need, helpful avenues are found.

A minister must never become overconfident of his own skill in the use of any technique of pastoral care. If he does, he soon begins to depreciate and think irreverently of the personalities of those with whom he deals. He begins to " play on their souls," which causes them to turn on him to rend him. Shakespeare describes such careless irreverence in Hamlet's dialogue with Rosencrantz and Guildenstern, who had been sent to lure his secret from him. He begged Guildenstern tauntingly to play upon a flute that he offered him. But Guildenstern said: " I have not the skill. . . . These cannot I command to any utterance of harmony." Then, with much vehemence, Hamlet replies:

Why, look you now, how unworthy a thing you make of me! You would play upon me, you would seem to know my stops, you would pluck out the heart of my mystery, you would sound me from my lowest note to the top of my compass; and there is much music, excellent voice, in this little organ, yet cannot you make it speak. 'Sblood, do you think that I am easier to be play'd on than a pipe? Call me what instrument you will, though you can fret me, you cannot play upon me.[19]

[19] *Hamlet,* Act III, Scene 2.

Chapter VIII

The Pastor as a Minister of Introduction

As the years have added new perspective to the kinds of relationships described in the foregoing pages, three major impressions stand out in my mind as both indigenous to and primary in the values of the Christian pastor. First, he not only *represents* God as he is revealed in Jesus Christ through the Holy Spirit; he actually *introduces* people to the God and Father of our Lord Jesus Christ. He does this through his teaching and pastoral care, both as preacher and shepherd. In this sense, he is an evangelist in the best sense of the word, i.e., he is personally acquainted with the Lord Jesus Christ and he wants his friends to " come and see him " who brought all that he himself ever did to focus with a whole new meaning, calling, and destiny. Secondly, the Christian pastor, therefore, is at work meeting new people and establishing durable and creative relationships with them. Human relationships, once formed, cannot be broken; they can only be changed into more creative ones or deteriorate into indifference or destructiveness. Therefore, the Christian pastor is like Bunyan's " Mr. Faithful." He establishes covenants with people and keeps them. He is sensitive to and scientifically informed about the processes that human relationships undergo in time.

But as the Christian pastor becomes durably related to persons, he, in the third place, introduces them to each other and to persons who can enable them to help themselves by providing them with the rich resources that friendship, professional skills, and clinical experience can afford them. Thus the pastor both multiplies his own service to parishioners and other counselees and at the same time creates a bond of service between himself, his church, and other professional persons in and out of the church. I call this his "ministry of introduction," a ministry that is an alchemy in human relationships. It takes the unsightly, seemingly valueless, and even detrimental stuff of human suffering and turns it into a whole new world of significant and committed persons for the one who is in distress. As one handicapped person, made so in an unfortunate accident, put it: "I met five lifetime friends through this awful thing that happened. It doesn't change what happened, but it has gone a long way toward making what happened worth a lot to me."

In the former edition of this book, I called this ministry of introduction the ministry of referral. However, use of the word "referral" itself creates some bad side effects in the minister's mind, and especially in the mind of the inexperienced theological student. The minister and student often take the easy way out and make quick, irresponsible referrals. This grows out of a feeling of inadequacy, the harassed feeling of being hurried and busy that hovers over all that ministers do, and preoccupation with other things the minister enjoys better. To "refer" the person both assuages the conscience and leaves the minister feeling that he has helped the person. In reality, his own relationship has simply deteriorated to the point that the person does not "bother" him anymore.

Another bad side effect of the idea of "referral" is that the minister is likely to feel that once this is successfully done, there is nothing left for him to do. Especially is this true of psychiatric referrals and referrals to marriage counseling services. Consequently, the pastor does not continue to give emotional support, reinforce the person's trust in his other counselors, and be a spiritual confidant, a fellow sufferer in the ministry of prayer with and for the person. That which the minister can uniquely be and do becomes much more apparent when the psychotherapeutic work is being done by other professional people. "Referral" often leaves the minister, the patient, and the other professional person feeling that "there is nothing now left for the minister to do." But being a friend, a "common denominator," before, during, and after such professional services have begun, taken place, and ended is the unique identity of a minister who is durably related to people.

Another side effect of the idea of referral is that it carries with it the connotation of sickness, pathology, and acute emergency for many who hear it. It does not include the sheer joy that comes from introducing one friend to another, of relating a new convert to a small group of persons with similar interests, of getting people with questions together with people who might have a few of the answers, of introducing people with shared interests or stations in life — such as two musicians or two widows, or two working girls who each need a roommate with whom to share an apartment.

In order to offset these bad effects of the idea of "referral," I have chosen to call attention here to "the ministry of introduction" of the Christian pastor. We can turn to the New Testament for an example of what is meant by "the ministry of introduction."

Possibly the most outstanding example of a "minister of introduction" was Barnabas, "the son of encouragement," told about in the book of The Acts. He it was who introduced the apostle Paul to the Christian community. His efforts failed when he introduced Paul to the church at Jerusalem. But apparently he kept a durable relationship of even warmth and acceptance with the apostle Paul. It was several years later before he succeeded in introducing Paul to the church at Antioch. We might surmise, also, that he introduced John Mark to Paul, and, although they had their differences, all three of them maintained a continuing relationship to one another.

Likewise, the letters of Paul are replete with greetings to friends, introductions, and intercessions. The whole letter to Philemon is devoted to the pastoral care of a new convert who also happened to be a slave.

The minister does his work in a widely varied context of persons who are devoted to helping others and trained in ways of doing so. He therefore should be daily at work at getting acquainted with these persons who can serve those whom he serves. When he goes to a new community a systematic church survey of the community as a whole will get him in touch with many persons, groups, and institutions. His lay leadership can do much to introduce him first to the membership of the church, then to the leadership of the community who may not be in the church of which he is pastor, and then to persons who are especially in need of the ministry of the church and its pastor. A living organism of " known persons becoming known to each other " is thus built through pastoral attention, considerateness, and care. The pastor's own isolation is thus overcome in his concern for others.

The Christian pastor cannot work alone. He does not minister to his flock without soon finding that he is not the only person in the community who is concerned with the welfare of his parishioners. Nor is he alone in the depth of his devotion to people, in the clarity of his sense of mission in the world, and in the favor of those to whom he ministers. Within the context of the Christian community in even a small city may be found *many* ministers who have " gifts that differ " accordingly from those of the pastor of the congregation, such as employers, landowners, teachers, lawyers, medical doctors, psychiatrists, social workers, clinical psychologists, and — most important of all — parents. In the rural community, the consolidated school staff, the athletic coach, the county agent, the home demonstration agent, the general medical practitioners, and parents offer in a less complex manner, similar ministries.

Often the fascinating vocations of these people pull them away from rather than bind them more closely to the church. The mechanistic education of many highly trained specialists sometimes has driven a wedge between their present way of life and the original sense of mission with which they started, and which often was stimulated by the church. Many times the careless neglect and unfriendly harshness from the pastors of these valuable persons have further alienated them from a vital Christian activity. But most of all, they have not been made to feel that their skill and resources are indispensable necessities for the total witness of the church to the community. They have often in ignorance thought of the church as the one-man activity of the pastor rather than as the cooperative teamwork of all the members in a ministry to the total personality of individuals according as each man has need.

Therefore, the Christian pastor's responsibility, upon having come to a new community, is to make friends first with his fellow shepherds, i.e., the other pastors of the community regardless of denomination; secondly, with the physicians, surgeons, psychiatrists, pediatricians, and gynecologists in the community; thirdly, with the social workers, heads of institutions, and public-school teachers; fourthly, with the parent-teacher organizations and child-care agencies. And, of course, the parent of any child should be considered by the pastor as his greatest ally or his potentially most effective opponent in the spread of the gospel. These are all members of a " community team " of healing helpfulness to people. As a general rule, they, like the minister, are passionately devoted to what they are doing. Almost any pastor can gain their respect by showing an intelligent, informed, and careful devotion to the same people to whom they also minister daily. As he becomes acquainted with them himself, he in turn becomes a " minister of introduction " of these persons who need their care. He " bridges " the gaps between the professions and represents their inseparability from each other. At the same time he communicates a realistic and creative witness of his church and its ministry to the professional persons themselves.

The minister soon learns the drastic limitations of his abilities to help people, even though he is no more limited than other trained workers who are circumscribed in their own particular ways. Then he discovers that it is not so important that he himself help a parishioner as it is that the parishioner's own personal energies be so strengthened that he can help himself. When the pastor discovers how to lay hold of the resources of all those about him (especially the resources of " those who are of the household of faith ") he will be less likely to become "weary in well-doing." And he will find his most loyal friends among those comrades on the "community team."

The minister is responsible, in the presence of a wealth of community resources for helping people, for more than he himself is capable of and trained to do for people. He is also obligated to see that they get the help of other professional workers who are equipped to help them with specialized difficulties. It is just as important that a pastor see that a person gets help as it is for him to give that help himself.

For instance, a pastor in a small county seat received a letter from a soldier in occupied Japan. The soldier was distressed over the economic welfare of his wife and children, who lived about ten miles out in the country from the town in which the pastor lived and worked. The soldier had tried other avenues of learning about the needs of his wife, who would not write him about the health and economic status of the family. The pastor was much too busy in his own community at the time to give personal attention to the man's request. He knew, too, that he might not be able to give the assistance needed, even if he should visit the home. Instead of going himself, therefore, he asked a social caseworker in the county welfare department (who was a devoted member of his church) to investigate the matter. She did, and having discovered the needs of the family to be acute, brought the welfare resources of the community to their rescue.

In order that a pastor may take his place with confidence on such a "community team" he needs specific guidance on the ministry of introduction. He needs to know something of the indications as to *when* he should introduce a person to another professional worker. He needs to know some of the methods and the hazards involved in making such introductions. He needs to know the resources of his own community well enough, and he should stay in a community long enough, to establish a working understanding with other members of the "community team."

Recognition of the Need for the Ministry of Introduction

The pastor needs to ask himself in every situation of pastoral care and personal counseling, " Is this parishioner in need of help other than the specific ministry that I am commissioned and equipped to offer him? " The question may be answered both generally and specifically.

General Indications of the Need for Additional Help

1. *Lack of available time.* The minister generally tries to introduce a parishioner to others when he knows that more time and attention will be required than he has to offer. For instance, a pastor may have the necessary training to carry through with deeper-level counseling over a period of weeks and months. Nevertheless, his program at that moment may be so heavy that he cannot give adequate attention to the person. He may be planning to be out of the community, or he may be so involved in other responsibilities that he cannot possibly find the time necessary to do what needs to be done. Then he will need other trained persons whose time will be available. This may mean that he will ask the individual to see an assistant, another pastor, a marriage and family counselor, a psychiatrist, or a social worker. The person to whom the needy individual is sent will be determined entirely by the kind of problem in need of solution and the kind of persons available for the assistance he needs. No specific rule can be devised.

2. *Social and emotional involvement.* Another general consideration on the ministry of introduction is that many ministers can be too socially and emotionally involved with an individual to supply the kind of help needed in a given situation. One instance can be cited. A student pastor in a part-time pastorate in the suburbs of a large city sought to counsel with two married couples in his church. All four persons were active members of his church, having places of important leadership. They were contemplating trading wives and husbands in a double divorce and remarriage arrangement. Before they did so, they brought their confusion to the pastor, who sought to

deal with the problem directly, without help. The whole church became involved, and the problem culminated in the pastor's resignation from the church. If the pastor had known that the trouble was too involved for him to handle alone, he could have introduced the couples to marriage and family counseling agencies in the nearby city. There they would have received expert help. Neither he nor the church would have been hurt so deeply. At the same time, the service of the marriage and family counseling agency would likely have built a durable relationship between their personnel and the church.

3. *Lack of specialized training.* In the third place, the pastor generally seeks additional help for parishioners whose problems require specialized treatment that the pastor has not been trained to give. This can be an easy way of avoiding the responsibility of dealing with the more serious troubles within a congregation. However, even the most highly trained pastors can be identified by their ability to know the limitations of their equipment for dealing with special difficulties.

Specific Indications of the Need for Additional Help

1. *Physical illness.* The parishioner who is physically sick, or who *thinks* that he is physically sick, needs the help of a good doctor. The pastor should be thoroughly informed as to the medical help available, both in his community and in the larger region in which he lives. Especial attention should be given to the availability of specialized diagnostic and therapeutic services in medical centers. The cost of such treatment, the various services of clinics, and the distances of the clinic from the person who needs it are practical problems to be confronted. Usually, if a parishioner is already under the care of a physician, the pastor should by all means confer with that physician before he takes any important step in counseling with the person about his or her spiritual difficulties. If the person does not have a medical doctor at the time, the pastor is at liberty to suggest the names of doctors whom he himself knows and with whom he has a working understanding.

2. *Mental illness.* The parishioner who is manifestly psy-

chotic needs medical help. As has already been suggested, these persons quite often come to the attention of a minister *before* they go to a doctor. If a person is threatening suicide, if he is dangerous to the personal safety of other people, if he is not amenable to reason but is deluded and irrational, or if he shows any of the less obvious signs of mental disease, he needs the care of a doctor. If the pastor is acquainted with the family of the person, he may seek tactfully to instruct the closest of kin as to the seriousness of the situation. In doing so, the pastor should avoid "diagnosing" or treating the person's difficulty himself. The extent of his ministry will be directly dependent upon the cooperation of the family and the availability of psychiatric help.

However, a pastor in a community where there are no psychiatric facilities, and where the general practitioners are extremely old and/or poorly trained, faces the heavy responsibility of doing for the patient what he can. He does it "with fear and trembling," taking care to do no harm. The situation of a pastor in the event that a psychiatrist *is* available is much like his situation in relationship to a surgical patient: *Before* and *during* the illness, his best help is offered in establishing the confidence of the patient and his family in the doctor's trustworthiness. His ministry *after* the illness is primarily that of helping the person to find himself in a place of security after his recovery.

3. *The problem of the unmarried mother.* The unmarried mother needs the help of the minister's wife, the medical resources of the area, and the guidance of a family service organization in addition to the personal ministry of a pastor to her and her family. The maternity homes established by the Salvation Army and the Florence Crittenden Homes for unmarried mothers meet an acute need here. It is very difficult for a minister to deal with the problem of unmarried mothers without the cooperation of physician, social caseworkers, and many others. The minister and his wife can provide a secure and trustworthy relationship while the girl moves from one to another of the many persons she needs. He has, as has already

been indicated, been her spiritual director in rediscovery of the love and forgiveness of God. In the present, he can be her minister of introduction to others who can serve her.

4. *The problem of the alcoholic person.* Another concrete example of the need for multiple sources of help are the alcoholic persons and their families, with whom every pastor deals. As Dean Sperry has pointed out: " Hitherto ministers have regarded drunkenness as a moral scandal and a vice. They looked to the mourners' bench at a revival meeting as the safest and surest cure. It is only fair to say that this remedy has worked in many classic instances. But today ministers are beginning to realize that there is a point beyond which drunkenness becomes a bodily disease, and the moral resolutions of penitence may well need the fortification of sober medical treatment." [1] Likewise, the reliability of the methods of the Alcoholics Anonymous groups has been demonstrated, and a minister is wise to depend upon the help of these men in dealing with acute alcoholism.

5. *Economic disability.* The poverty-stricken person, in need of economic assistance, is another for whom the pastor usually relies upon the expert casework assistance of welfare agencies. Much harm has been done to people who were given economic assistance by well-meaning persons who did not know how to get the facts and foundation for wisely doing so. The pastor and his church should be participants in the general welfare program of the community, both in terms of giving support and in terms of relying upon the guidance of these agencies in the care of destitute persons. The personnel of these agencies are trained to meet the needs of hungry, naked, and shelterless people. If they are not trained to do so according to wisdom and tenderness, the pastor should be held in enough confidence among the people of the community to be heard when he suggests the need for more adequate workers. The church, of course, will have ways and means of meeting the emergency economic needs of its own members. If a dependable family in

[1] Willard L. Sperry, *The Ethical Basis of Medical Practice* (Paul B. Hoeber, Inc., 1950), p. 23.

the community should lose their house and other belongings by fire, the fellowship of the church should be strong enough to keep the family from too much hardship. If a long-term chronic need appears in some family (such as a mother being left a widow with several small children and no relatives to turn to), the pastor may confer with the community service organizations and make a plan whereby a consistent and intelligent program of help can be offered cooperatively. Pastors do well to seek the advice of the welfare agencies as to *how* a family or an individual can be helped without taking away their self-respect and causing them to lose personal initiative.

6. *Other areas of need.* Many other specific situations can be named in which a pastor needs the help of people to whom he may introduce parishioners who come to him for guidance. Young people seeking work may be referred to employers, young persons seeking premarital counseling will be introduced to doctors, and those seeking guidance about adoption of children will be helped through both doctors and social agencies. Parishioners making educational plans will be referred to college and university authorities, and veterans with specific difficulties will be guided to Government agencies that have been established for such purposes. Charles F. Kemp has prepared an unusually thorough booklet on the ways and means whereby pastors can draw upon community resources.[2]

The Process and the Methods of the Ministry of Introduction

The process of the ministry of introduction and the methods used in carrying through with that process determine to a large extent the amount of good the person gains by the referral.

[2] Charles F. Kemp, *The Pastor and Community Resources* (The Bethany Press, 1960).

Recognizing Limitations

Wittenberg rightly observes that the first step is the pastor's own recognition of the problem.[3] It can be added that the pastor must recognize not only the nature of the parishioner's difficulty but also his own obligation to diffuse and distribute the responsibility when he becomes overextended. Naturally, he can overdo this: he can feel so inadequate in the presence of even the most trivial problem that he runs for cover when he sees the first sign of suffering. Or he may simply not want to be bothered at all and pass the buck to someone else. But ordinarily the pastor is overconscientious instead. He mistakenly feels that he should have the resources within himself and from his knowledge of the Bible and religion to solve any and every problem that arises. In such an instance, the pastor who recognizes his need for help has made a real step in his understanding of himself.

Interpreting the Person's Problem to Him

The second step in calling in the help of other professional people is to interpret the person's own difficulty to him. A young man comes to his pastor and describes many physical symptoms such as headache, loss of appetite, and sleeplessness. He says, however, that these are all caused by his fears that he is going to " do something " at night to hurt his wife, and by his fear that he is losing his mind. He breaks down, cries profusely, and falls all over the chair, writhing with anxiety. After calming the man, the pastor gets a little more of the story, discovering that the man is hearing strange voices " out of nowhere." Obviously the man needs help, but the pastor recognizes his own inability to minister to him without the help of a good psychiatrist. Therefore, in a persuasive and suggestive manner, the pastor says to him: " You have had these feelings pile up during the rapid events of the past few weeks. You have not been married long; you are facing new responsibilities; you have had several misunderstandings with those who are very close

[3] Wittenberg, *op. cit.*, p. 90.

to you; you are afraid of what you think; you are upset, nervous, and have not slept or eaten properly. I think you realize that you are not in any frame of mind to think through your problems clearly or to make any important decisions at this time, until you have regained your health of body and spirit." This is a commonsense interpretation of the man's trouble, aimed at suggesting to him the idea that he does not just *think* he is sick, but that he really *is* sick and needs help in addition to that which the pastor can offer.

Confessing Limitations

The third step in a ministry of introduction is the pastor's confession of his own limitations and his explanation of the need for the help of the professional person to whom he hopes to send the individual. Great care should be exercised here. When a pastor says: "There is nothing I can do to help you," he has literally pronounced doom upon the person, for he represents God to the person. He should preface his confession of his limitations with a confident assurance of the things he *can* do. In the case cited above, the pastor went on to say to the person: "Of course, your health is the most important thing to you at this present moment. I can be your faithful friend and talk with you about your relationship to God. I can pray with you and keep you reminded of God's love and sustaining power. I will stand by you. But your health needs the attention of a doctor. I know that you cannot be your best spiritual self as long as you are ill in your total being. You need to go to a doctor, who can give you treatments that will relax you and restore your perspective, who can talk with you about your ideas and feelings after you have rested awhile. A good psychiatrist can help you with your troubles." The pastor added, "Maybe I could help by talking to your wife also." Fortunately, the pastor found the wife cooperative, and he was able to help the patient to accept the fact that he was a sick man and to understand the necessity for psychiatric help.

Introducing the Other Professional Person

The fourth step in the ministry of introduction is that in which the pastor gets the parishioner in touch with the other professional person. This is usually done by telephone, but occasionally is done personally. Sometimes, if the situation is not one that involves emergency action, a letter will do. In the case mentioned above, the name, address, and telephone number of the psychiatrist were given to the patient and his wife. It is a helpful and meaningful ministry for the pastor on occasion to go with the person in need to the office of the doctor, the social worker, etc. This man was admitted to a hospital the next day and received treatment. At this stage, the most important necessity is that the pastor " transfer " whatever confidence the parishioner may have in him as a pastor to the professional person. He will find it necessary to reassure both the patient and the family after this order: " I have known this doctor for some time. I know from observing him that he is trustworthy and deserves your complete confidence. Now that you are in his care, be sure to depend upon him and his guidance without too much fear. He is a good man, and shares the same ideals that you and I share in God." Simple honesty requires that the pastor do his best to know persons about whom he can sincerely say such things.

Showing Concern While Not Interfering

The fifth phase of such a ministry includes cooperative concern and a minimum of interference on the part of the pastor. The person must not feel that the pastor is " trying to get rid of him." In the case under discussion, this was avoided by directly reassuring the patient, by following his progress by telephoning his wife, and by visiting him during his hospitalization. The process of reassurance could have been aided by letters, as well.

In referring a patient to a psychiatrist, the pastor does the doctor a great service by writing him a letter in which he gives a brief summary of the facts that he knows about the patient's situation. This summary should include a word about how this parishioner came to the attention of the pastor, a concise description of the number and nature of conversations the pastor has had with him, a description of his problem *in the same words that he himself used,* insofar as is possible, and a statement of the facts that the pastor may know about the life history of the parishioner. The summary may be followed by another paragraph in which the pastor gives his own interpretation in *nontechnical language* of the life situation of the person; lengthy letters are not indicated in most cases.

The case of a psychiatric cooperation has been cited here because it is the most difficult type of situation with which a pastor has to deal, and because requests come more often as to how to introduce a person to a psychiatrist. Tender persuasion and strong suggestion are necessary in most cases of this kind. However, some of the most important ministries of introduction come under much happier circumstances. A pastor introduces a strange couple to other couples in the church as friends. He writes a letter of introduction for a college freshman to one of his own former professors. He introduces a jobless young man to a prospective employer whom he knows. He introduces a skeptic or an avowed atheist to a professor of philosophy. He *may* even introduce a young man and a young girl! They may even become husband and wife. Who knows! But more than this, the pastor as an evangelist is always at work introducing people to Jesus Christ.

Following Up

The final phase of the ministry of introduction is the follow-up. This corresponds to the phase of follow-up and experimentation characteristic of all good counseling.

A procedure of this kind, skillfully executed, leaves the pastor's hands free for a definitely religious ministry in the life of his people. He can rely upon the resources of his community to help him in such a way that he can do a distinctive task without being a "jack-of-all-trades and master of none," dabbling in this, that, and the other and not "sticking to his own last"

— the reconciliation of men with God. Nevertheless, this does not relieve him of the responsibility of knowing enough about the work of the other members of the community team to be able to function smoothly in relation to them.

The question may be properly raised at this point, "What should be done in case a person does not want to cooperate with efforts to call in outside assistance?" An instance of this is the sixty-five-year-old woman who constantly sought the help of the church with her financial difficulties. She had no family except a sick brother, had no work, wandered about the city begging, would call the wealthier members of the church by telephone and ask them for help. If they did not do what she wanted them to do, she would threaten to kill herself, call them profane names, and become incensed with anger. She was the first seeker for help who came to the attention of every new pastor.

One of the pastors, when she came to him, listened carefully to her story and asked her to come back to see him the next day. In the meantime, he called the city relief agencies and discovered that she had a sixteen-year record with them. She had an epileptic brother and was considered by the agencies to have "epileptoid personality traits" herself. They suggested that the pastor ask her to return to see them, and that the church itself contribute what it could to the total program of medical and financial relief that the agency would plan for her.

When the woman returned the next day, the pastor, after having conferred with the social service committee of the church (which had long since lost patience with her), asked the woman to return to the social agency. He said to her: "The church plans to help you if you will cooperate with us in the program we have outlined for you. I have talked with the family service organization and asked them to study your whole financial problem. I have told them that we will do for you what they suggest. We will pay our funds directly to them, and they will add whatever else you need." The woman became irate and refused to cooperate. It finally became necessary for her to be institutionalized in a state hospital. However, the pastor had no hand in this. Two of the lay leaders of the church took the case of the elderly widow to two physicians and arrangements for her commitment were completed. The state hospital, which formerly would have had little but custodial help to offer her, now has an extensive geriatric rehabilitation program. It has two chaplains for the pastoral care of the patients. The members of the Woman's Missionary Union visit with the woman regularly.

But there is a limit beyond which a pastor cannot go in trying to help people. He does them harm when he tries to overrule their objection to being helped. Remembering this will help a pastor to be objective at the same time that he will do all that can be done to meet people's needs. He is forced to give his time and energy to people who cooperate.

Anton T. Boisen is fond of saying that the pastor deals with three groups of people: First, there are those who are capable of taking care of themselves, and will get along nicely regardless of the care the pastor gives them. Secondly, there are those who will become progressively worse, regardless of the care and attention the pastor can offer them, and will not profit by anything he does for them because they do not want to be helped. Thirdly, there are those who stand at the crossroads, and the outcome of their lives will be *largely determined* by the patient efforts of a pastor in his ministry to them. Of course, this is a loose but very valuable generalization. The pastor is under obligation to devote his time, energy, and equipment where they will do the most good. The parable of the sower and the seed and the parable of the wheat and the tares can be appreciated best by the veteran pastors who see the magnitude of human suffering and the finitude of their own abilities in the light of the eternal wisdom of God.

Appendixes

Appendix A

Criteria for Evaluating Effective Pastoral Care

The earlier years of experimentation in the field of pastoral care represented a group of pastors who were concerned with success and failure in pastoral care and counseling. This was the focus of much writing in the field. Success stories were recounted. In reaction against this, stories of failures were studied for the purposes of correction. But in both instances the focus of concern was success and failure. These were the two criteria for evaluation.

Contemporary pastoral care in the mid-sixties, however, has begun to devote more attention to a sharper definition of criteria for evaluation than success and failure. The following criteria are suggested as questions for the pastor to ask himself in evaluating a given record of pastoral ministry. Appendix B provides suggestions as to how these records can be kept.

1. *Has the pastor formed a faithful and durable relationship of pastoral care?*

The pastor's effectiveness is measured primarily by his ability and willingness to establish a faithful and durable relationship to the individual and/or his family. Does he follow through with his covenants, and are his covenants formed clearly and explicitly as to what he intends to be with and to do for this individual? This faithful and durable relationship of care is characterized, as C. S. Anderson Scott has said, by *attention, considerateness,* and *concern.*

2. *Is the pastor both capable of and willing to function in a distinctly pastoral identity?*

How does the pastor feel about being seen as a pastor? Does he function appropriately as a pastor? Can he communicate within this identity with a personal rather than institutional orientation? Is he self-centered about his identity as a pastor? Or, is this identity an instrument of ministry in relation to the person?

3. *Does the pastor actively clarify, define, and implement the specific structure of his pastoral relationship?*

There are formal, informal, dual (formal and informal), and confused relationships within any working day of a pastor's relationships. Therefore, the pastor must be at the work of clarifying and defining his context of ministry. The pastor must be able to move creatively with the person on the level on which they are actually related — as a friend, as a supporting and sustaining comforter, as a teacher, in brief pastoral dialogue, or in longer term pastoral counseling, etc. His effectiveness as a pastor is largely determined at times by his willingness and ability to relate at these different levels.

4. *Is the pastor able to evaluate his own work with neither a need to avoid any self-criticism, on the one hand, nor the need to become unduly discouraged as a " failure " on the other hand?*

Here the very fallacy of the " success image " and the " failure image " in pastoral care must be brought into self-criticism.

5. *Is the pastor responsive to the emotional atmosphere of the relationship, sensitive to the patterns of emotional reaction, and willing to converse personally in terms of these?*

The patterns of hostility, detachedness, dependency, withdrawnness, suspiciousness, manipulativeness, despair, apathy, etc., provide the tonal and emotional atmosphere of both sides of the pastor-parishioner relationship. To what extent is the pastor sensitive to this and in what way is he responsive to it?

6. *Does the pastor appreciate the personal background and developmental pilgrimage behind the presented difficulties?*

The effective pastor takes time to listen. He follows the leads of the person into the background and the developmental history of a given difficulty and of the person's life as a whole. This makes an understanding pastor. This understanding is an important criterion of pastoral effectiveness. People ask: " Does he really understand me? "

7. *Does the pastor take initiative and appropriately involve the responsible persons of the caring fellowship of the church by diffusing and distributing responsibility to them?*

The pastor cannot effectively work in isolation. Nor should he relieve the people of his church of the responsibility of caring for one another. This is one of his most effective ways of being a pastor. In this he exercises his identity as a " pastoral director " of a caring fellowship.

8. *Does the pastor relate himself and the person or persons whom he is serving to other significant people in the parishioners' lives?*

The family, the personal friends, the lay mentor figures, other pastors than the pastor himself, other professional persons such as doctors, lawyers, social workers, public-school teachers, and employers are allies of the pastor. A criterion of effective pastoral work is the willingness and ability of the pastor to function as a fellow minister along with these other persons.

One way of using this evaluation scale is to rate each item on a scale from zero to twelve, making zero " unacceptable " and twelve " exceptional," somewhat as follows:

SCALE FOR EVALUATION

12	Exceptional
11	Excellent
10	Superior
9	Above Average
8	Good
7	Average
6	Acceptable
5	Fair
4	Below Average
3	Poor
2	Inferior
1	Barely acceptable
0	Unacceptable

Appendix B

Records of Pastoral Work

Records can become an end in themselves and thereby blight the ministry of a shepherd. But when they are used as a means of keeping a check on oneself and as a means of pastoral research in themselves, they become a guide to a richer understanding of people. As Washington Gladden has said: " Every minister can be and must be an original investigator. Genuine laboratory work is demanded of him. . . . Firsthand knowledge is imperative." The method whereby he accomplishes this is by keeping a carefully recorded analysis of his face-to-face ministry to people.

The working pastor will find need of about four kinds of records:

Statistical Records

Ministers have always felt the necessity of keeping a record of the names, ages, dates, and places, of marriages, funerals, and baptisms at which they have officiated. Many ministers also keep a record of their sermon titles and of the places where they have preached these sermons. These records are of great value for reference and prevent embarrassment when certain occasions arise.

The pastor, however, will profit all the more by keeping a careful record of the following items:

1. Visits to the homes and places of business of his people:
    a. Initial visit.
    b. Follow-up visits.
2. Visits he makes to hospitals and other institutions:
    a. Initial visit.
    b. Follow-up visits.

243

3. Visits his people make to his home or study, seeking his personal counsel:
   a. Initial visit.
   b. Return visits.

This sort of record may be kept very simply in an anonymous fashion by placing three sheets in the back of a pastoral notebook and tabulating them in this fashion. Or a brief card file may be kept, which will include a new entry every time a new person is contacted within the scope of a given year.

The advantage of a record like this is that it keeps a gauge on the type of ministry the pastor is rendering, whether it is one in which people come to him or one in which he must seek them out. Again, the pastor can keep a check on the relative degree of extensiveness and intensiveness with which he is functioning with his people. He may be touching a great many people superficially in only one initial interview, or he may be swinging to the other extreme of spending too much time with a relatively few people and neglecting the larger needs of more people.

Brief Pastoral Notes

Another type of record is the sort that identifies the kind of problem the persons present; whether the pastor visits them or is visited by them is of no consequence in this type of record. Here the pastor simply lists the major kinds of requests that experience has taught him will most often come. One extensive study listed them this way:

Evangelism and the care of new converts
Vocational decisions
Premarital counseling
Physically ill
Dying
Bereavement
Alcoholics and their families
Mentally ill and their families
Child-care problems
Adolescents and their adjustment
The stresses of middle adulthood
Problems of later maturity

Of course, he may add many others as time goes along; also, he may discover that many of these thorny problems may be present in one person who comes to him. His problem in knowing where to list such a person will consist in determining the dominant, over-ruling difficulty that the person is facing.

This type of record can best be kept on a card with a brief pastoral note as to the date and the sort of complaint the person presented. If the pastor is in a small church, a confidential note-book with a leaf for each person in the community serves better. In such a case, a "progressive note" sequence can be kept.

CONVERSATION SEQUENCE RECORDS

The pastor will occasionally want to keep a record of his ministry to one individual — a record that comes as nearly as possible to re-calling everything that happened in the conversation sequence. The reasons for this sort of record are manifest: In the first place, the pastor's work with the person may have been of a controversial nature, and the pastor will want to have a complete record of his dealings with the person. An example of this would be an inter-view with a young theological student on a controversial point of theology. If there is ever any question, the pastor will not need to tax his memory for the facts. Secondly, and more important, the pastor will learn as much about the person as he attempts to recall the sequence of the conversation as he did while he was talking to the person face-to-face. He will have a means of criticizing his own work with the person. If he does not have a faculty of self-criticism, this process may bring one to birth. The pastor can find no more thorough way of self-instruction in the art of pastoral counseling than this.

Abundant examples of this type of history may be found in books by Dr. Russell L. Dicks such as *And Ye Visited Me* (Harper & Brothers, 1939). *The Art of Ministering to the Sick,* by Dicks and Richard Cabot (The Macmillan Company, 1936), is another ex-ample. Of course, *Casebook of Non-directive Counseling,* by Wil-liam U. Snyder and others (Houghton Mifflin Company, 1947), is a phonographically recorded report on such histories. More recent ones are Seward Hiltner's book, *The Counselor in Counseling* (Ab-ingdon Press, 1960), and Newman S. Cryer and John M. Vayhinger, *A Casebook in Pastoral Counseling* (Abingdon Press, 1962). These are of exceptional value, also, to the pastor. Case histories of this sort are not used by this author because a wealth of such data can be found elsewhere and because of the introductory nature of this book.

The Pastoral History Letter

Another practical use of records is in the pastor's ministry of introduction. Quite often he will lead a person to go to a doctor, a social agency, or another pastor and need to write that worker a letter concerning the referral. Such a letter should be a succinct, one- or two-page typewritten letter that includes all the pertinent facts concerning two things: (1) the chronological sequence of life-history events as far as they are known to the pastor, (2) the course of the relationship that the pastor has had to the person.

Such a letter should carefully keep facts separated from *interpretations*. In this letter the pastor is first of all a good reporter. He does not editorialize. *After* the facts have been stated, then an interpretive paragraph by the pastor himself becomes very appropriate and in order.

These letters will go into the pastor's confidential file as he continues in his ministry.

Conclusions

A word needs to be said about taking notes during a conference with a person. This writer has found that such a procedure is like using notes in preaching: it gets in the way of the relationship. Likewise, the pastor fails to discipline his attention to recall the material later if it is needed for records.

Finally, records of pastoral work, apart from anonymous statistical records, should be kept completely out of sight and access of other people. The pastor should exercise great care in keeping such material from those who are closely associated with him: secretaries, assistant pastors, education directors, and even members of his own family. However trusted these persons may be, it is unavoidable that information which they have not themselves earned the right to know will give them their attitudes toward persons in the community. Furthermore, unguarded slips of the tongue are well-nigh impossible to prevent.

Appendix C

A Systematic Program of Reading

The following is a selected and descriptive bibliography of books that can be read for maximum benefit. Careful distinction should be drawn between books that a pastor studies himself and those he uses by handing to his people. No good physician hands his patient an anatomy book or a treatise on differential diagnosis! These are books for the pastor's own edification as a professional person. Books that can be handed to parishioners and other counselees are discussed and listed in the book *Where to Go for Help*, by Wayne E. Oates, and published by The Westminster Press, 1957. A more recent volume of a similar but more restricted nature is Samuel R. Laycock's *Pastoral Counseling for Mental Health*, Abingdon Press, 1961.

THE PSYCHOLOGY OF RELIGIOUS EXPERIENCE

Allport, Gordon, *Becoming: Basic Considerations for a Psychology of Personality*. Yale University Press, 1955. Psychology here is concerned with the power that the goals and spiritual strivings of man have to shape the destiny of his selfhood.

—— *The Individual and His Religion*. The Macmillan Company, 1950. The leading psychologist at Harvard University gives a reflective, positive, and full-orbed understanding of the positive realities in the religious sentiments.

Argyle, Michael, *Religious Behavior*. London: Routledge and Kegan Paul, Ltd., 1958. A synoptic survey of recent research on religious attitudes toward age, sex, marital status.

Boisen, Anton, *The Exploration of the Inner World*. Harper &

Brothers, 1952. A combined autobiographical and research volume that stands alongside James' *Varieties of Religious Experience* as a classic in the psychology of religion. Also to be read in relation to this is Boisen's complete autobiography, *Out of the Depths*, Harper & Brothers, 1960.

James, William, *Varieties of Religious Experience.* One of the timeless documents on religious experience every pastor should read.

Oates, Wayne E., *The Religious Dimensions of Personality.* Association Press, 1957. A comprehensive summary and textbook of the psychology of religion, quoting primary sources extensively. Concluding chapter on a Christian understanding of personality.

Strunk, Orlo, *Religion: A Psychological Interpretation.* Abingdon Press, 1962. A brief volume interpreting religion in terms of the very recent form of psychology known as "phenomenological psychology." Readable and provocative.

—— ed., *Readings in the Psychology of Religion.* Abingdon Press, 1959. A series of papers gleaned from classical and contemporary sources concerning the psychology of religion. A "must" for reference purposes.

Tournier, Paul, *Escape from Loneliness,* tr. by John S. Gilmour. The Westminster Press, 1962. A penetrating analysis of both the psychology and the religious dimensions of loneliness and the quest for community. Especially helpful in understanding communication problems in marriage.

—— *The Meaning of Persons,* tr. by Edwin Hudson. Harper & Brothers, 1957. Tournier is a Swiss physician who has taken a specifically Christian stance in his therapy. This book is a reflective discussion of the meaning of persons as contrasted with the social roles they fill as "personages."

Theological Foundations of Pastoral Care

Hiltner, Seward, *Preface to Pastoral Theology.* Abingdon Press, 1958. Using the "shepherding perspective" as a central focus, Hiltner develops a systematic theology of pastoral care as it is related to the total field of theological inquiry.

Niebuhr, H. Richard, *The Purpose of the Church and Its Ministry.* Harper & Brothers, 1956. A disciplined overview of the identity and function of the minister as a channel of love of God and neighbor in the context of the church.

Oates, Wayne E., *The Bible in Pastoral Care*. The Westminster Press, 1953. The pastor's basic attitude toward understanding of and intimate acquaintance with the Scriptures is part and parcel of his practice of pastoral care. This is the burden of this discussion.

—— *Christ and Selfhood*. Association Press, 1961. Man's birth into and struggles within the Christian life as a self before God are related to the Person of Christ in his incarnation, anointing, death, and resurrection, and in his promise and gift of the Holy Spirit. Man's experience of sin, meaninglessness, loss of a clear sense of destiny, and his tendency to stagnate spiritually are discussed in this context.

—— *Protestant Pastoral Counseling*. The Westminster Press, 1962. The central conceptions of both Protestantism generally and the Free-Church tradition within Protestantism particularly become the data for developing an ordered theology of pastoral care in this book.

Roberts, David E., *Psychotherapy and a Christian View of Man*. Charles Scribner's Sons, 1950. A Christian philosopher who underwent psychotherapy himself distinguishes between dynamic and static understandings of salvation. He brings the great affirmations of the Christian faith into critical encounter with psychology.

Southard, Samuel, *Pastoral Evangelism*. Broadman Press, 1962. The minister's identity and function as an evangelist are discussed fully from a historical, theological, and pastoral point of view in this volume. Pastoral care and evangelism are united.

Thurneysen, Eduard, *A Theology of Pastoral Care*, tr. by Jack A. Worthington, Thomas Wieser, and others. John Knox Press, 1962. A translation of a Swiss theologian's understanding of pastoral conversation as the communion and communication of the Word of God, especially as it is related to Reformed theology. This author is a close associate of Karl Barth.

Tillich, Paul, *The Courage to Be*. Yale University Press, 1952. Through the use of this "method of correlation," Tillich discusses the distinctions between the anxieties that are inherent in and those that are alien to human existence.

Williams, Daniel Day, *The Minister and the Care of Souls*

Harper & Brothers, 1961. A systematic theologian explores the
"Christological heart" of the work of the caring pastor and
sets forth basic theological principles for the practice of pastoral care.

THE IDENTITY OF THE CARING PASTOR

Baxter, Richard, *Gildas Salvianus: The Reformed Pastor* (abridged
from original edition), ed. by John T. Wilkinson. London:
Epworth Press, 1939; 2d ed., 1950. Lest the pastor think of
the pastoral care of his people as a new invention, he should
read this seventeenth century Baptist pastor's understanding
of pastoral care.

Hiltner, Seward, *The Christian Shepherd*. Abingdon Press, 1959.
Recurrent problems of caring relationships are discussed in
a very informative and helpful way. Social class-climbing,
theological and ecclesiastical rebellion, and many other problems are set within the presuppositions of Hiltner's *Preface to
Pastoral Theology*, Abingdon Press, 1958.

——, and Lowell G. Colston, *The Context of Pastoral Counseling*.
Abingdon Press, 1961. The work of a minister in first a church
and then a psychological counseling center is studied for comparison and contrast of the influence of these contexts on his
work. Now in paperback.

Hulme, William, *The Pastoral Care of Families*. Abingdon Press,
1962. An overview of the theology and practice of pastoral
care of families by a Lutheran minister.

Johnson, Paul E., *The Psychology of Pastoral Care*. Abingdon Press,
1953. An interpretation of the crises of human existence —
grief, marriage, illness, parenthood, etc. — with special attention to the wealth of psychological data useful to the minister.

Oates, Wayne E., ed., *The Minister's Own Mental Health*. Channel
Press, Inc., 1961. Thirty papers of a reflective, analytical, or
research nature in which the common theme of the emotional
problems and needs of the minister himself are discussed.

Oman, John Wood, *Concerning the Ministry*. London: SCM Press,
Ltd., 1936. A sensitive and informed treatment of the ministry
in its spiritual depths and in terms of the pastor's own spiritual
resources. An inspiring book to be read by the candidate for
the ordination to the ministry.

Sherrill, Lewis J., *The Struggle of the Soul*. The Macmillan Company, 1951. Each age-stage of human development is discussed, giving the minister a wholesome synthesis of Biblical, theological, and psychological understanding of the pilgrimage of man from birth to old age. Now in paperback.

Sperry, Willard L., *We Prophesy in Part*. Harper & Brothers, 1938. Lyman Beecher lectures, 1938. Salty wisdom of an older minister which will help the pastor see some of the vagaries and half-baked enthusiasms of pastors in a clever perspective.

Storer, James Wilson, *The Preacher, His Belief and Behavior*. Broadman Press, 1953. Sermons to pastors, wisely put and profoundly searching of the motives of the minister.

PASTORAL CARE IN RELATION TO THE BEHAVIORAL SCIENCES

Adler, Alfred, *What Life Should Mean to You*, ed. by Alan Porter. Little, Brown & Company, 1931. A popular statement of Adler's point of view, written by Adler himself. Very readable and inspirational.

Boisen, Anton, *Religion in Crisis and Custom*. Harper & Brothers, 1955. The social dimensions of religious experience in reaction to great crises of the community, such as depression and war, are astutely assessed here.

Erikson, Erik, *Identity and the Life Cycle* (Vol. I, No. 1, Psychological Issues Monograph Series). International Universities Press, Inc., 1959. An influential volume on the development of personality. The author uses language and concepts that are easily translated without distortion into the work of everyday life, into religious meaning, and into homiletical frames of reference.

Frankl, Viktor, *The Doctor and the Soul*. Alfred A. Knopf, Inc., 1955. A Viennese psychiatrist who survived Nazi concentration camps traces the causes and explains the treatment of many emotional maladies, relating them to the struggle for spiritual meaning in life.

Havighurst, Robert J., *Human Development and Education*. Longmans, Green & Co., Inc., 1953. A highly useful handbook for interpreting the developmental tasks of people at various stages of life.

Loomis, Earl, *The Self in Pilgrimage*. Harper & Brothers, 1960. A

psychoanalyst gives a religious interpretation of the development of personality.

Menninger, Karl, *Theory of Psychoanalytic Technique*. Basic
Books, Inc., Publishers, 1958. A highly readable statement of
the theory and practice of psychoanalytic psychiatry.

Rogers, Carl, *Client-Centered Therapy*. Houghton Mifflin Company, 1951. The definitive revision of Rogers' previously described nondirective psychotherapy.

Sullivan, Harry Stack, *The Psychiatric Interview*. W. W. Norton
& Company, Inc., 1954. A thorough discussion of the process
of interviewing disturbed persons.

Specialized Problem Areas

Bergler, Edmund, *Homosexuality*. Hill & Wang, Inc., Publishers,
1956. A psychiatrist with an unabashed ethical and personal
commitment to the Christian faith discusses this very thorny
pastoral problem of homosexuality.

Bernard, Jessie, *Remarriage*, The Dryden Press, 1956. The com-
plexities of remarriage of widows, widowers, and divorced
persons are discussed in detail by a sociologist of the family.

Clinebell, Howard, *Understanding and Counseling the Alcoholic*.
Abingdon Press, 1956. The best single volume on the pastoral
psychology and care of the alcoholic.

Douglass, Paul F., *The Group Workshop Way in the Church*. Association Press, 1956. The genius of Baptist life has been in the
small group, the face-to-face fellowship. This book brings scientific know-how to bear on the problem of how these groups
work and learn together.

Duvall, Evelyn, *In-Laws: Pro and Con*. Association Press, 1954. A
combined statistical study and interpretation of the problems
and the solutions as they arise in the in-law situation.

Irion, Paul E., *The Funeral and the Mourners*. Abingdon Press,
1954. The psychological factors in the funeral situation, the
pastoral follow-up of the mourners, and the cultural dimensions of grief are thoroughly discussed by this author.

Johnson, Wendell, *People in Quandaries*. Harper & Brothers, 1946.
The science of semantics made clear in terms of the ways in
which language both conceals and reveals human distress.

Oates, Wayne E., *Premarital Pastoral Care and Counseling*. Broad-

man Press, 1958. A succinct discussion of premarital counseling as done by a Baptist pastor and his congregation.

Pike, James, *If You Marry Outside Your Faith.* Harper & Brothers,
1954. Do not let this author's wild remarks on other subjects
detract from his excellent discussion of the interfaith marriage
in this book. He wrote this before he became a bishop. It is
carefully done.

Ross, Murray G., and Hendry, Charles E., *New Understandings of
Leadership: A Survey and Application of Research.* Association
Press, 1957. A popular but thoroughly sound treatment of the
psychology of leadership. Helpful in understanding the power
struggles in your church.

Southard, Samuel, *Counseling for Church Vocations.* Broadman
Press, 1957. The specific task of the minister in counseling persons who are entering full-time service within the churches is
the topic of this book.

Sullivan, Harry Stack, *The Interpersonal Theory of Psychiatry.*
W. W. Norton & Company, Inc., 1953. This is the most valuable single volume on psychiatry for the minister. The author
sees people as persons and not as " cases."

Vincent, Clark, *Readings in Marriage Counseling.* Thomas Y.
Crowell Company, 1957. An extensive compilation of excellent
journal articles on marriage counseling. Detailed attention is
given to a wide range of problems the pastor meets.

———— *Unmarried Mothers.* The Free Press of Glencoe, 1961. A scientific study of the problems and distresses of unwed parents.

Warner, W. Lloyd, and others, *Social Class in America.* Science Research Associates, Occupational Information Division, 1949.
A working research handbook to give a pastor some index to
the stresses of social class competition and quiet desperation
among his people.

Westberg, Granger, *Minister and Doctor Meet.* Harper & Brothers,
1961. A popular treatment of medical-ministerial cooperation.
Very useful in pastors' seminars and in discussions with individual doctors.

Young, Richard K., *The Pastor's Hospital Ministry.* Broadman Press,
1954. A basic book on the care of the critically sick, the hospitalized, the bereaved. Especially helpful in discussing the
" healing team " and the relations of the minister to other professions.

Indexes

Author Index

Subject Index

Alcoholism, 17, 60, 83, 152, 176, 229
Ambivalence, 200 f., 209 f.
Appointments, 194 f.

Bereavement, 36 ff., 39, 49, 147, 165
Bible, 9 ff., 52, 59 f., 72 ff., 89 f., 113, 152, 171 f., 215 f.
Bibliographical helps, 154, 247 ff.
Birth, 12 ff.
Brief pastoral dialogue, 181 ff., 214 f.

Catharsis, 166 f.
Church, the, 66 ff., 125 ff.; as a community of the Holy Spirit, 62; as a context for counseling, 58; a disciplined, 128 ff.; as a fellowship, 38, 53, 98; responsibilities of, 26 ff., 34 f.; as a teaching agency, 109 ff.; at worship, 120 ff.
Clinical pastoral training, 28, 33, 95, 154, 190 f.
Communication, 28, 104 ff., 198, 218
Confession, 40, 91, 172 ff.
Continuity of experience, 6 ff.
Conversion, 15 ff.; progressive, 16 ff.; regressive, 17
Counseling, conditioning factors

in, 137 ff.; directive, 179 f., 184, 207 f.; nondirective client-centered, 149, 187 ff., 202 ff.; preparation for, 184 ff.
Crises, 1 ff., 10 ff., 42, 165 f.
Criteria for pastoral effectiveness, 239 ff.

Death, 32, 36 ff., 39 ff., 165
Depression, 155 f.
Divorce, 25 ff., 42, 60, 76 ff., 152

Evangelism, 18 f.

Family therapy, 151
Fear, 31 f., 217
Follow-up, 216 ff., 234 f.

Gossip, 217 f.
Grief, 37 f., 164 ff.
Group counseling, 14, 91, 109 ff., 163 f.

Holy Spirit, 42, 48, 59 ff., 64 f., 97, 112, 219

Identification, the law of, 55 ff., 80 ff.
Identity, 3, 6, 20, 28, 99 ff.
Idolatry, 49 f.
Insight, 208 ff.
Interpretation, 57, 178, 213 f., 231 f.

257